TEN SIMPLE KEYS TO LIVING

A LIFE ABLAZE

RICK RENNER

A Life Ablaze: Ten Simple Keys To Living on Fire for God
ISBN: 978-1-68031-423-6
Copyright © 2020 by Rick Renner
P. O. Box 702040
Tulsa, OK 74170-2040

Published by Harrison House
Shippensburg, PA 17257
www.harrisonhouse.com

6 7 8 9 10 / 25 24 23 22 21
6th printing

Editorial Consultants: Cynthia D. Hansen and Rebecca L. Gilbert
Text Design: Lisa Simpson, www.SimpsonProductions.net

DEDICATION

I dedicate this book to my precious friend and fellow minister, Sergei Vasilevich Ryakhovsky. When God called my family to move to the former Soviet Union in 1991, He had already designed this covenant relationship that Sergei and I have now shared for so many years. It was a God connection from the beginning — one that has not only enriched our own lives personally, but that has also impacted churches, pastors, leaders, and believers throughout this vast region of Russian-speaking people.

I've been privileged to personally know many notable spiritual leaders, but Sergei Vasilevich Ryakhovsky's consistent spiritual fire for the things of God is a particularly remarkable source of inspiration to me. For this reason, I dedicate this book, *A Life Ablaze*, to this powerful man of God, whose life that is so ablaze with spiritual fire has mightily influenced untold numbers of people for the Kingdom of God throughout the territory of the former USSR.

CONTENTS

CHAPTER 8

ABLAZE WITH HOLINESS **281**

CHAPTER 9

ABLAZE WITH HUMILITY **319**

Acknowledgments

It is my custom to acknowledge those who have helped me put the truths I write about into print. Some of my books are larger and require more help; other books are smaller and require less participation from others. But regardless of each book's size, I find every person's role to be vital in the process, and I am thankful for each one.

So first, I wish to express my thanks to Vincent Newfield and Becky Gilbert for their respective editorial contributions to the early stages of this book. I'm also grateful for the valuable insights and fine-tuning editorial skills Becky added to the later stages. In addition, I want to thank Andrell Corbin for adding her rich editorial input to this book. Finally, I want to say thank you to Cindy Hansen for her excellent editorial work and thoughtful questions that helped me articulate many important points in this book. As has been true for years, Cindy's input with her editorial mind and her ministry heart was a great blessing to me as this book was being written.

Furthermore, I want to express thankfulness to my publisher, Don Nori, and to Brad Herman and the entire team at Harrison House, all of whom work so professionally to help get my books into the hands and hearts of those who are hungry for the spiritual truths God has entrusted me to communicate.

Last but certainly not least, I am thankful to Denise, our sons, and our Moscow leadership team who carefully listen as I formulate ideas and concepts that I eventually put into print for people around the world to read. Your thoughtful responses mean so very much to me, and I am thankful that God called us as a team to serve the Body of Christ.

Never lag in zeal
and in earnest endeavor;
be aglow and burning with the Spirit,
serving the Lord.

— Romans 12:11 *AMPC*

Let us not allow slackness to spoil our work
and let us keep the fires of the spirit burning,
as we do our work for God.

— Romans 12:11 *Phillips*

CHAPTER 1

A LIFE ABLAZE

Do you struggle to keep the fire of the Holy Spirit burning in your heart as it may have burned earlier in your life? Do you sometimes feel like all that is left are a few small glowing embers — and that perhaps even those embers are starting to die out and become cold? If this description hits close to home as you evaluate your Christian walk, I have two questions to ask you:

- How do you stoke the embers of the fire within you so that it begins burning red-hot in your heart again?
- Once you have that fire burning hot and bright, how do you sustain and *grow* the intensity of that inner fire for the rest of your time on this earth?

How do you stoke the embers of the fire within you so that it begins burning red-hot in your heart again?

NO FUEL, NO FIRE

In this book, I want to speak to you about the different kinds of fuel you need to stay spiritually ablaze. But to begin with, I want to tell you a story from our family's earliest days in the former USSR that will demonstrate my point about doing whatever is necessary to *keep the fire burning*.

In the early years just after we moved to the former USSR, my wife Denise and I purchased an apartment in the heart of our city for our family to live in. But when we purchased it, it was abandoned and in miserable condition. Honestly, it was so ruined that it should have been condemned. It was a morass of mold, collapsed ceilings, and plaster falling off the walls. But we could see what it *could* be with lots of hard work, so we purchased it and went to work restoring it. After the restoration was complete, that apartment became as elegant as it had been nearly 100 years earlier.

When the work was finished, the walls were covered with fine wallpaper and magnificent chandeliers hung once again from giant, hand-carved medallions in the center of the ceilings. The giant-sized crown molding that was wrapped around the ceilings of each room had been meticulously restored. Every room had intricate, new parquet floors to match those that had existed before the Revolution. And the nine fireplaces — one for each big room and in each bedroom — were the most magnificent features of the apartment. Once restored, those fireplaces looked like they belonged in a museum.

But although our apartment had been restored, every other apartment in that big building still remained in a state of devastation and abandonment. Eventually the entire building would be beautifully restored, but when we moved into our apartment, the other apartments and the central staircase of the building looked like something that had been bombed in World War II. The stairs were navigable, but those areas had been so long abandoned that derelicts actually slept in our entryway.

City authorities told us a city-wide heating system would be connected to the building before winter, so in anticipation we installed new pipes in the walls to carry the heat to every room. But as the weather turned cold and winter approached, it became apparent that the promised heat was not coming that year and that our family would be living in freezing temperatures inside that apartment. This was a serious problem, because this was very far north and the city became *very* cold in winter.

I realized we'd have to use those lavish, museum-quality fire-places to provide heat for our family, as much as I didn't want to do it. It would be a necessity for surviving the harsh winter. But transporting wood was very difficult because the apartment was in the very center of that historic city and there was no nearby source of wood. In desperation, our three sons came up with an innovative idea about where to get wood so our family would have heat for the winter. When it's really cold, it's a good time to get creative, and our sons thought of something Denise and I would have never thought of in a million years.

The apartment directly below us was abandoned and destroyed by years of neglect. It is impossible to exaggerate its horrible con-dition. No one owned it at that point, so it had continued to deteriorate. In fact, we learned that the many previous residents of the apartment we purchased had contributed to its sad demise. When we purchased the apartment, our bathroom floor had a hole next to the toilet where men had "missed" the toilet bowl for so many years that the urine had eaten a hole through the floor! For years urine had dripped into the apartment below us.

That huge empty apartment below us was so destroyed that *nothing* could be salvaged from it. Walls were half gone; fireplaces were destroyed and crumbling; windows were broken; and the winter wind was blowing through it. The broken window frames and shattered glass windowpanes were especially bad for us because our apartment was located directly above, and we could feel the effect of the freezing winter wind blowing through the apartment beneath our floor. Our building was constructed from brick and plaster, so our apartment held on to that "cold" almost like it was a refrigerator!

The floors of that apartment below us had once been covered with splendid, expensive parquet with all types of inlaid exotic woods and intricate designs. But now those floors were warped and ruined from water leaks and the long-term acid effects of urine. The parquet was bowed by water damage; it was half ripped up; and it was lying in heaps of irreparable, shattered pieces all over that apartment.

One freezing early morning, Denise and I were pondering what to do with the cold temperatures getting worse by the day. Suddenly our three sons jumped up, put on their coats, dashed out the door, and disappeared as if they were on an urgent mission. When they reappeared some time later, they jubilantly walked through the door of the apartment with heaping armloads of 100-year-old parquet flooring that they had gathered from the floor of the devastated apartment below us.

Denise and I watched with shock as the boys piled that old historic parquet into each of our magnificently restored fireplaces and then worked on each pile until a fire was blazing strong. That wood was so old and dry that it began quickly popping and burning — and soon the brick and plaster walls of that apartment began to warm up in every room, fueled by wood flooring from the apartment below that our sons had collected and used as fuel for the fire.

When the fire started to die down and it felt like the temperatures were dropping, we'd open the metal doors to the fireplaces to see if the fire was going out. If we saw that there was nothing left but embers, the boys would quickly put on their jackets, rush down two flights of steps to the abandoned apartment below, and rip up more flooring (which any eventual buyer would have had to replace anyway).

Soon the boys would be back with armloads of ruined antique parquet flooring. They would first break the dry-rotted parquet into smaller pieces; then they would shove the pieces through the fireplace doors into the fire, and almost immediately the house would start warming up again.

That winter we kept our apartment constantly warm because of the blazing heat that was produced in our fireplaces from the antique flooring of that downstairs abandoned apartment. As long as wood was on the fire, we knew we would have heat. But if there was no wood left to burn, or if only embers remained, it was certain that the fire would go out *unless* we took action. *Fuel was essential to keep those fires going in our fireplaces.*

It's just a fact that when fuel of any sort is depleted, fire eventually goes out.

Often there was enough wood to keep the fire burning, but the embers needed to be stoked — moved around and repositioned with a long poker. We'd insert that long iron rod into the fireplace and rigorously rake the embers back and forth and side to side to provide more oxygen and keep the fire burning longer. In fact, if we didn't regularly stoke those embers and fan the flames, we discovered that the fire could go out even if there *was* enough wood to keep it burning. Those embers had to be tended to regularly to keep the fire going. *We learned that it takes lots of attention and work to keep a fire burning bright.*

It's just a fact that when fuel of any sort is depleted, fire eventually goes out.

When it was my turn to stoke the embers, at times I'd reflect on the apostle Paul's words to Timothy in Second Timothy 1:6, where Paul wrote, "Wherefore I put thee in remembrance that thou *stir up* the gift of God, which is in thee by the putting on of my hands."

The words "stir up" are from the Greek word *anadzoopureoo*, a triple compound of the Greek words, *ana, zoos,* and *pur.* The word *ana* carries the idea of *repeating an earlier action* or *doing something again.* The word *zoos* is from the word *zao,* which means *to be enthusiastic, to be fervent, to be passionate, to be vigorous, to be wholehearted,* or *to be zealous.* The word *pur* is the Greek word for *fire.*

It must be noted that in Classical Greek, fire was *a life-giving force.* Fire was used on the hearths of every ancient home to keep people warm; it was used in matters related to the divine and supernatural; and it was used as a force to defeat enemies. Fire was central to life and considered essential for one's existence. In fact, human life is unsustainable without fire — a point that I'll address in just a moment.

But when these three Greek words are compounded, they form the Greek word *anadzoopureoo* — the very word Paul used in Second Timothy 1:6 when he told the younger minister to "stir up" the gift of God that was in him. It implies that the fire in Timothy's heart had ebbed to embers or was on a low burn. That is the reason Paul told Timothy to begin to passionately and rigorously *stoke* and *stir up* the gift of God in his life. Paul was telling Timothy that just as one would stoke the embers of a fire in a hearth or fireplace, it was time for the younger minister to take action. Paul was commanding Timothy to reach within himself and to begin *to rekindle*, or *kindle anew*, the fire in his heart.

At the time Paul wrote to Timothy, this young man was surrounded by a great deal of chaos and confusion because of the intense persecution that was taking place at that time. It is probable that the younger minister was physically and emotionally exhausted from dealing with an onslaught of problems and that his own spiritual fire was beginning to wane. That is why Paul told him to take action before the fire inside him that burned for the things of God went out completely.

Paul was commanding Timothy to reach within himself
and to begin *to rekindle*, or *kindle anew*,
the fire in his heart.

In other words, Timothy needed to open the door to his heart, look inside to determine the condition of his inward fire, and then take action to stir up the gift of God inside him. Like a person would stoke the coals in a fireplace, Timothy was being called to stir the embers and then "put more wood on the fire."

This would not occur accidentally. Timothy would have to be intentional and proactive to keep that flame burning. But if he would heed Paul's command, that inward fire — which was beginning to wane — would blaze once again in the core of Timothy's spiritual being.

In those early days of living in the former Soviet Union, our family learned the lesson that if we wanted to have heat, we would have to become proactive in making it happen. We had to find fuel; we had to carry it upstairs; we had to open the fireplace door; we had to put the fuel on the fire; and we had to stoke the fuel regularly throughout the day to *keep* it burning. We knew we'd reap a lot of cold, unnecessary discomfort — and even serious trouble — should we decide to neglect what was happening deep in those fireplaces.

If we discovered that the fire had ebbed too low and the coals of wood were turning cold and hard — that we had "hit a low burn" — we would have to begin the process all over. So the choice to be proactive was wiser than reaping the consequences produced by negligence. The truth is, we made the choice to do whatever was required to stay warm — because otherwise, we knew we'd freeze!

It is the same for you. If your spiritual fire is at a low burn or close to going out, it's time for you "to stir up" the gift of God that is inside you. You cannot depend on someone else to do the stoking and stirring for you. It is so vital that you take responsibility to look inside yourself, to determine your fuel supply, and to do whatever you must to stir your spiritual embers and keep your fire burning.

If you'll ask the Holy Spirit, He'll show you how to open the door to your heart and take an honest look on the inside to assess your condition and need. Then you must let Him show you the steps to take and the kinds of fuel you need to activate and fully utilize in your life. You are called to consistently stir up those embers and fuel that fire so you will remain a blazing inferno for Jesus!

If your spiritual fire is at a low burn or close to going out, it's time for you "to stir up" the gift of God that is inside you. You cannot depend on someone else to do the stoking and stirring for you.

WHAT WOULD THE WORLD BE LIKE WITHOUT FIRE?

What would the world be like without fire? Have you ever thought about it? The short answer is that life would be very *primitive*. Without fire, humankind would only have the moon and stars as a light source at night. For early humans, fire was essential to extend the day, provide heat, ward off predators and insects, illuminate dark places, and facilitate cooking. Long before gas and electricity were invented, people totally depended on fire for light, for heat, and for *survival*.

Without fire, there is no light in the dark, no heat in winter, no cooking of meat or baking of bread, no burning bricks, no smelting ore — basically, no civilization. The discovery of fire was one of the greatest discoveries ever made in humanity, and we can't imagine life *without* fire. Fire was needed to create tools and make weapons, and the energy produced by fire was essential for constructing buildings and making machines fueled by the engines of the Industrial Revolution. Finally, fire determined the outcome of two world wars and the ultimate emergence of super-powers in the geopolitical realm.

Today we still use fire to create technology and to make the world a more comfortable place to live. Fire still burns coal and oil to make electricity. In fact, if we were to remove fire from the world, life would be similar to living on the moon! There would be no electricity, no warmth, and no cooked food. Shelter, agriculture, and technology in general would not be able to progress without fire. Without fire, technology would be impossible to create. Metal is shaped to make wires and phones by the use of heat derived from fire. Without metal, no electricity could be transported to facilitate a host of functions needed to keep civilization running.

Fire! We must have it for survival, for development, and for progress! Likewise, we must have *spiritual fire* if we are to move forward in the advancement of God's purposes and in the fulfillment of His great plan!

Wesleyan minister Samuel Chadwick eloquently stated the importance of staying ablaze with spiritual fire. He wrote, "Spirit-filled souls are ablaze for God. They love with a love that glows. They serve with a faith that kindles. They serve with a devotion that consumes. They hate sin with fierceness that burns. They rejoice with a joy that radiates. Love is perfected in the fire of God."[1]

Fire! We must have it for survival, for development, and for progress! Likewise, we must have *spiritual fire* if we are to move forward in the advancement of God's purposes and in the fulfillment of His great plan!

---

[1] Samuel Chadwick quote, *Christian Quotes*, https://www.christianquotes.info/quotes-by-author/samuel-chadwick-quotes/.

So in light of this, I want to ask you...

HOW IS YOUR SPIRITUAL FIRE BURNING?

For you to be effective spiritually and truly fulfilled in life, it is absolutely essential that you remain ablaze with spiritual fire! Perhaps you can remember a time when your heart was literally *ablaze* with a passion for the things of God — but if you were honest with yourself, you'd admit that since that time, the fire has diminished. If that describes your walk with God, have you taken the time to consider:

- What happened along the way to diminish or quench that fire that once burned so brightly?
- What should you have done differently to keep it burning — and what can you do right now to stoke those glowing embers and get your inner fire blazing again?

John Wesley, founder of the Methodist Church, wrote about his own personal concerns regarding the fire of God eventually waning. He noted, "My fear is not that our great movement, known as the Methodists, will eventually cease to exist or one day die from the earth. My fear is that our people will become content to live without the fire, the power, the excitement, the supernatural element that makes us great."[2] Considering the state of the modern Church, Wesley's concerns seem to have been well-founded.

Oh, it's so very vital that we determine to stay ablaze with the Spirit and power of God! And that is what I want to help you with in this book. The chapters that follow in this book are

[2] Ron Brooks, "The Language of Ministry and Calling: Jeremiah," *Church Awakening*, https://churchawakening.com/the-language-of-ministry-and-calling-jeremiah/.

intended to help you identify and embrace the different types of key spiritual fuels you need to remain burning strong for God every day of your life.

In First Thessalonians 5:19, the apostle Paul admonished us, "Quench not the Spirit." Since Paul told us not to quench the Spirit, it means the Holy Spirit *can* be quenched — *which we do not want to do*!

But what does the word "quench" mean in this verse? This word comes from the Greek word *sbennumi*, which means *to extinguish, smother, suppress, douse, put out, snuff out*, or *quell*. It is most often used in the context of *extinguishing a fire by dousing it with water*. In some places, it means *to evaporate* or *to dry up*.

There's no doubt about what Paul is trying to tell us — that if we ignore the Holy Spirit's voice long enough and often enough, eventually we will become spiritually hardened and will no longer be able to hear Him when He does try to speak to us. It will be like His voice *evaporates* or *dries up*, and we will hear it no more.

What a terrible tragedy that is when it happens — but it happens all the time within the Church. Whether Christians realize it or not, if they make a practice of hardening themselves to the Holy Spirit's voice, they separate themselves from the life-giving power of the Gospel that He was sent to unveil and reveal to their hearts — and to perform as a manifested reality in their lives.

If you've ever seen a campfire, you know that its flames can burn very bright and hot. But what happens if someone keeps throwing water on the coals? Initially it will only *dampen* the heat of the flames. But if the person continues to throw water on the flames, eventually that water will *quench, smother*, or *put out* the fire altogether.

> If we ignore the Holy Spirit's voice long enough
> and often enough, eventually we will become spiritually
> hardened and will no longer be able to hear Him
> when He does try to speak to us.

Let me encourage you to never allow cold water to be thrown on the flames of your heart. Do not quench the Spirit! Instead, do everything you can to throw more fuel onto the fire of your heart! When you adopt the attitude that you're going to start fueling your fire, consistently utilizing to the fullest all the fuels God provides, I guarantee you that your inner man will burst into spiritual flames! But you are the only one who can choose to "add the fuel" and "stoke the coals" to keep the Holy Spirit's fire burning brightly in your life.

Before you continue in this book, I encourage you to make a serious commitment before the Lord that you will stay ablaze with God's holy fire for the rest of your days on this earth. Then open your heart to learn more about what is required to do just that. As you learn about the ten types of fuels that will help you stay on fire, set aside time with the Lord to ask Him for His help and *His* strategies as you purpose to add more of each type of fuel to your fire. Then determine to do whatever the Spirit of God tells you to do to keep your inner man burning like a spiritual inferno!

> When you adopt the attitude that you're going to start
> fueling your fire, consistently utilizing to the fullest
> all the fuels God provides, I guarantee you
> that your inner man will burst into spiritual flames!

Think About It

1. It takes a steady supply of fuel to sustain a blazing fire. If your spiritual fire is close to flickering out, it's time to consider how and even why you have neglected "to stir up" the gift of God within you.

   Can you detect where you have given inadequate attention to your own fuel supply? Have you allowed the Word of God and prayer to dwindle in your life because of preoccupation with worldly activity? Have you shifted your attention and become nonchalant in your regard of the Holy Spirit and His voice? What are some practices you need to reinforce in your life to maintain a strong, fiery life in God? The choice to be proactive is wiser than remaining inactive and reaping the consequences of negligence.

2. Inconsistency in spiritual practices and disciplines produces a dullness that may go unnoticed — until you need the power of God to manifest through you. Then, sadly, when you reach for the fire you once knew, you find that the bright flame you vividly recall but left unattended has long since gone out.

   Are you trying to live today based on the memories of your spiritual state yesterday? Memories of the former fire in your life carry no heat forward. The past is over. Each day you must advance in God, or you will actually slip backward into old weaknesses. It's time to bring your spiritual account current. Repent and do your first works again. Rekindle fresh fire on the altar of your heart.

3. Passion and patience go hand in hand to maintain a fiery pursuit of God's plan for your life. The assignment God needs you to accomplish will require you to retain focus and fervency, regardless of circumstances. This means you will need to cultivate habits that will help you not only start strong but also *finish* strong. Wisdom and a steady fuel supply will prevent you from starting with a bang, only to end with a fizzle.

Consider your ways. Do you really know yourself? People are quick to speak of their strengths — which at times are actually idealized or even imaginary! But do you know your own weaknesses? It's important for you to identify and then to eradicate your weak spots through a systematic application of discipline — especially when you don't feel like it.

CHAPTER 2

ABLAZE WITH GOD'S WORD

T he first essential fuel for keeping your spiritual life fiery hot is the consistent intake of the Word of God. This first fuel is absolutely key, because it is foundational to all the other types of fuel we will be discussing in this book. In fact, one of the clearest evidences that a believer is truly on fire for Jesus Christ is his or her undeniable and unquenchable appetite for the Bible.

But even more than fuel, the Bible *itself* is fire — infused with the fiery presence of the Holy Spirit who inspired men to write it. This is confirmed in Jeremiah 23:29, where God declared, "Is not My word like as a fire?..." When God's Word blazes in the human heart, it drives out darkness, provides illumination, brings warmth and fervor into the places that have grown cold, burns away dross, and spreads its flames into the lives of those who are touched by its power.

Nothing can compare to the intense burning effect of the Word of God in the heart of a believer. Jeremiah referred to this when he wrote, "...His *word* was in mine heart as *a burning fire* shut up in my bones..." (Jeremiah 20:9).

Have you ever sensed God's Word like a burning fire shut up in your bones? Have you ever felt its flames ignited within your spirit as you read the Bible? Have you ever sensed the Holy Spirit melting away hardened places in your soul that had grown calloused or indifferent as you put your whole heart into reading His Word?

> When God's Word blazes in the human heart,
> it drives out darkness, provides illumination,
> brings warmth and fervor into the places
> that have grown cold, burns away dross,
> and spreads its flames into the lives
> of those who are touched by its power.

The supernatural impact of God's Word is seen in the reaction of two disciples who were visited by the resurrected Jesus as they walked to the city of Emmaus. In Luke 24:15, the Bible tells us, "And it came to pass, that, while they communed together and reasoned, Jesus himself drew near, and went with them." Verse 27 says, "And beginning at Moses and all the prophets, he [Jesus] expounded unto them in all the *scriptures* the things concerning himself."

Just before Jesus disappeared from the two on that road, Luke 24:31,32 relates what happened next: "And their eyes were opened, and they knew him; and he vanished out of their sight. And they said one to another, Did not our heart *burn* within us, while he talked with us by the way, and while he opened to us the *scriptures*?"

Notice that their hearts "did burn" as Jesus spoke of the Scriptures to them. The word "burn" is translated from a Greek word that means *to ignite*, *to be set on fire*, *to burn*, or even *to be consumed with fire*. The verse actually carries the following ideas:

- "Did not our hearts feel *ignited* within us as he talked with us...?"

- "Did not our hearts feel *set on fire* within us as he talked with us...?"

- "Did not our hearts *burn* within us as he talked with us...?"

- "Did not our hearts feel *consumed with a burning blaze* within us as he talked with us...?"

While Jesus "opened the scriptures" to the two disciples as they walked down the road together, the living Word entered their hearts and *burned* within them. This makes me think of the words of Martin Luther, who said, "The Bible is alive; it speaks to me. It has feet; it runs after me. It has hands; it lays hold of me."[3] You see, there is nothing to compare to the effect of God's Word as it reaches out to grip your spirit man with its convicting power and then to ignite you spiritually from the inside out.

The great American evangelist, D. L. Moody, wrote of how the Bible has the supernatural ability to literally speak to us. He said, "In our prayers, we talk to God; in our Bible study, God talks to us, and we had better let God do most of the talking."[4]

---

[3] Martin H. Manser, ed., *The Westminster Collection of Christian Quotations* (Louisville, KY: Westminster John Knox Press, 2001), p. 21.
[4] R. A. Torrey, *The Importance and Value of Proper Bible Study* (New York: Fleming H. Revell Co., 1921), p. 29.

These words of Moody powerfully remind us that if we'll silence our minds and let the words of the Bible enter our spiritual ears and hearts, those words will come *alive* inside us in the same way the Scriptures were ignited and burned in the hearts of the disciples who walked with Jesus on the road to Emmaus (*see* Luke 24:13-32).

There is nothing to compare to the effect of God's Word
as it reaches out to grip your spirit man
with its convicting power and then to ignite you
spiritually from the inside out.

Like a lighted match put to kindling, when the fire of God's Word is lit in the heart, it sets the heart *on fire*. The power of His Word brightly burns within us when we throw the door open to that divinely energized flame and welcome its cleansing into our lives to bring change.

THE FIERY EFFECT OF GOD'S WORD IN THE HEART

The Bible is like fire in so many ways when it is allowed inside the human heart. For example, as fire purifies metal, the Word of God purifies our consciences. It renews our minds, illuminates our spirits, and drives away darkness. Its brilliant light exposes areas in our lives that need to be changed.

God's Word brings us warmth and comfort in times of difficulty. Oh, how I love to think of the warmth that the Bible brings to my heart! There is no medication that soothes the soul like His Word. Like the warmth and comfort I feel when I draw near to the glowing warmth of a fireplace, the Word of God warms my heart when I sit before it and allow its life-giving truth to permeate my being.

I have discovered time and again that when I draw near to the Bible, it comforts me. There are no words to adequately express the warmth and comfort the Bible brings to me or to *anyone* who makes room for its life-giving presence in his or her life.

Like the warmth and comfort I feel when I draw near
to the glowing warmth of a fireplace, the Word of God
warms my heart when I sit before it and allow
its life-giving truth to permeate my being.

In addition to bringing us comfort, the fiery impact of God's Word also awakens us to areas of our lives that need to be transformed by His Spirit.

The English preacher, Charles Haddon Spurgeon, spoke often of this fiery effect of the Word of God. He noted that if a person puts his finger in fire, he quickly feels the effect of the fire. Likewise, Spurgeon noted, a person immediately knows he has come into contact with the presence of God when his or her spirit is touched by the powerful, fiery truth of God's Word.

A believer will sense the effect of God's Word if he allows the flames of its truth to erupt in his heart. When that believer hears the Scriptures expounded by the anointing of the Holy Spirit, or when he reads the Bible to take it by faith into his heart, its supernatural power is *unleashed*. And when that happens, that person's heart, will, thoughts, emotions, and memories are all touched by God's power as if by fire.

The life in those words awakens the recipient to receive a greater measure of God's presence into his life in the divine process of transformation. And as that Christian drills deep and by faith taps into the divine power and presence contained in the Holy Spirit-inspired words in the Bible, the spiritual force that is released can change *anything*!

Fire has *melting power*. And those who are willing to let the Word of God do its deeper work will see stubbornness and unbelief melting away in their lives. Even the stony hearts of those who seem to let nothing move them can melt like wax when they come under the influence of the anointed Word. The hardest heart has been known to melt when it comes near the intense heat of the spiritual fire released by the Word of God.

Fire is used in the natural world to burn garbage, among other things. Likewise, when the Bible is ingested into the soul, its divine fire identifies, ignites, and consumes debris that needs to be expunged from a person's life. That fire also ignites new life in areas of a person that have grown indifferent and resistant to God's will.

Furthermore, when your heart is truly set ablaze and you continue to yield to that spiritual process, the fire of God's Word will keep on brilliantly burning, spreading throughout your entire system as long as you surrender to its transforming work. Just keep allowing that consuming fire to burn off any "chaff" left in the soul that hinders your spiritual progress and see what God will do!

When the Bible is ingested into the soul,
its divine fire identifies, ignites, and consumes debris
that needs to be expunged from a person's life.

This is why English theologian John Stott said, "We must allow the Word of God to confront us, to disturb our security, to undermine our complacency, and to overthrow our patterns of thought and behavior." The word "allow" in that statement is important. We must choose to yield to the fiery effect of God's Word working in us — because that process is not always comfortable, to say the least, as it blazes a fire so strong that it incinerates those things that are displeasing to the Spirit and need to be removed. When everything is said and done, only the Word of God has the power to permanently transform a life!

FIRE PURIFIES, ILLUMINATES, AND EMPOWERS

Fire is a *purifier*. And when the Bible is given entrance into the heart and acted upon by faith, it takes on that characteristic of fire as it begins to do its purifying work in us.

The psalmist wrote of the purifying effect of God's Word in Psalm 119:9 when he said, "Wherewithal shall a young man *cleanse* his way? by taking heed thereto according to *thy word*." In John 15:3, Jesus spoke of the cleansing quality of God's Word when he said, "Now ye are *clean* through the *word* which I have spoken unto you." In Second Corinthians 7:1, Paul also wrote of the way the Holy Spirit uses the promises of God's Word to take us into greater levels of sanctification and purity. Paul wrote, "Having therefore these *promises*, dearly beloved, let us cleanse ourselves from all filthiness of the flesh and spirit, perfecting holiness in the fear of God."

Throughout history, fire has also been a source of *illumination*. Likewise, when the words of the Bible are allowed into the heart and soul, those divinely inspired words illuminate our paths. This is why Psalm 119:105 says, "Thy *word* is a *lamp* unto my feet, and a *light* unto my path." Psalm 119:130 further says, "The entrance of thy *words* giveth *light*...."

When the Bible is received and believed, it acts in the same way that a lamp provides light for a darkened room in the natural realm. God's truth that is embraced shines light into every sphere of life, bringing understanding and enlightenment and eradicating the ignorance that governs darkened minds.

The Scriptures are God's lamp, designed to give continuous light to a people or society that would lie in darkness if the source of that light was removed. Only the light of God's Word drives away spiritual darkness — which is why demonic forces hate the Light *and* the Light-bearers!

God's truth that is embraced shines light
into every sphere of life, bringing understanding
and enlightenment and eradicating the ignorance
that governs darkened minds.

When the Word of God is heeded, embraced, and believed, it continuously shines its brilliant light into the dark, murky places of our lives. Whenever any person reads and gives heed to God's Word, allowing its powerful light to shine into his or her life, that light will dispel spiritual darkness.

History has proven this to be true, not only in the past, but even in this present time. Entire nations where darkness once ruled are being changed because of the penetrating light of God's Word. When the Bible is proclaimed, believed, and applied, it eradicates spiritual darkness, ignorance, disease, inequality, poverty, and racism. The Bible is a life-enhancer for all who benefit from its shining light.

Those who reject the Word remain in darkness, but those who embrace it are delivered from spiritual darkness and ignorance. These blessed ones are thrust into light that illuminates the path for all who love the Word and preach its truths. The Bible provides freedom for the mind, strength and resolve for the will, healing for the body, vision for a bright future, and light for the path ahead.

Within the covers of the Bible are all the answers for every problem man could ever face. The Bible can bring new life to hearts, establish order to confused minds, and refresh souls that are being rocked by emotion.

When God's Word is decreed from a person's mouth that is connected to a believing heart, that Word has a life-changing and yoke-destroying effect. There is power in the Word of God that even the devil cannot deny!

Fire *empowers* the mightiest engines to operate! Likewise, when the Bible is ignited in the heart, it supernaturally empowers those who take it deeply into themselves. Just as fire empowers engines to operate, scriptures that are released in a believer's life unloose supernatural energy and power to enable him to rise above himself and to master whatever challenge he may be facing.

A hallmark verse of my own personal life is Ecclesiastes 8:4, which says, "Where the word of a king is, there is power...." I vow before you that when God's Word is received as the all-authoritative word of our divine King, it imparts power beyond imagination and transforms weaklings to do feats beyond their natural capacity!

Those who previously felt weak and insufficient are suddenly energized when the power of God's Word is released into their lives. In fact, the truths of Scripture will impart supernatural strength to a believer to do *whatever* God has commanded him or her to do.

Psalm 119:28 marvelously depicts the powerful effect of God's Word to divinely energize a person who otherwise would feel physically or emotionally weak. When the psalmist was confronted with his own humanity, he knew that the Word would strengthen him to rise above it. That is why he said, "...*Strengthen* thou me according unto *thy word*."

> I vow before you that when God's Word is received
> as the all-authoritative word of our divine King,
> it imparts power beyond imagination
> and transforms weaklings to do feats
> beyond their natural capacity!

The role of the Bible cannot be underestimated in the life of a believer. In fact, the amount of spiritual fire one has burning at his core is directly related to how much of God's Word he plants in his heart.

This is why J. C. Ryle, a prominent evangelical Anglican bishop during the 1800s, pleaded to his readers, "I call upon you not to forget the book of the soul. Do not let newspapers, novels, and romances be read, while the prophets and apostles be despised. Do not let the exciting and sensual swallow up your attention, while the edifying and the sanctifying can find no place in your mind."[5]

---

[5] J. C. Ryle, *Thoughts for Young Men* (Shawnee, KS: Gideon House Books, 2015; originally published 1865).

R. A. Torrey — evangelist, pastor, educator, and writer — further stated, "Ninety-nine Christians in every hundred are merely playing at Bible study; and therefore ninety-nine Christians in every hundred are mere weaklings, when they might be giants."[6]

When Christians could be spiritual giants, they are often weaklings because they have ignored the source of fuel that could empower them to be mighty!

When Christians could be spiritual giants,
they are often weaklings because they have ignored
the source of fuel that could
empower them to be mighty!

Friend, there is nothing to compare to the powerful effect of God's Word when it is taken by faith into the heart and put into action.

As Martin Luther famously wrote in his hymn, "A Mighty Fortress Is Our God," a single word of the Bible is sufficient to trounce even the forces of hell:

> **...And though this world, with devils filled,**
> **Should threaten to undo us,**
> **We will not fear, for God hath willed**
> **His truth to triumph through us.**
> **The Prince of Darkness grim —**
> **We tremble not for him;**
> **His rage we can endure,**
> **For lo! His doom is sure —**
> ***One little word*** [of God] ***shall fell him....***

---

[6] Fred Sanders, *How God Used R. A. Torrey: A Short Biography as Told Through His Sermons* (Chicago: Moody Publishers, 2015).

Jesus Was the Word Made Flesh

Jesus was the Word made flesh among us (*see* John 1:1,2,14). And when we love God's Word and allow its fiery truth to burn within us, we are actually coming ablaze with Christ Himself.

We should continually assess how we are honoring or dishonoring the Word of God, the kind of space we make for the Word in our lives, the amount of time we spend daily in the Word, and how well we obey what the Word says. All these are signs that reveal the type of relationship we have with Jesus. In John 14:15, Jesus said, "If ye love me, keep my commandments." In other words, how much we love Him is evidenced by how we respond to His Word.

It is impossible to separate the Word of God from Jesus, for He is the Word made flesh. How you treat the Bible is a reflection of your level of intimacy with Him. If you neglect the Bible because you don't think you have time for it, in actuality you are unintentionally ignoring your relationship with Jesus.

How you treat the Bible is a reflection
of your level of intimacy with Him.

Jesus *is* the Word! He was conceived by the Spirit in the womb of Mary as she received the Word of God into her heart (*see* Luke 1:38). He was the living Word made manifest (*see* John 1:14). He launched His ministry with the Word of God (*see* Luke 4:16). And as you read the four Gospels — Matthew, Mark, Luke, and John — it is clear that everywhere Jesus went, He spoke the Word of God with power and authority. It flowed from Him because He was the Word of God.

Matthew 4:23 says, "Jesus went about all Galilee, teaching in their synagogues, and preaching the gospel of the kingdom, and healing all manner of sickness and all manner of disease among the people." The word "teaching" in this verse is translated from the Greek word *didasko*, which is a word that emphatically alerts us to the fact that Jesus was expounding the Bible in those meetings! When those in synagogues heard Jesus, they were amazed and dumbfounded, even *aghast*, because they had never heard the Scriptures illuminated so powerfully.

Luke 4:36 (*NLT*) says it this way: "...The people exclaimed, 'What authority and power this man's words possess! Even evil spirits obey him and flee at his command!'" Although listeners had heard the Old Testament expounded many times in their synagogues, they had never heard it as Jesus delivered it. Of course, He was the Word of God, and when He spoke, a river of powerful truth flowed from the lips of the Living Word Himself. As He spoke, truth was revealed on a level they had never heard before.

Jesus' sermon texts are explained by the usage of the Greek word *didasko* in Matthew 4:23. In this case, it indeed refers to the systematic teaching of Scripture. This tells us that Jesus' text was not focused on politics, economy, or other popular themes of the day, although the Bible deals with many of these topics. When Jesus opened His mouth, it was the Word of God itself that flowed from His lips. The Master Teacher seized each opportunity to open the Scriptures and nourish souls and spirits.

Jesus was the Word made flesh (*see* John 1:14). God's Word was Jesus' identity — and as a result, His entire public ministry was devoted to flooding men's souls with the words of His Father as He taught and preached for anyone who had ears to hear them.

ADDICTED TO THE WORD

The apostles ministered side by side with Jesus for three years and watched how He ministered the Word of God. As Jesus' disciples, the apostles learned to replicate what He did. So when the New Testament Church began in the book of Acts, they continued to do exactly what they saw Jesus do. He was their Example.

God's Word was Jesus' identity — and as a result,
His entire public ministry was devoted
to flooding men's souls with the words of His Father
as He taught and preached for anyone
who had ears to hear them.

Therefore, since Jesus focused on the Word of God with miraculous results, the apostles also went about preaching and teaching the Word of God — and they experienced the same miraculous results. Jesus dedicated Himself fully to the Word and to delivering it to others. The apostles did the same thing as the Early Church was getting on its feet. This is why Acts 2:42 tells us:

And they [early believers] **continued steadfastly in the apostles' doctrine and fellowship, and in breaking of bread, and in prayers.**

The word "steadfastly" means to *persevere consistently*. It carries the idea of *very intense focus and hard work*. This tells us that when the early believers came together in those early meetings, they really set their hearts to listen and to learn from the apostles as the Word of God was preached and taught to them. They wanted the Word to ignite their hearts and souls and become ablaze inside them! This word "steadfastly" pictures *constant diligence* and *effort that never gives up.*

The word for "steadfastly" carries such a strong meaning that it actually signifies those early believers were *addicted* to the teaching of the apostles. They were so enthralled with it and so ignited by it that they gathered to hear and receive it every day (*see* Acts 2:46).

When we hear the word "addiction," we usually think of that word in a negative context. But consider the fuller meaning of the word "addiction" for a moment. If a person is addicted to drugs, he can't get by without the substance to which he is addicted. If an addict goes without that substance for a period of time, he feels the absence of it and can even get sick from the lack of it. A serious addict can't live without the substance of his addiction.

Keep that in mind as we consider the word "steadfastly" in Acts 2:42. Those early believers literally craved the apostles' teachings. They were addicted to the apostles' teaching of God's Word and to the transformative effects of that teaching in their lives. It nourished them, healed them, and empowered them. Their lives were radically changed as the Word was poured into them. They became so addicted to the powerful exposition of God's Word that they gathered every day to receive a daily dose of the Scriptures.

This is the kind of passion God wants us to have for the Bible in our lives. He wants us to burn with desire for the depths of the Word. It doesn't matter how much of the Bible you already know, it holds depths of revelation truth that you have never experienced, and its voice is beckoning you to come deeper into its waters.

As John Owen, an English church leader and theologian, stated, "In the divine Scriptures, there are shallows and there are deeps; shallows where the lamb may wade, and deeps where the elephant may swim."[7] The depth to which we plunge into the Scriptures depends entirely upon us. But if we are willing, Christ is calling us to go deeper and deeper into unfathomable depths of the Bible that will satisfy the hungry heart like nothing else can do.

It doesn't matter how much of the Bible
you already know, it holds depths of revelation truth
that you have never experienced, and its voice
is beckoning you to come deeper into its waters.

Furthermore, God doesn't just want us to take an occasional dip into these divine waters. He actually wants us to be like those early believers in Acts 2, *persevering consistently and never letting up* in our pursuit of the Scriptures. God wants every Christian — and that means you — to intensely focus on the Word of God and crave it with the intensity that an addict craves his next fix.

The biblical pattern in the book of Acts also reveals that if we will give the Word of God a preeminent position in our lives, we also put ourselves in a position for the miraculous to take place. Where God's Word is honored, embraced, and declared, the Holy Spirit supernaturally works to confirm it with supernatural signs and wonders!

THE WORD PRODUCES WONDERS

In the last chapter, we saw that where the Gospel is preached, the power of God is ignited. We can also see in the Word that where the Bible is taught in authoritative power, this, too, triggers a release of God's power in the Church.

---

[7] *The Life, Thought, and Writings of John Owen*, JohnOwen.org/quotes.

A. B. Simpson, the Canadian preacher, theologian, author, and pioneer of global missions, said, "The religion of the Bible is wholly supernatural."[8] If you want to experience the supernatural work of the Holy Spirit in your life, you must make the authoritative teaching of the Bible a priority. Where the Word is declared in power, it sets the atmosphere for the miraculous to take place.

Jesus taught the Word with authority, which resulted in signs and wonders. The apostles preached the Word exactly as Jesus had preached, and it also resulted in a supernatural working of the Holy Spirit as He confirmed the Word with signs and wonders. Mark 16:20 says, "…They went forth, and preached everywhere, the Lord working with them, and *confirming the Word with signs following….*"

Where the Word is declared in power,
it sets the atmosphere
for the miraculous to take place.

Never forget that the book of Acts is not merely a history book; it is a *pattern* book. As you follow the pattern in the book of Acts, you will see that early believers continued steadfastly in the apostles' teaching. They were addicted to that teaching. In fact, they continually craved *more* of it. And in the midst of this season of intense hunger for God's Word, Acts 2:43 tells us what followed: "…Many wonders and signs were done…." Signs and wonders occurred concurrently with the early believers' intense focus on the anointed proclamation of biblical truth.

---

[8] A. B. Simpson, *Days of Heaven on Earth: A Daily Devotional To Comfort and Inspire* (Chicago: Moody Publishers, 1984), May 14.

This was not just an atypical instance that occurred in the early days of the Church. The pattern revealed in Acts 4:31 shows us that when believers were gathered together for prayer and the Word was proclaimed, the supernatural once again took place. In fact, there was so much power manifested during that prayer meeting that "the place was shaken where they were assembled together...."

The word "shaken" literally means *to shake, teeter, wobble,* or *reel.* The physical building and all those inside it shook, teetered, wobbled, and reeled as the power of God manifested! I want to ask — have you ever been in a meeting where you saw people fall under the power of the Holy Spirit? You might answer yes, and that's wonderful — but have you ever witnessed *an entire building* shaking because of the level of power that invaded it during a corporate prayer meeting?

In Acts 6, as the narrative continues, we read that a time came when deacons were chosen to oversee the daily distribution of food among the widows in the church at Jerusalem. After the apostles laid their hands on them and prayed, verse 7 says, "And the word of God increased; and the number of the disciples multiplied in Jerusalem greatly; and a great company of the priests were obedient to the faith."

Notice that it says, "the word of God increased." Immediately following that verse is Acts 6:8, which says, "And Stephen, full of faith and power, did great wonders and miracles among the people." Once again, we see that signs, wonders, miracles, and powerful manifestations occurred during a time when the anointed proclamation of the Word of God was on the increase!

Then in Acts 8, we find Philip ministering the Word to an Ethiopian official in a royal chariot. Acts 8:30-35 tells us that as Philip shared from the book of Isaiah with this noble Ethiopian, the miraculous again followed the anointed declaration of God's Word. After the Ethiopian was saved and water-baptized, Philip was supernaturally translated to the coastal town of Azotus.

The biblical pattern lets us know that this was no accident. The supernatural event coincided with the anointed proclamation of the Word of God. The pattern in the book of Acts shows that God's miraculous power is unleashed when His Word is declared by the anointing of His Spirit!

We see this over and over throughout the four gospels in the life of Jesus and throughout the book of Acts. Wherever the Word is taught or preached with authority, it is followed with divine supernatural activity.

The pattern in the book of Acts shows that God's miraculous power is unleashed when His Word is declared by the anointing of His Spirit!

Of course, the greatest miracle of all is that moment when a person is born again. We can never minimize the miraculous nature of this event. But there is no question about it — when the Word of God is believed, embraced, and declared with authority and power, there is a response from Heaven, as witnessed in Scripture and throughout history. Signs, wonders, miracles, and healings are unleashed!

The Word of God is a mighty sword wielded by the Holy Spirit! He uses that divine "sword of the Spirit" to slice open lost men's hearts, attack the works of Satan, and perform divine surgery on every category of people who are afflicted in any way. The Word of God — which is the sword of the Spirit — is the instrument the Holy Spirit uses to heal, restore, and make people whole.

Hebrews 4:12 (*AMP*) makes this abundantly clear:

For the word of God is living and active and full of power [making it operative, energizing, and effective]. It is sharper than any two-edged sword, penetrating as far as the division of the soul and spirit [the completeness of a person], and of both joints and marrow [the deepest parts of our nature], exposing and judging the very thoughts and intentions of the heart.

Satan knows the life-transforming power that is locked inside the Bible. That's why he fights so hard to get believers and churches to back away from it. He lures them to water it down, modify it, or even eliminate it. (*Note:* I discuss this demonic attack in-depth in my book *How To Keep Your Head on Straight in a World Gone Crazy*. I urge you to obtain that book and read it.)

The Word of God is a mighty sword
wielded by the Holy Spirit!
He uses that divine "sword of the Spirit"
to slice open lost men's hearts,
attack the works of Satan,
and perform divine surgery on every category
of people who are afflicted in any way.

Satan knows that if he can coax believers to back off the Bible and stop declaring it in authority and power, the supernatural work of the Holy Spirit will diminish. One always follows the other, because the anointed declaration of Scripture always goes hand in hand with signs and wonders following.

Some suggest that the Bible is outdated and that its voice is no longer applicable to our times. But as English preacher Charles Spurgeon said, "Nobody ever outgrows Scripture; the book widens and deepens with our years."[9] Likewise, I want to tell you that the times and culture may fluctuate and change, but the voice of Scripture never changes. And the deeper you delve into the Word, the more you will discover that it is impossible to outgrow it.

D. L. Moody challenged his listeners and readers, "If I utter a syllable that is not justified by the Scriptures, don't believe me. The Bible is the only rule. Walk by it and it alone."[10] American pastor and author A. W. Tozer wrote of the never-ending relevancy of the Bible when he said, "The Bible is not only a book which was once spoken, but a book which is *now* speaking."[11]

> The times and culture may fluctuate and change,
> but the voice of Scripture never changes.

The Bible is as relevant as ever; it is indeed a book that is now speaking. Like the disciples on the road to Emmaus, you will find the words of the Bible begin to burn inside you as you purpose to take it deeper into your spirit.

MY PERSONAL WORD ON THIS SUBJECT

As a founding pastor of several significant churches and leader of a ministry with a global outreach to many parts of the world, I am able to speak to this with a level of authority. And I strongly

---

[9] *The Charles Spurgeon Sermon Collection,* https://www.thekingdomcollective.com/spurgeon/.

[10] D. L. Moody, *The Way Home* (Chicago: The Bible Institute Colportage Assoc., 1904), p. 94.

[11] A. W. Tozer quote, "Quotes," *Tony Cooke Ministries,* https://www.tonycooke.org/quotes/.

affirm that a passion for the Word of God — *the Bible* — must first be alive in the hearts of spiritual leadership if it is to be ignited in those who follow them.

We who hold positions of spiritual leadership *must* demonstrate love and honor for the Scriptures and impart that same love and honor to the people we are charged to lead. We are called to herald the truth in such a way that it makes people hungry, stirring their appetite for more knowledge and understanding of the Scriptures and a deeper relationship with Jesus. We must read and study God's Word with serious minds and with committed, steadfast hearts. A surface "skim" will not do. To unlock the power that resides in the words the Bible contains, we must delve *deeply*. It must be our lifelong aim to understand the Word more comprehensively and to perceive ever more clearly what God is saying to us in it.

This I how I view my life task. My God-appointed pursuit is to grow ever deeper in my understanding of God's Word, to never depart from the eternal truths contained in it, and to convey to others its life-giving, transforming power through the work of the Holy Spirit. Any spiritual leader who deviates from this has departed from his principal task to be God's voice to the Church and in the earth.

It must be our lifelong aim to understand the Word
more comprehensively and to perceive
ever more clearly what God is saying to us in it.

World-renowned evangelist Billy Graham noted the importance of the Bible when he said, "If you are ignorant of God's

Word, you will always be ignorant of God's will."[12] But how many people struggle to find God's will today? The wrestling would cease in most cases if they would align themselves with the voice of Scripture.

The majority of what Christians need to know — or at least the principles needed to answer their questions — are clearly provided in the Bible. Instead, Christians search for answers by reading book after book or by listening to one preacher after another, often never finding what they are seeking. Yet if they would just open the Bible and read it — *and then actually believe what they read!* — they would find the answers they endlessly seek. God's answers belong to anyone who will open his or her Bible and dig into it.

Harry Ironside — Bible teacher, preacher, theologian, pastor, and author — said this: "It is well to remember that reading books about the Bible is a very different thing to searching the Word for oneself."[13] Famed missionary Jim Elliot said, "Why do you need a voice when you have a verse?"[14]

How many people struggle to find God's will today?
The wrestling would cease in most cases if they
would align themselves with the voice of Scripture.

If we take God's Word into our lives as our most important fuel, it will release its divine blazing fire inside us to internally change us. The Holy Spirit will then work to authenticate that

---

[12] Franklin Graham, *Billy Graham in Quotes* (Nashville: Thomas Nelson, 2011), "Billy Graham on God's Will."
[13] H. A. Ironside, *Proverbs and Song of Solomon* (Grand Rapids, MI: Kregel Academic, 2006), p. 23.
[14] Jeffrey Farmer, *Small Church, Excellent Ministry: A Guidebook for Pastors* (Eugene, OR: Wipf and Stock, 2017), p. 6.

fiery force with supernatural demonstrations of His power, just as the biblical pattern shows that He has done throughout history wherever the Word has been declared with the bold confidence of faith that what God says is altogether true.

Only the Word can bring the answers people seek to be internally changed or to see supernatural wonders released in their lives and the lives of those around them. D. L. Moody lamented the absence of power in the Church and pinpointed the reason for it when he said, "The reason why we have so little success in our teaching is because we know so little of the Word of God."[15] And A. W. Tozer emphatically stated, "Nothing less than a whole Bible can make a whole Christian."[16]

This means if we want people to be made whole, we have to give them the Bible, for it is the divine instrument that will bring them to wholeness. If we really want to see the miraculous presence of God in our lives, we must do what the early Christians did. As we fearlessly preach the Word, the power in that Word will bring the supernatural presence of God into manifestation.

GIVE THE WORD CENTER STAGE

Because I am privileged to travel all across the world to teach God's Word in conferences, seminars, and churches, I've been able to acquire a global view of what is happening in the Church at large.

What I see in many churches is very disturbing. Although I encounter wonderful churches with a passion for the Word of God, I also see that many people in the Body of Christ are

---

[15] Dwight Lyman Moody, *The New Sermons of Dwight Lyman Moody* (New York: Henry & Goodspeed, 1880), p. 342.
[16] A. W. Tozer, *Of God and Men* (Chicago: Moody Publishers, 1960, 2015), Chapter 18.

becoming biblically illiterate. Not only do these Christians not know elementary facts, such as the books of the Bible, primary biblical characters, and well-known Bible stories, but they are unschooled in basic Christian doctrines. The verse-by-verse teaching of the Bible has often been replaced by motivational and inspirational preaching. These types of preaching have merit. But if this is all people hear, it eventually results in people remaining ignorant about the most basic Bible truths. As Hosea 4:6 says, people are "…destroyed for lack of knowledge…."

"Nothing less than a whole Bible
can make a whole Christian."
— *A. W. Tozer*

Study the history of many of the traditional, denominational churches, and you'll discover that when those churches first began, they declared the Word of God with fire! The pulpit — the place from which the Word was taught — was the center of activity because nothing held a higher position than the authoritative voice of the Bible. In earlier days, the declaration of Scripture was strong and those denominations blazed with the power of the Spirit. But along the way, many denominations shifted their focus from the teaching of the Bible to religious rites, rituals, and liturgy.

Every time the anointed proclamation of the Bible takes a second seat to these other elements of man's tradition and preference, history shows that the power of the Holy Spirit begins to diminish and the supernatural activity of the Holy Spirit begins to subside in the Church. Many traditional churches even have pulpits that are shifted to the side of the stage rather than holding center stage, subliminally revealing that the Word of God is no longer central in that setting but has become secondary in importance.

So I want to ask you — what is center stage in the church you attend? Is it the anointed declaration of the Word, as it was in Jesus' ministry and as is shown in the pattern in the book of Acts, or has the Word been replaced by something else? If the focus has shifted from a bold stand on the infallible Word of God to something else, what has taken its place as the central focus? And if there *has* been a shift, a question of great importance is this: Do you still see the same supernatural manifestations of the Holy Spirit that were witnessed earlier when the emphasis was on a solid foundation of Bible truths?

An example of a shift in many churches is the focus from the Word to an emphasis on music and worship. Anointed music and worship are powerful fuels in the life of a believer or in a healthy church, as I will show you in Chapter 6. But this type of shift in emphasis actually results in a *lower* level of worship. Music may temporarily stir emotion, but the diminishing of the Word's importance in that body of believers will eventually result in a loss of God's power being manifested.

There is no doubt that anointed music and worship provides important fuel to help bring us into a spiritual atmosphere where the Holy Spirit is free to work. But this is *not* equivalent to the proclamation of the Bible. If you face challenges and trials along the way in your walk with God, you need the *Word* to stand on, not music, no matter how spiritual. The only foundation strong enough to hold you steady in times of trouble is the Word of God.

There is nothing more important than believing, embracing, and declaring the Word of God, and only His Word is strong enough to build our lives upon. The Bible must always be the *primary* focus, not the *secondary* focus. The bold and anointed proclamation of the Word must be emphasized in teaching and preaching if our lives are going to be changed from the inside out and if we are going to experience a supernatural working of the Holy Spirit in the Church.

The only foundation strong enough
to hold you steady in times of trouble
is the Word of God.

Never forget that the Word of God and the power of God go hand in hand. If you remove God's Word, it will result eventually in the diminishing of God's supernatural activity in the life of a church and in your personal life.

So in conclusion, I want to ask you — since the Bible is itself a fire that ignites us, and since it is a fuel that triggers a divine release of power in your life, what place in your life are you giving the Bible? The answer to that question may give you insight into the reason you are experiencing power or *a lack of* power in your own walk with God.

Remember those words of A. B. Simpson: "The religion of the Bible is wholly supernatural." If you want the supernatural power of God to be a part of your life, the Bible must be central — for wherever the Word is authoritatively proclaimed, embraced, believed, and acted upon, the power of God is released!

But let's go on to see the next vital fuel you need to keep the fire of God burning strongly and brightly in your heart. I'm referring to the fire that explodes inside you when you devote yourself to *prayer*. Get ready — because when you learn how to pray effectively the way Scripture teaches, your prayers will literally detonate the power of God in your life, in the lives of those you are praying for, and in the midst of any situation you will ever face or any environment you will ever find yourself in!

THINK ABOUT IT

1. What priority do you give to reading the Bible each day? The value you ascribe to the Word of God reflects the quality of your fellowship with God. Every time you allow the Bible to take second place to other activities, you make less room for the supernatural power of God to operate in your life.

   When you are faced with challenges or life decisions, does the Bible hold the preeminent influence and authority in your life? Or do you confer with people and search out trending opinions? Do you neglect to read the Bible daily because you think you don't have time for it? Your answers to these questions are a direct link to the level of power you are experiencing in your own walk with God. What adjustments does your own heart prompt you to make in order to increase your awareness of a greater measure of God's presence in your life?

2. God's Word is a two-edged sword that will both comfort and confront you. The fiery impact of the Word will comfort you with the assuring warmth of His life-giving promises. Its transformative fire will also confront the cold, hardened, and unresponsive places in your heart — purifying your conscience and illuminating your mind.

   The words you think on and speak not only build the foundation of your life, but also shape the atmosphere around you while laying track for the future before you. Do you seize each opportunity to saturate your soul with the Word of God, or are you valuing other words above His?

3. God upholds all things by the word of His power (*see* Hebrew 1:3). Is God's Word what you rely upon to hold you steady when the pressure is on? Do you continually fuel yourself on words of healing so that when your health is challenged, the word of his power keeps you unshaken? Do you maintain a regular intake of God's Word regarding wisdom and prosperity so that when lack or financial insufficiency threaten you, the word of His power emboldens you to expect God's hand to guide you into a wealthy place?

Give the word of God's power permission to make your thoughts agreeable to His will so He can set you on fire as you walk together.

CHAPTER 3

ABLAZE WITH PRAYER

L et's continue our study on the kinds of fuels that cause believers to sustain their spiritual fire throughout their time on this earth — and that cause a church to blaze strongly in power and effectiveness for generations.

The next type of fuel — one that is absolutely vital in keeping the fire burning *hot* — is *prayer*. Throughout history, individuals and congregations who lived ablaze with the power of God were devoted to prayer. And the same is true for today — a key fuel to ignite the Church and sustain its fire for God in these last days is *a vibrant, consistent prayer life.*

Nothing can replace prayer as the essential fuel we must add *and keep adding* to keep our spiritual fire burning. Prophetic minister Leonard Ravenhill stated this so powerfully: "No man is greater than his prayer life. The pastor who is not praying is playing; the people who are not praying are straying. We have many organizers, but few agonizers; many players and payers, few pray-ers; many singers, few clingers; lots of pastors, few wrestlers; many fears, few tears; much fashion, little passion; many interferers, few intercessors; many writers, but few fighters. Failing here [in prayer], we fail everywhere."[17]

THE GOD WHO HEARS AND ANSWERS!

In Jeremiah 33:3, God extends an extraordinary invitation with great promise to every Christian who will hear His voice:

Call unto me, and I will answer thee, and show thee great and mighty things, which thou knowest not.

To call unto God is a reference to passionate prayer. And according to this verse, if we do our part in prayer, God will show us great and mighty things that are astounding — beyond what the natural mind can comprehend. This task of calling unto God is the glorious assignment He has given to every individual believer and to the Church as a whole.

"No man is greater than his prayer life.
The pastor who is not praying is playing;
the people who are not praying are straying."
— *Leonard Ravenhill*

The Early Church believed this verse with all their hearts, and because they believed it, they called unto God. As a result, He heard them and answered their prayers. A study of the book

---

[17] Leonard Ravenhill quote, "Quotes and Sayings About Intercession," *Famous Quotes and Sayings,* https://quotessayings.net/topics/intercessors/.

of Acts shows that early believers passionately prayed and God responded positively with mighty demonstrations of His power.

A. C. Dixon, a well-known Bible expositor, said, "When we depend upon organizations, we get what organizations can do; when we depend upon education, we get what education can do; when we depend upon man, we get what man can do; but when we depend upon prayer, we get what God can do."[18]

Early Christians depended on the power of God, and they regularly called on Him to move among them. As a result, they consistently experienced the power of God on a miraculous level as the power of darkness was driven back. This explains why Samuel Chadwick wrote, "The one concern of the devil is to keep Christians from praying. He fears nothing from prayerless studies, prayerless work, and prayerless religion. He laughs at our toil, mocks at our wisdom, but he trembles when we pray."[19]

I like how author Max Lucado said it: "When we work, we work; but when we pray, God works."[20] Oh, how we must learn to lean upon God in prayer! We must not lean on our own efforts, for it's only as we press into God's presence in prayer and call out to Him that we activate His promise to answer us with mind-boggling power and answers that are beyond our natural ability to comprehend.

I recall the words of E. M. Bounds, who also wrote about the power that is released through prayer. He stated, "What the

---

[18] A. C. Dixon quote, "Prayer," *Tony Cooke Ministries*, https://www.tonycooke.org/free_resources/messages/quotes/quote6.html.

[19] Samuel Chadwick quote, "Prayer and Mission Quotations," *World Mission Prayer League*, https://wmpl.org/quote/the-one-concern-of-the-devil/.

[20] Ruthie Jacobsen, *The Difference Is Prayer* (Hagerstown, MD: Review and Herald Publishing Assoc., 1998), p. 8.

church needs today is not machinery or, better, not new organizations or more and novel methods, but men whom the Holy Spirit can use — *men mighty in prayer.* The Holy Spirit does not flow through methods, but through men of prayer."[21]

It's only as we press into God's presence in prayer
and call out to Him that we activate His promise
to answer us with mind-boggling power and answers
that are beyond our natural ability to comprehend.

When we study the book of Acts, we find that the Early Church had no machinery or equipment on which to rely. Realizing their total dependency on God, these early believers pressed into prayer. The result was a release of torrential power that enabled the followers of Jesus Christ to take the Gospel to the ends of the known world in that age.

Let's turn our attention again to the book of Acts. As I have told you, Acts is not merely a history book, but it is also *a pattern book* to show us how God worked throughout the centuries and still works in the Church today.

In the book of Acts, we see a pattern of powerful prayer that God established among early believers right from the start. As you will see, early Christians' lives were literally *ablaze* with prayer. They prayed at *all times* of day and night and in a variety of locations about *everything* that concerned them.

Let's take a look at how, when, and where it is recorded that early Christians prayed and what resulted from their times of prayer. Let's begin in Acts chapter 1, where the Bible tells us that

---

[21] E. M. Bounds quote, "Quotes on Prayer," *ACTS413 Ministries*, https://www.acts413.net/quotes.

a group comprised of 120 followers of Jesus were gathered in an upper room and that they "all continued with one accord in prayer and supplication" (Acts 1:14).

For ten consecutive and concentrated days, those followers of Jesus earnestly prayed as they waited for the promise of the Father to be poured out upon them. Then when the Day of Pentecost finally came, God moved in response to their prayers and sent the promised baptism in the Holy Spirit. True to the divine promise in Jeremiah 33:3, when Jesus' followers called unto God, He positively responded by showing them *great and mighty things*!

Then in Acts 3:1, we read that Peter and John were on the way to the temple for the regularly scheduled "hour of prayer" when they encountered an opportunity for God to manifest His healing power through them. A crippled man was miraculously raised up who had been lame for 40 years. In the words of Jeremiah 33:3, Peter and John called unto God, and He responded by showing them *great and mighty things*!

Then we come to Acts 4:31, where we find Peter and John returning to a gathering of believers in a private home after being interrogated by the Jewish leaders in Jerusalem. It says, "When they had prayed, the place was shaken where they were assembled together; and they were all filled with the Holy Ghost, and they spake the word of God with boldness." In the words of Jeremiah 33:3, these believers called unto God, and He responded by showing them *great and mighty things*!

Moving forward, we come to Acts 8 where we find that this pattern of prayer continued wherever those early Gospel preachers went. Again, Peter and John were praying, but this time they were in Samaria, laying hands on new Christians and praying for them to receive the baptism in the Holy Spirit. Again, God heard and answered the apostles' prayers as God moved mightily upon the Samaritans and they were gloriously filled with the Holy Spirit (*see* Acts 8:14-17). In the words of Jeremiah 33:3, they called unto God, and He responded by showing them *great and mighty things*!

In Acts 9, we read of a disciple named Ananias. As Ananias prayed, the Lord spoke to him in a vision and instructed him to go pray for Saul (whose name would later be changed to Paul). In the vision, Ananias understood that when he laid hands on Saul, Saul would receive his sight and would be baptized in the Holy Spirit. Ananias obeyed what he heard in prayer, and it came to pass just as the Lord had told him. Saul's eyes were opened, and he was baptized in the Holy Spirit. In the words of Jeremiah 33:3, Ananias and Saul called unto God, and God responded by showing them *great and mighty things*!

Moving on to Acts 10, we see Cornelius, a devout Roman centurion "...that feared God with all his house, which gave much alms to the people, and prayed to God always" (v. 2). The Bible tells us that while Cornelius was praying, an angel of God appeared to him. The angel directed Cornelius to send for the apostle Peter, who would bring him and his family the message of the Gospel. The centurion obeyed, and he and his family received salvation and the baptism in the Holy Spirit. God gloriously moved among them! In the words of Jeremiah 33:3, he called unto God, and He responded by showing Cornelius and his family *great and mighty things*!

Passionate prayer is also found in Acts 12:5, where we read that believers had gathered to pray for Peter because he had been thrown in prison by King Herod. The verse says, "...Prayer was made without ceasing of the church unto God for him." They called to God, and He responded to their prayers by sending an angel to Peter's prison cell — who miraculously unlocked Peter's chains and opened the prison doors to set him free. In the words of Jeremiah 33:3, these early believers called unto God, and He responded by showing them *great and mighty things*!

The pattern of prayer among the Early Church continued, and when we come to Acts 13:2, we find elders in the church at Antioch praying to seek God's will and direction. As they prayed, the Holy Spirit — speaking through the gift of prophecy — directed those elders to separate Paul and Barnabas from the rest of the group to begin taking the Gospel to people in distant lands. Because the elders had yielded to the Holy Spirit's leading in a season of intense prayer, they understood that it was time for Paul and Barnabas to be launched into their apostolic ministries. In the words of Jeremiah 33:3, they called unto God, and He responded by showing them *great and mighty things*!

From the beginning to the end of the book of Acts, we see example after example of believers calling to God, and God clearly and powerfully answering their prayers. Every time they called out to Him, He answered and showed them *great and mighty things*. Indeed, whenever prayer is offered fervently from the heart, the results are *always* mighty!

PRAYER WAS A PRIORITY

We know from the book of Acts that prayer was a top priority to the early believers. Acts 2:42 says, "And they continued *steadfastly* in the apostles' doctrine and fellowship, and in breaking of bread, *and in prayers*." As we saw earlier, the word "steadfastly" is the Greek word *proskartereo*, which describes someone (or a group of people) who *perseveres consistently, intensely focusing and working hard at something*. It really pictures *effort that never gives up*.

The use of this word tells us that First Century believers were *intensely focused on* and *completely committed to* prayer. Prayer was not something they tried to fit into their schedules. It was a priority to them. They fully understood that if they'd call out to God, He would hear them and show them mighty answers beyond their natural understanding. For this reason, they put great importance on their responsibility to pray.

Likewise, if we are going to see God move mightily among us today, it is essential that we sincerely call out to Him in fervent, faith-filled prayer. The type of prayer I am describing will require sustained focus. If we want New Testament results, we must do what the early believers did as they continued steadfastly in prayer.

First Century believers were *intensely focused on* and *completely committed to* prayer.
They fully understood that if they'd call out to God, He would hear them and show them mighty answers beyond their natural understanding.

The apostles learned to pray from the example they saw in Jesus. Evangelist D. L. Moody said, "We are not told that Jesus ever taught His disciples how to preach; but He taught them how to pray."[22]

Prayer was the centerpiece of Jesus' own ministry. Scripture shows that He often withdrew from the company of others to

---

[22] D. L. Moody, "Prevailing Prayer Requires Faith," *Great Preaching on Prayer*, Curtis Hutson, ed. (Murfreesboro, TN: Sword of the Lord Publishers, 1988), p. 111.

spend time with the Father in prayer at any time of day or night. And just as the disciples did with so many aspects of Jesus' ministry, they replicated what Jesus did by making prayer a daily discipline in their own lives; then they passed this prayerful emphasis on to the Early Church.

PRAYER AS A POWERFUL ACT
OF YIELDEDNESS AND SURRENDER

But I want to comment on the word "prayer" that is used in Acts 2:42. It is the Greek word *proseuche*. This particular word in its various forms is used 127 times in the New Testament and is the most common word translated "prayer." It is this very word that Paul used in Ephesians 6:18 when he wrote, "Praying always with all prayer...." In both instances — in Acts 2 and Ephesians 6 — the word "prayer" is taken from the Greek word *proseuche*.

This word *proseuche* is a compound of the words *pros* and *euche*. The word *pros* depicts something that is *upfront, close,* or *face to face.* As used in the context of prayer, it pictures *intimate contact.*

The second part of the word *proseuche* is *euche*, which is a Greek word that describes *a wish, desire, prayer,* or *vow.* The word *euche* was originally used to depict a person who made some kind of a vow to God because of a need or desire in his or her life. This individual would vow to give something of great value to God in exchange for a favorable answer to prayer.

A perfect example of this can be found in the story of Hannah, the mother of Samuel. Hannah deeply desired a child but was not able to become pregnant. Out of great desperation and anguish of spirit, she prayed and made a solemn vow to the Lord.

The vow Hannah made is recorded in First Samuel 1:11. She prayed, "O Lord of hosts, if thou wilt indeed look on the affliction of thine handmaid, and remember me, and not forget thine handmaid, but wilt give unto thine handmaid a man child, then I will give him unto the Lord all the days of his life, and there shall no razor come upon his head...."

First Samuel 1:19,20 tells us what happened next: "And they [Hannah and her husband, Elkanah] rose up in the morning early, and worshipped before the Lord, and returned, and came to their house in Ramah: and Elkanah knew Hannah his wife; and the Lord remembered her. Wherefore it came to pass, when the time was come about after Hannah had conceived, that she bare a son...."

In exchange for receiving the precious gift of this son, Hannah vowed that her young boy would be devoted to the work of the ministry. Technically, this was a type of *euche*, for by making this commitment, Hannah gave her most valued and prized possession to God in response to His answering her prayer.

Quite frequently in Old Testament times, people seeking an answer to prayer would offer God a gift of thanksgiving in advance. This was their way of releasing their faith in the goodness of God and thanking Him for His favorable response to their prayer requests.

Before a person verbalized his prayer, he would set up a commemorative altar and offer a sacrifice of thanksgiving on that altar. Such offerings of praise and thanksgiving were called "*votive offerings*" (derived from the word "vow"). This votive offering was similar to a pledge, for it was the person's promise that once his prayer was answered, he would return to the altar to give an additional offering of thanksgiving to God.

All of this information sets the backdrop for the Greek word *proseuche*, which was used more than any other word for "prayer" in the New Testament. Acts 2:42 is just one example, where this word was used to describe the prayers that the early believers regularly offered to God.

What a picture this paints of prayer! Certainly it tells us several important things about the subject. First, the word *proseuche* tells us that prayer should bring us face to face and "eyeball to eyeball" with God in intimate fellowship. Prayer is more than a mechanical act or a formula to follow. It is a vehicle that lifts us to a place in the Spirit where we can enjoy close, intimate fellowship with God.

The idea of sacrifice is also associated with this word for "prayer." This word portrayed an individual who so desperately desired to see his request answered that he was willing to surrender everything he owned in exchange for the answer to his prayer. Clearly this word "prayer" describes an altar of sacrifice and consecration built in the place of prayer, upon which a person entirely yields his life to the Lord.

Although the Holy Spirit may convict our hearts of areas that need to be surrendered to His sanctifying power, He will never forcibly take these things from us. Thus, this particular word for prayer points to a place of decision and consecration — an altar where we freely commit our lives to God in exchange for the fullness of His life.

Because the word *proseuche* has to do with these concepts of surrender and sacrifice, this tells us that God obviously desires to do more than merely bless us. *He wants to change us.*

This particular word for prayer
points to a place of decision and consecration —
an altar where we freely commit our lives to God
in exchange for the fullness of His life.

Thanksgiving was also a vital aspect of the Greek word *proseuche*, so commonly translated "prayer." We therefore know that when we offer a genuine prayer in faith, we should never stop short and fail to thank God in advance for hearing and answering our prayers. Thus, this Greek word *proseuche* refers to much more than making a simple prayer request. It is also the act of *surrender*, *consecration*, and *thanksgiving*.

In my own life, there have been many times I've asked God to do something for me, but in every case, I first had to come to a place of surrender. In truth, every time I pray, I am aware of more that I need to give to the Lord — a deeper place of surrender that He is calling me to. It is rarely about physical belongings, but rather about private matters of the heart and soul.

This should be true with each one of us. There is always more to surrender as each day the Holy Spirit reveals areas of our lives that we need to yield more fully to Him.

That is really the essence of what this word *proseuche* means. Like Hannah, we reach a place of surrender where we are willing to give something of great value to God and He gives something back to us.

But returning to Acts 2:42, we find that the believers in those early years of the Church were totally committed to prayer (*proseuche*). Every time they assembled to pray, they would come to the altar they had built in the spiritual realm, where they surrendered themselves to God once again in exchange for His supernatural power and presence. And each time they willingly laid their lives on that altar, His presence and power was precisely what they received.

There is always more to surrender as each day
the Holy Spirit reveals areas of our lives
that we need to yield more fully to Him.

Christian leader and author Charles Swindoll said, "Prayer is an investment. The time you dedicate to prayer isn't lost; it will return dividends far greater than what a few moments spent on a task ever could."[23]

The Early Church understood the importance of prayer; that's the reason they continued steadfastly in it. Today many church leaders study all the latest church-growth trends and do all that they know to help their churches grow — but nothing is more powerful than the act of prayer, both personal and corporate. This explains why D. L. Moody said, "My friends, if we are going to do a great work for God, we must spend much time in prayer; we have got to be closeted with God."[24]

PRAYER COMES IN MANY FORMS

There's something else I believe is important to note in Acts 2:42. It says, "They continued steadfastly in...*prayers*." The Greek word is in the plural form, indicating that the believers were doing a great deal of praying. They were meeting with God and each

---

[23] Charles R. Swindoll, *The Owner's Manual: The Essential Guide for a God-Honoring Life* (Nashville, TN: Thomas Nelson, 2009), p. 98.
[24] Steve Miller, *D. L. Moody on Spiritual Leadership* (Chicago: Moody Publishers, 2004), p. 78.

other daily, surrendering themselves to Him and His purposes, expecting to experience His power and presence in exchange.

Today many church leaders
study all the latest church-growth trends
and do all that they know to help their churches grow —
but nothing is more powerful than the act of prayer,
both personal and corporate.

Not only were these believers offering a large quantity of prayers, but they were also praying *many types* of prayers.

To assist us in maintaining victory, God has given the Church various kinds of powerful prayer. The apostle Paul confirmed this in Ephesians 6:18: "Praying always *with all prayer* and supplication...."

Notice the phrase "with all prayer." These words are taken from the Greek phrase *dia pases proseuches*, and it would be better translated "...with all *kinds of* prayer...." Ephesians 6:18 (*NIV*) actually says, "And pray in the Spirit on all occasions *with all kinds of prayers and requests*...." In other words, it's not "one prayer fits all." There are different kinds of prayers for different situations, and we have to learn how and when to operate in each of them.

The New Testament uses six different Greek words for prayer that are available for our use. Some sources may list more than these six; however, those additional words primarily have to do with worship or are prayer words that were used only by the Lord Jesus Christ. But God has given six specific kinds of prayer that pertain to us as believers.

Each one of these six forms of prayer is different from the others, and each form of prayer is also continually at our disposal to use in our fight of faith. The basic types of prayer found in the New Testament can be categorized as follows:

1. The Prayer of Surrender and Consecration

This is the Greek word *proseuche*, which is the one we have just examined up close. As mentioned earlier, this is the most common word for prayer used in the New Testament.

2. The Prayer of Petition

The Greek word *deesis* is the second most used word for "prayer" in the New Testament. This word essentially describes *a person's cry for help*. It is a humble recognition of our insufficiency and continual need for God. The word "supplication" in Ephesians 6:18 is the word *deesis*. This word and its various forms are translated "prayer and petition" more than 40 times.

3. The Prayer of Authority

In this case, the word "prayer" is taken from the Greek word *aiteo*, which means *I ask* or *I demand*. It describes someone who knows what he or she needs and authoritatively asks God for it. The word *aiteo* primarily deals with tangible needs, such as food, shelter, clothing, and the like.

4. The Prayer of Thanksgiving

The word "prayer" is also sometimes translated from the Greek word *eucharistia*, which is a combination of the words *eu* and *charis*. It basically describes *wonderful feelings and good sentiments that freely flow up out of the heart in response to something or someone*.

Paul used the word *eucharistia* in First Thessalonians 5:18 when he wrote, "In everything *give thanks*: for this is the will of God in Christ Jesus concerning you." This verse tells us it is God's will that we use the prayer of thanksgiving in every aspect of our lives.

5. The Prayer of Supplication

This form of "prayer" is derived from the Greek word *enteuxis*. This word *enteuxis* and its various forms are used only five times in the New Testament. It often is translated as the word "intercession." However, it does not necessarily refer to intercession as most people understand it. The word *enteuxis* carries the idea of *falling into the presence of the Lord* or *freely enjoying fellowship in the presence of the Lord*. It signifies a wonderful, intimate form of prayer that includes access to freely petition for "grace to help in time of need" (*see* Hebrews 4:16).

6. The Prayer of Intercession

In this instance, we are looking at the word "prayer" that is translated from the Greek word *huperentugchano*. It is the rarest of all the words used and only appears once in the entire New Testament. We find it in Romans 8:26: "Likewise the Spirit also helpeth our infirmities: for we know not what we should pray for as we ought: but the Spirit itself [Himself] *maketh intercession* for us with groanings which cannot be uttered."

The phrase "maketh intercession" is translated from this Greek word *huperentugchano*. It means *to fall in on behalf of someone else and to come to their rescue*. It exclusively describes prayer done by the Holy Spirit Himself on our behalf.

These are six different types of prayer specifically referred to in the New Testament that are given to the Church. Each form of prayer is to be used at different times for different situations.

SIMPLY CONTINUE

In Colossians 4:2, Paul instructed us to "continue in prayer, and watch in the same with thanksgiving."

The word "continue" in this verse is so very important. It is translated from the Greek word *proskartereo*. It is the same Greek word translated "steadfastly" in Acts 2:42. The word *pros* means *close, upfront, intimate contact with someone else*. The word *kartereo* means *to be strong, to be stout, to bear up*, or *to be steadfast*. As used in Colossians 4:2, it portrays *a strong, robust, "never-give-up" type of leaning toward an object*.

This does not describe someone who offers a quick prayer and is done. This paints a picture of a person or congregation who is *tenaciously pressing into the Spirit realm, busily engaged in activities that will help bring the object of his or her desires to fruition*. They want something so desperately that they are *pressing toward it* and are *resolute* in their determination not to give up until they have received the answer to their prayers.

J. Oswald Sanders was the General Director of Overseas Missionary Fellowship and an author of more than 40 books, an elder statesman, and a worldwide conference speaker. Sanders made this powerful statement about the apostle Paul's life of ministry and prayer: "It is obvious that Paul did not regard prayer as supplemental, but as fundamental — not something to be added to his work but the very matrix out of which his work was born. He was a man of action because he was a man of prayer. It was probably his prayer even more than his preaching that produced the kind of leaders we meet in his letters."[25]

---

[25] J. Oswald Sanders quote, "Quotes About Prayer," *AZ Quotes*, https://www.azquotes.com/author/ 17730-J_Oswald_Sanders/tag/prayer.

Paul's words in Colossians 4:2 plainly mean that prayer cannot be an add-on to life's schedule. It must be a central fixture in what we do if we are going to see the power of God move in our lives and churches. This is why R. A. Torrey said this: "We are too busy to pray, and so we are too busy to have power. We have a great deal of activity, but we accomplish little; many services, but few conversions; much machinery, but few results."[26]

Peter Marshall was a Scots-American preacher who was the pastor of the New York Avenue Presbyterian Church in Washington DC and at one time the Chaplain of the United States Senate. Marshall expressed his heart to the Lord about prayer when he said, "Forgive us for thinking that prayer is a waste of time and help us to see that without prayer our work is a waste of time."[27] Oh, that we would comprehend the need to come into the Father's presence daily and call out to Him to move among us!

I am also reminded of the words of S. D. Gordon, a prolific writer who was active in the latter part of the Nineteenth and the early Twentieth Centuries. Gordon wrote, "The real victory in all service is won in secret beforehand by prayer."[28]

> Oh, that we would comprehend the need
> to come into the Father's presence daily
> and call out to Him to move among us!

[26] Craig Brian Larson and Brian Lowery, *1001 Quotations That Connect* (Grand Rapids, MI: Zondervan, 2009), p. 33.
[27] Peter Marshall quote, *Great Thoughts Treasury*, http://www.greatthoughtstreasury.com/author/peter-marshall.
[28] S. D. Gordon, John Wesley, E. M. Bounds, and Andrew Murray, *How To Live a Life of Prayer: Classic Christian Writers on the Divine Privilege of Prayer*, "The Real Victory" by S. D. Gordon (Uhrichsville, OH: Barbour Publishing, 2018).

We must learn to press into the realm of the Spirit and to continue in prayer — *robustly*, *steadfastly*, and *tenaciously* calling out to God for Him to answer us in great and mighty ways (*see* Jeremiah 33:3). If we want to see results in prayer, we have to *continue in prayer*.

Jesus prayed all the time. It was an ongoing way of life for Him — not something He did just before He ate, before He went to bed, or when He attended the synagogue. And He instructed His disciples to continue in prayer. Luke 18:1 says, "He spake a parable unto them to this end, *that men ought always to pray*, and not to faint."

The apostle Paul prayed all the time, and he encouraged believers, both then and now, to "pray without ceasing" (1 Thessalonians 5:17). James, the brother of Jesus, was also a man of prayer. Church history records that James prayed so much that his knees became like those of a camel — calloused from constant kneeling in prayer.[29]

We also must be committed to prayer — especially if we are going to experience the strong presence of God in these last days. If we choose not to pray, we must understand that this is a choice that will leave us with a lack of God's power. Scottish evangelist and teacher Oswald Chambers said that unless "…you learn to fling the door wide back and let God in, you will work on a wrong level all day; but swing the door wide open and pray to your Father in secret, and every public thing will be stamped with the presence of God."[30]

---

[29] Saint Jerome, trans. by Thomas Halton, *On Illustrious Men* (Washington DC: The Catholic University of America Press, 1999), p. 7.
[30] Patrick Morley, *Pastoring Men: What Works, What Doesn't, and Why It Matters Now More Than Ever* (Grand Rapids, MI: Zondervan, 2019), p. 215.

We must learn to press into the realm
of the Spirit and to continue in prayer —
robustly, *steadfastly*, and *tenaciously* calling out to God
for Him to answer us in great and mighty ways.

Abiding in prayer releases the supernatural power and presence of God in our lives. It stamps us with God's miraculous presence! If we try to do things without Him, we'll become merely a human organization fueled by human effort. We have to make the decision to do whatever is necessary to cultivate a passion for prayer. It's the *only* way we will continually stay ablaze with the Spirit of God!

15 THINGS WE ARE COMMANDED TO PRAY ABOUT

When it comes to prayer, one particular question is frequently asked: "What are we supposed to pray about when we pray?" If you begin to develop a prayer life, it won't be long until you'll be led supernaturally in your praying. But to begin with, I can give you 15 specific things the Bible commands us as believers to pray about:

1. For God's will to be done on earth

2. For physical provision

3. For us to be delivered from evil

4. For us to forgive those who have wronged us

5. For spiritual leaders

6. For governmental leaders

7. For all who are in authority

8. For a peaceable life

9. For preachers of the Gospel

10. For open doors for the Gospel

11. For those who have been saved through our influence or ministry

12. For believers who are physically sick

13. For believers who are living in sin

14. For Israel to be saved

15. For the peace of Jerusalem

Let's take a look at each one of these and read the scriptural context in which they are presented.

First, in the passage known to many as the Lord's Prayer, Jesus commanded us to pray for *God's will to be done on earth.* In Matthew 6:9 and 10, Jesus instructed us, "After this manner therefore pray ye: Our Father which art in heaven, hallowed be thy name. Thy kingdom come. Thy will be done in earth, as it is in heaven."

Second, we are to pray for *physical provision.* Jesus prayed in Matthew 6:11, "Give us this day our daily bread." This verse confirms that it is right and appropriate to ask God for our basic needs to be met each day. He knows very well that we have need of these things before we even ask (*see* v. 32), yet He leads us to ask.

Third, we are to pray for *deliverance from evil.* In verse 13, Jesus prayed, "And lead us not into temptation, but deliver us from evil...."

Fourth, we are to pray for *the ability to forgive those who have wronged us.* This prayer is vitally important. In fact, it's so important that in this passage alone, Jesus included three verses explaining the necessity for forgiveness. In verse 12, He said, "And forgive us our debts, as we forgive our debtors." Then to emphasize how critical it is for us to forgive others, Jesus said in verses 14 and 15, "For if ye forgive men their trespasses, your heavenly Father will also forgive you: but if ye forgive not men their trespasses, neither will your Father forgive your trespasses." In order to forgive those who have wronged us, we must pray for God to give us His grace and ability to forgive.

Fifth, we are commanded to pray for our *spiritual leaders.* In Second Thessalonians 3:1 and 2, the apostle Paul said, "Finally, brethren, pray for us, that the word of the Lord may have free course, and be glorified, even as it is with you: and that we may be delivered from unreasonable and wicked men: for all men have not faith." So Paul was saying to the believers in Thessalonica, "Hey, pray for us! We're your spiritual leaders, and we desperately need your prayers." Your spiritual leaders would include your pastor(s), elders, deacons, and anyone else in a position of church oversight. All your spiritual leaders need *your* prayers.

Sixth, seventh, and **eighth**, we are commanded to pray for *all people in authority*, for *governmental leaders*, and to *live a peaceful life.*

In First Timothy 2:1 and 2, Paul wrote, "I exhort therefore, that, first of all, supplications, prayers, intercessions, and giving of thanks, be made for all men; for kings, and for all that are in authority; that we may lead a quiet and peaceable life in all godliness and honesty."

According to this passage, we are to pray for government officials, such as kings, presidents, senators, congressmen, governors, and so forth, as well as all who are in positions of authority. Please notice Paul *didn't* say, "Pray for the leaders you like and the ones you voted for." He said we are to pray for *all* leaders. This is not an option, nor is it a suggestion. It is a *command*.

Paul *didn't* say, "Pray for the leaders you like and the ones you voted for." He said we are to pray for *all* leaders. This is not an option, nor is it a suggestion. It is a *command*.

Why does God want us to pray for all our leaders? One of the greatest reasons is "...that we may lead a quiet and peaceable life in all godliness and honesty" (1 Timothy 2:2). Another reason of equal importance is found in verse 4 (*NLT*). Revealing the heart of God, Paul wrote that He "...wants everyone to be saved and to understand the truth." God loves everyone and doesn't want anyone to perish (*see* 2 Peter 3:9). Thus, He wants us to pray for all who are in authority to be saved. Paul then added, "For this is good and acceptable in the sight of God our Savior" (v. 3). Heartfelt prayer for people in authority greatly pleases our Heavenly Father.

Ninth, God directs us to pray for *people who preach the Gospel*. This is also found in Second Thessalonians 3:1,2.

Tenth, we are told in Colossians 4:3 (*NIV*) to pray for *open doors for the Gospel*. Writing to the church in Colossae, Paul said in essence, "Don't forget to pray for us, too, that God will give us many opportunities to preach about His secret plan — that Christ is also for you Gentiles."

Eleventh, our prayer agenda should include praying for *people who have been saved through our ministry*. Just before going to the Cross, Jesus lifted a prayer to the Father that is recorded in John's gospel. In John 17:9, He said, "I pray for them; I pray not for the world, but for them which thou hast given me, they are thine." He then spent the remainder of the chapter praying for those who had been saved through His ministry, as well as those who would be saved through the ministry of His disciples, establishing a clear pattern for us to pray for those who get saved through our efforts.

Twelfth, we are to pray for *fellow believers who are physically sick*. In James 5:14 and 15, James wrote of this type of prayer: "Is any sick among you? Let him call for the elders of the church; and let them pray over him, anointing him with oil in the name of the Lord. And the prayer of faith shall save the sick, and the Lord shall raise him up...."

Thirteenth, the Bible tells us to pray for *believers who are living in sin*. First John 5:16 (*NLT*) informs us that "if you see a Christian brother or sister sinning in a way that does not lead to death, you should pray, and God will give that person life...." We need to remember that none of us is beyond the reach of temptation and sin. We need people to pray for us. Therefore, we need to pray for others.

Fourteenth, in Romans 10:1, the apostle Paul wrote that we need to pray for *the salvation of the nation of Israel*. This verse reveals Paul's heart cry: "Brethren, my heart's desire and prayer to God for Israel is that they might be saved." Paul was himself a Jew — "of the stock of Israel, of the tribe of Benjamin, a Hebrew of the Hebrews..." (Philippians 3:5). His heart broke for his fellow Israelites so deeply that he was willing to be eternally separated from Christ if they could be saved (*see* Romans 9:2,3)!

God wants you and me to earnestly pray for the salvation of the Jewish people as well.

Fifteenth, we are to pray for *the peace of Jerusalem*. King David said in Psalm 122:6, "Pray for the peace of Jerusalem: they shall prosper that love thee." This prayer is unique in that it comes with a promise: Those who love the Lord and His chosen city enough to pray for it will be personally blessed.

These are 15 specific things for which we are commanded to pray in Scripture. If you have ever wondered for what or for whom to pray, now you have a detailed, biblical list that will help you pray what's on God's heart. This is *not* all-inclusive, but these 15 points will give you a good starting place to fill your time when you begin to develop a discipline for prayer. And believe me, when you get started, it won't be long until you begin to supernaturally pray for many things that are not included in this list, because the Holy Spirit will lead you in your praying!

WHEN ARE WE TO PRAY?

Now that we have outlined what God wants us to pray for, another question often comes to mind: *When am I supposed to pray?* For the answer to this question, let's look once again at Ephesians 6:18, where Paul wrote, "Praying always with all prayer and supplication in the Spirit...."

In Ephesians 6:18, Paul used the phrase, "Praying always." The word "always" is taken from the Greek phrase *en panti kairo*. The word *en* would better be translated *at*. The word *panti* means *each and every*. It is an all-encompassing word that embraces *everything, including the smallest and most intricate of details*. The last word in the phrase is *kairo*, which means *times* or *seasons*.

When all three of these words are combined to form *en panti kairo*, the phrase would be more accurately translated, *"at each and every occasion," "every time you get an opportunity,"* or *"at each and every possible moment."* In other words, what Paul was trying to communicate is this: *"Every time you get the opportunity, no matter where you are or what you are doing, seize the opportunity to pray!"*

In my personal life, I do my best to remain in a constant attitude of prayer. D. L Moody said, "We ought to see the face of God every morning before we see the face of man."[31] This is good advice, so the first thing I do every morning is pray, even before I get out of my bed.

I do my best to stay in a state of prayer. I pray as I walk through my house; I pray as I drive my car. I pray as I get a cup of coffee, and once I have my coffee, I pray on my way to the living room where I sit in my chair to read my Bible. Before I open it, I'm praying and asking for God to speak to me. And while I'm reading the Word, I'm silently whispering, "Lord, speak to me and open my eyes to truths that my heart needs to hear."

When I sit at my desk, before I open and read my emails or read messages on my phone or devices, I pray, "Lord, help me today with everything I am about to read." When I am about to teach or preach, I pray, "Lord, help me be the best I can be and communicate truth in the simplest way that people can hear and understand." In fact, I am praying *right now* as I write this book you're reading.

If I need to go somewhere, I pray before I get in my car. I pray for safety and protection while I am driving. Before I get up to preach, I pray. While I am preaching, I whisper prayers to

---

[31] Luis Palau, *God at the Center: Habits for Spiritual Growth* (Grand Rapids, MI: Our Daily Bread Ministries, 2015).

the Lord. After I preach, I stop to pray and thank God for His anointing and for the transformation He brings into the lives of the hearers.

Before I meet with someone, I pray: "Lord, give me wisdom and insight as I meet with this person. Help me be what I need to be for him." Throughout my day, I am *"praying always."* This includes praying in tongues — a very vital part of my personal prayer life.

If someone comes to my mind, I take it as a signal to pray for that person. As the names and faces of people rise in my spirit, I pray for them. I pray for people individually and by name. I lift up government officials, our ministry partners, our team, our ministry, our sons and their wives and children — and on and on as the Holy Spirit brings people to my mind. I also pray for Denise and me.

And at the end of every day as I lie in bed before I fall asleep, the last thing I do is pray. My last request of God every night is that He gives me peaceful sleep. I often pray Psalm 4:8 (*NLT*), which says, "I will lie down in peace and sleep, for you alone, O Lord, will keep me safe."

I am sharing all of this with you because I want you to see that in regard to prayer, you can pray *anytime, anywhere,* about *anything.* You can seize every moment you can to pray. By maintaining an attitude of prayer, it will keep you in a constant state of peace, and you can maintain this prayerful attitude every hour of every day. It may take time for you to cultivate this habit, but it is not difficult to do — and it is worth the effort because it brings the presence and power of God into your day.

David Martyn-Jones was a Welsh Protestant minister and leader in the British evangelical movement in the Twentieth

Century who served as the minister of Westminster Chapel in London for 30 years. Martyn-Jones said, "Man is at his greatest and highest when upon his knees he comes face to face with God."[32] It is so vital that we see our lives, families, churches, cities, and nations changed through the power of prayer.

If prayer truly is this essential, it is so deeply regretful that the modern Church has relegated it as a side issue. Surely this is a significant reason why so many believers and churches lack divine power. What makes all of this even more regretful is found in the profound words of Billy Graham: "Heaven is full of answers to prayer for which no one ever bothered to ask."[33]

Leonard Ravenhill summarized the state of the modern Church when he said, "I grant you that to our modern Christianity, praying is foreign."[34] So let's take this to heart and make sure that you and I are not numbered among the prayerless saints who are so abundant in the Church today.

"Heaven is full of answers to prayer for which
no one ever bothered to ask."
— *Billy Graham*

Maintaining a prayerful attitude includes a continual surrendering of yourself to God in exchange for His presence and power in your life. When you commit yourself to such a holy pursuit, you'll find that your decision is one that radically transforms your

---

[32] Daniel Henderson, *Transforming Prayer: How Everything Changes When You Seek God's Face* (Grand Rapids, MI: Bethany House, 2011), Intro.
[33] Franklin Graham and Donna Lee Toney, *Billy Graham in Quotes* (Nashville: Thomas Nelson, 2011), p. 30.
[34] Leonard Ravenhill quote, *Quote Master*, https://www.quotemaster.org/ q906bed37601869443e131b04d7ee1f7d.

life — because you've opened the way for God to be involved in everything you do!

PRAYER IS A DECISION

If you want to really burn with the Holy Spirit and remain alive, vital, and strong your entire life, you must make the decision to add the fuel of prayer to your life. It's imperative that you make the quality decision to cultivate a passion for prayer. You won't always feel like praying. In fact, most of the time you *won't* feel like praying. But prayer doesn't depend on your feelings, because it is put into practice by a decision of your will.

Your flesh will resist doing what you have read in this chapter because it does not want to develop the discipline of prayer. But as you choose to mortify your flesh by the power of the Holy Spirit, your own spirit will soar to heights and depths you've never known before.

So stir up your passion for prayer! Make the decision, "I'm going to learn how to maintain an attitude of prayer throughout each day. With God's help, I'm going to pray *'every time I get the opportunity, at each and every possible moment.'* And I'm not going to give up until I see what God has said come to pass!"

We started this chapter on prayer with Jeremiah 33:3, where God extends an extraordinary invitation with great promise to every Christian who will hear His voice. In that verse, He says, "Call unto me, and I will answer thee, and show thee great and mighty things, which thou knowest not."

Today if you will hear God's voice, He is calling you to an intimate walk with Him, fueled by an undying passion to commune with Him in prayer. According to Jeremiah 33:3, if you will do your part in prayer, God will show you great and mighty things that transcend natural understanding — for He is the One "…that is able to do exceeding abundantly above all that we ask or think…" (Ephesians 3:20).

Today if you will hear God's voice,
He is calling you to an intimate walk with Him,
fueled by an undying passion
to commune with Him in prayer.

That, friend, is the marvelous, miraculous realm that God wants you to experience by calling out to Him in fervent prayer! This is the glorious assignment He has given to every individual believer and to the Church as a whole.

As I close this chapter, I want to leave you with words about prayer written by two of the great generals of the faith. First, I want to assure you that when you pray, God's voice and power will respond to your faith-filled prayers. Pastor, author, and missionary Andrew Murray emphasized this truth, saying, "Prayer is not monologue, but dialogue. God's voice in response to mine is its most essential part."[35]

I conclude with another powerful statement made by Leonard Ravenhill: "A man may study because his brain is hungry for knowledge, even Bible knowledge. But he prays because his soul is hungry for God."[36]

---

[35] Andrew Murray, *Collected Books on Prayer*, "With Christ in the School of Prayer" (New Kensington, PA: Whitaker House, 2013), p. 592.
[36] David George, *The Daily Thought Shaker* (Bloomington, IN: WestBow Press, 2014), p. 233.

Is your soul hungry for God? If so, it's time to throw another log on the fire of your heart and let the fuel of prayer cause your inner man to become an inferno blazing with the presence and power of God. God desires to move, but He is first waiting for you to call out to Him, expectant for Him to show you great and mighty things that your natural mind cannot imagine or comprehend!

"A man may study because his brain
is hungry for knowledge, even Bible knowledge.
But he prays because his soul is hungry for God."
— *Leonard Ravenhill*

THINK ABOUT IT

1. Of all that the disciples observed in the life of Jesus, it is of note that they didn't ask Him to teach them to preach or to perform miracles — they asked Jesus to teach them how *to pray*. Prayer was the centerpiece of Jesus' ministry. As a result of the disciples following the Master's lifestyle of prayer, dynamic power blazed through their lives on a regular basis. They taught others to pray likewise until the power of God shook buildings, changed cities, unlocked prisons, and raised the dead!

   That same power is available to you today if you will pray. What is *your* pattern of prayer? Is prayer a continual stream of communion between you and the Father? Do you inquire of the Lord often about matters great or small? Or do you spend so much time talking or worrying about situations that you barely pray at all? Prayer always releases the power and the presence of God. If you desire to experience more of God's presence, yield more of your time and attention to Him in prayer.

2. God has extended an extraordinary and very personal invitation. He desires to express His heart and to reveal His mind to you. In Jeremiah 33:3, He said: "Call unto me, and I will answer thee, and shew thee great and mighty things, which thou knowest not." God desires to communicate with you, to be known by you. He longs to move on your behalf. But He waits for you to express your desire as He has expressed His.

Have you accepted the divine invitation? Are you calling out to Him in hungry anticipation? He will surely respond to your prayer in ways that exceed your greatest expectation.

3. Prayer is a vital fuel to ignite and invigorate your spiritual life by connecting you to the Source of Life Himself. To pray is not only to commune with God from your heart; in prayer, you also collaborate with God regarding the desires of His heart when you pray according to His will. We are instructed to pray without ceasing (*see* 1 Thessalonians 5:16). To maintain an attitude of prayer throughout the day is as easy as to breathe without ceasing, for it is simply the release of a continual acknowledgment and honor of God in all things.

How often do you give yourself to communing with the Father in prayer? Do you watch daily at His gates in prayer, acknowledging Him and inclining your ear to hear from Him daily? A lifestyle of ongoing prayer is an unfolding experience of the power, the strength, and the manifested presence of God. It is also entirely attainable if that is your desire and you refuse to extinguish the flame of prayer in your life.

CHAPTER 4

ABLAZE WITH
THE HOLY SPIRIT

An absolutely crucial form of fuel that ignites fire in the heart of a believer or a church is the supernatural work of the Holy Spirit. In fact, if you study Church history throughout the ages, you will discover that the supernatural element of the Holy Spirit was in operation.

The Holy Spirit indeed *is* the fire that keeps the Church — and its individual members — strengthened and ablaze with the glory and power of God. To the degree that God's people consistently embrace the ten types of essential fuels that we discuss in this book, *He's the fire that comes.*

What I'm describing is so important that Andrew Murray emphasized, "Men ought to seek with their whole hearts to be filled with the Spirit of God. Without being filled with the Spirit, it is utterly impossible that an individual Christian or a church can ever live or work as God desires."[37]

In the earliest days of the Church, as recorded in the book of Acts, the early believers understood their complete dependence upon the Holy Spirit and they lived ablaze with His power. They healed the sick, cast out demons, raised the dead, and testified to the living reality of Jesus Christ as the miraculous abounded among them. As a result, darkness was driven back and the Gospel was established in the hearts of those who had been formerly gripped by darkness. The Early Church was literally ablaze with the divine energy of the Holy Spirit!

Unfortunately, much of the Church today operates without the supernatural involvement of the Holy Spirit. A. W. Tozer described this dilemma in the modern Church when he so aptly said, "If the Holy Spirit was withdrawn from the Church today, 95 percent of what we do would go on and no one would know the difference. If the Holy Spirit had been withdrawn from the New Testament Church, 95 percent of what they did would stop, and everybody would know the difference."[38]

Many churches doctrinally believe in the supernatural work of the Spirit, but they don't experience much of it. Other churches believe that it was relegated to the past in the first years of the Christian era. I personally grew up in a wonderful church that was among those who believed the gifts of the Spirit were for a past age. I learned many foundational truths in my childhood church that positively impacted my life. However, we didn't believe the gifts of the Holy Spirit were for today, so we didn't experience them.

---

[37] Robert Campbell, "The 10 Most Profound Andrew Murray Quotes," *LogosTalk* (June 12, 2012), https://blog.logos.com/2012/06/the-10-most-profound-andrew-murray-quotes/.

[38] Dr. Michael Brown, "Who Changed Things?" *Christian Post* (February 17, 2014), https://www.christianpost.com/news/who-changed-things.html.

I can honestly testify that when it came to effort, the church of my youth would have won an award for commitment. Oh, I learned so much in that church that is still today ingrained in my spiritual deposition. But when it came to the supernatural dimension of the Holy Spirit's work, we greatly limited it in our midst. I personally never saw a miracle; I never heard of anyone who was supernaturally healed; I never heard a prophecy; I had no idea what a word of knowledge or a word of wisdom was; I had never heard of the discerning of spirits. And we generally looked down on people who spoke in tongues and dismissed them as being doctrinally off-base and emotionally unstable.

In our denomination, we gave our attention to the study of the Bible and using our natural talents to serve the Lord, which is essential and good. But I cannot personally remember a single sermon or conversation that focused on the supernatural activity of the Holy Spirit. Theologian Donald Gee said, "Doctrines about the Spirit are necessary and inevitable. But the all-important question is not what we mentally believe, but what we experimentally enjoy."[39] We certainly knew our doctrine, but I personally did *not* know the power of God on the experiential level that He wants every one of His children to know it.

This makes me think of the words of the great missionary, Hudson Taylor, who said, "We have given too much attention to methods, and to machinery, and to resources, and too little to the Source of Power, the filling of the Holy Ghost."[40] Oh, let us not be so focused on what we can do that we forget what only the power of the Holy Spirit can do through us! Let's open our hearts and allow the Holy Spirit to *move* so He can manifest His glorious power!

---

[39] Donald Gee, *God's Grace and Power Today* (Springfield, MO: Gospel Publishing House, 1936), Introduction.
[40] *Tongues of Fire: 50 Days Celebrating Pentecost Devotional* (New Kensington, PA: Whitaker House, 2019), p. 6.

D. L. Moody stated this so well when he said, "How easy it is to work for God when we are filled with His Spirit! His service is so sweet, so delightful; He is not a hard master. People talk about their being overworked and breaking down. It is not so. It is [over-worry] and care that wears people out. Why do so many workers break down? Not from overwork, but because there has been friction of the machinery; there hasn't been enough of the oil of the Spirit. Great engines have their machinery so arranged that where there is friction, there is oil dropping on it all the time. It is a good thing for Christians to have plenty of oil."[41]

Oh, let us not be so focused on what
we can do that we forget what only the power
of the Holy Spirit can do through us!

Moody also said, "The fact is, we are leaky vessels, and we have to keep right under the fountain all the time to keep full of Christ, and so have fresh supply." He added, "I believe this is a mistake a great many of us are making; we are trying to do God's work with the grace God gave us ten years ago. We say, if it is necessary, we will go on with the same grace. Now, what we want is a fresh supply, a fresh anointing and fresh power, and if we seek it, and seek it with all our hearts, we will obtain it."[42]

At the end of this book, I will tell you how to receive this glorious infilling of the Holy Spirit that so many have experienced and written about. This is an experience that is subsequent to the new birth and one that will totally change your life and set you on a new spiritual trajectory. The baptism in the Holy Spirit is a priceless gift promised to every child of God who will open his or her heart to

[41] Steve Miller, *D. L. Moody on Spiritual Leadership* (Chicago: Moody Publishers, 2004), p. 98.
[42] D. L. Moody, *Secret Power* (Global Grey; 1881, 2018), pp. 28-29.

receive it. It is truly an inestimable privilege and honor to receive this gift — a truth D. L. Moody emphasized when he said, "God commands us to be filled with the Spirit; and if we are not filled, it is because we are living beneath our privileges."[43]

The baptism in the Holy Spirit is a priceless gift
promised to every child of God
who will open his or her heart to receive it.

You are about to see in the following pages that in the four gospels, in the book of Acts, and throughout Church history, the Holy Spirit has supernaturally moved and worked anytime hearts are open and faith is released for His supernatural work to happen. When people are receptive to it, they experience the supernatural moving of the Holy Spirit.

But to really know this, let's take a journey through the Old Testament, through the gospels, and through the book of Acts to see how the Holy Spirit has moved and worked throughout the ages. It is especially important for you to see how early believers were affected when they blazed with fire as the Holy Spirit worked and manifested His powerful presence among them.

DIVINE MOVEMENT:
A PATTERN OF THE HOLY SPIRIT IN ACTION

In the opening verses of the Bible, we read, "In the beginning God created the heaven and the earth. And the earth was without form, and void; and darkness *was* upon the face of the deep. And

---

[43] T. J. Shanks, *D. L. Moody at Home: His Home and Homework* (New York: Fleming H. Revell, 1886), p. 255.

the Spirit of God *moved* upon the face of the waters" (*see* Genesis 1:1,2). In these verses, we see the Holy Spirit *moving* upon the face of the deep, which was upon the face of the earth. This first mention of the Holy Spirit in the Bible is very important, for it reveals the Holy Spirit in *movement*. From the beginning to the very end of the Bible, the Holy Spirit is always in *divine movement*.

When the Holy Spirit moved, creative and divine power was released, bringing order to the chaos that was upon the face of the deep. Thus, from the outset of the Scriptures, we find that the Holy Spirit was revealed as the creative power of God. And throughout the entire Bible, we read over and over again that when the Holy Spirit is present and begins to move, individuals are divinely empowered and creative power is supernaturally released.

We see this in the pages of the Bible when the Holy Spirit would come upon common people and they were divinely energized to accomplish uncommon feats. I must point out that when the Spirit is referred to in the pages of the Old Testament, He is never silent or motionless. He moves, He speaks, He enables, and He releases power to change people and circumstances. If we just focused on the Old Testament, we'd have sufficient evidence to convince us that the Holy Spirit's role in the earth is to bring the active power and voice of God into the earth as believers yield to Him.

The Holy Spirit's Movement
in the Ministry of Jesus

When you come to the four gospels, we find this same witness in the life and ministry of Jesus. As early as the angel Gabriel's announcement that Mary would become pregnant and bear the Son of God, we see the role of the Holy Spirit as one of divine activity. Mary asked Gabriel, "How shall this be, seeing I know not a man?" (Luke 1:34) Notice Gabriel's response: "And the angel answered and said unto her, The Holy Ghost shall *come upon* thee, and the *power* of the Highest shall *overshadow* thee: therefore also that holy thing which shall be born of thee shall be called the Son of God" (Luke 1:35).

The Holy Spirit is never silent or motionless.
He moves, He speaks, He enables, and He releases power
to change people and circumstances.

In this remarkable verse, we find that the Holy Spirit was going to *move* upon Mary — and as a result of His *movement*, the *power* of God would come upon her and she would *supernaturally* conceive Jesus in her womb. And this was only the beginning of Jesus' story in the New Testament.

When Jesus came to the Jordan River to be baptized by John the Baptist, Matthew 3:16 tells us, "And Jesus, when he was baptized, went up straightway out of the water: and, lo, the heavens were opened unto him, and he saw the Spirit of God descending like a dove, and lighting upon him." As a result of this *movement* of the Spirit upon Jesus, Jesus was supernaturally *empowered* by the Holy Spirit (*see* Luke 4:1). And we see that only *after* being filled with the supernatural, creative power of God through the Holy Spirit was Jesus then thrust into His earthly ministry.

We have seen in previous chapters that Jesus' disciples and the early believers duplicated Jesus in the way they loved souls and in their deep passion for the Word of God. But they also took Jesus and His ministry as the model for the Holy Spirit's work in the Early Church.

What Jesus did, what Jesus said, and how Jesus operated was the model for everything the early believers did as the Christian era began. Jesus demonstrated His need for the partnership of the Holy Spirit, and He allowed the Spirit's miraculous power to be released through His ministry. His disciples therefore clearly understood they needed the Holy Spirit's power demonstrated in their own lives and would not be able to do the work of God without it.

The New Testament book that contains the clearest record of the Holy Spirit's *movement* and His supernatural power at work is called the book of *Acts*. I find this interesting, because wherever the Holy Spirit is allowed to *move*, He *acts*.

Don't look at the book of Acts as a mere history book. Although it does contain history, it is even more importantly a *pattern book* to show us what should still be happening in the lives of believers and in churches today.

Where there is *no moving* of the Holy Spirit, there is no supernatural activity, no power, and no supernatural acts. The Bible shows that the Spirit is all about *action*. Especially in the book of Acts, we are shown a pattern of how the Spirit operates in the life of a believer and in the life of the Church.

The book of Acts makes it clear that when the Holy Spirit is allowed to *move*, His moving results in *power*. When the Spirit's power is released, that power unleashes the supernatural that does what the human mind and natural talent could never achieve.

This is so foundational to the work of the Holy Spirit that I would challenge you to find a place in the book of Acts where the moving of the Spirit occurs without some type of action or movement also taking place!

THE HOLY SPIRIT'S MOVEMENT
IN THE BOOK OF ACTS

In Acts 1:5, Jesus instructed His followers to wait together for the promise of the Father. Then in verse 8, Jesus told them that this *movement* of the Holy Spirit upon them would give them *power* to be witnesses to the uttermost parts of the earth. That word "power" is *dunamis*, which is the New Testament word for *explosive power*. But it is also the Greek word used to describe *the full might of an advancing army*.

The book of Acts makes it clear that when the Holy Spirit is allowed to *move*, His moving results in *power*.
When the Spirit's power is released, that power unleashes the supernatural that does what the human mind and natural talent could never achieve.

This means when the Holy Spirit's power is received, He releases the advancing power of God into the person who receives it. And it isn't a quiet, reserved, motionless power. The word "power" in Acts 1:8 (the Greek word *dunamis*) depicts an advancing power that is *mighty* and *explosive*.

The fulfillment of this occurred in Acts 2:4 when the Holy Spirit *moved* upon those who were gathered in that upper room in Jerusalem on the Day of Pentecost. It says that when the Spirit moved that day, those who were present "...were all filled with the Holy Ghost, and began to speak with other tongues, as the Spirit gave them utterance."

When the Holy Spirit's power moved in that upper room and filled the disciples, they were set ablaze with the fire of God as "tongues of fire" appeared over each one — and *immediately* the supernatural manifested. Those who had gathered in that room began to speak in miraculous languages and were so empowered that bystanders were dumbfounded by what they witnessed that day.

But this was only the first spark of the supernatural power of the Holy Spirit manifesting in those first days of the infant Church. Like a spreading flame, the power of God would burn in the Church throughout the book of Acts and throughout the Church Age wherever believers will allow the Holy Spirit to move and supernaturally work. From the very outset of the book of Acts, we learn that the Holy Spirit *moved* upon willing recipients and that His supernatural *power* enabled and energized early believers to go into all the world preaching the Gospel with signs following.

Furthermore, in the Bible and particularly in the book of Acts, we find that the Holy Spirit is rarely silent. When He descended into the upper room on the Day of Pentecost, no one wondered if He was present! Everyone there felt His presence, saw His fire, and experienced the miraculous evidence of His divine power.

> From the very outset of the book of Acts, we learn
> that the Holy Spirit *moved* upon willing recipients
> and that His supernatural *power* enabled
> and energized early believers to go into all the world
> preaching the Gospel with signs following.

By the standards of much of the modern Church, it was a rowdy moment! The place was filled with a loud sound from Heaven, and believers who were gathered there began to speak loudly in other tongues.

Those who are unfamiliar with supernatural demonstrations of God's power tend to think the Holy Spirit is only gentle and quiet. But the Bible shows that the Holy Spirit is rarely quiet and almost never silent — and that when He moves, His movement is visible and can often be tangibly felt.

The Bible shows that the Holy Spirit is rarely quiet and almost never silent — and that when He moves, His movement is visible and can often be tangibly felt.

Jack Hayford — pastor, author, and songwriter — wrote about the power of the Spirit that was imparted to the Church when the Holy Spirit came. Hayford wrote, "…When the Spirit comes, He is loaded with packages! He desires to release much more in us and through us than we could ever imagine."[44] Oh, how we need to pray that our hearts will be open so the Holy Spirit can move in our midst to release the full load of gifts and power that He wants to manifest among us!

A study of the entire book of Acts from the beginning to the end reveals that when the Holy Spirit moves, He produces powerful actions and performs the miraculous as spiritual gifts and manifestations are released.

This pattern continues in Acts 2:43, where we read that early believers were meeting together to hear the apostles expound from the Word of God. We learn from this verse that at that precise time, "…many wonders and signs were done…" among God's people. From this, we see that the miraculous events that occurred on the Day of Pentecost were not anomalies meant only for those who

---

[44] "Jack W. Hayford Quotes," *AZ Quotes*, www.azquotes.com/author/21822-Jack_W_Hayford.

were present in the upper room. Instead, the supernatural manifestations that swept into that upper room and then exploded out onto the streets of Jerusalem actually set a *precedent* and a pattern for the Holy Spirit's divine activity that would be repeated over and over in the book of Acts and then throughout the Church Age.

When we come to Acts 3, we read of a man who had been lame from birth. This man was instantly and miraculously healed when the Holy Spirit's presence *moved* upon Peter and John, empowering and emboldening them to command the man to rise up healed. Shortly after that, we read again in Acts 4:24-31 that believers gathered for concentrated prayer and that as they prayed, the Holy Spirit *moved* upon them. As a result, His presence and power so filled the place where they were meeting that the building they were in began to shake!

Then in Acts 5, we read that people from Jerusalem and the surrounding towns came to hear the Word of God. Because the Holy Spirit was *moving* so strongly in the midst of the people, the miraculous was taking place.

> **And believers were the more added to the Lord, multitudes both of men and women.) Insomuch that they brought forth the sick into the streets, and laid them on beds and couches, that at the least the shadow of Peter passing by might overshadow some of them. There came also a multitude out of the cities round about unto Jerusalem, bringing sick folks, and them which were vexed with unclean spirits: and they were healed every one.**
>
> **Acts 5:14-16**

The crowds wanted Peter to lay his hands upon them, but because there were so many sick people, it was physically impossible for the apostle to touch them all. However, the Spirit was *moving* so mightily that the people decided to lay the sick in beds on the street so the mere shadow of Peter would fall upon them. And that was enough. The power of the Holy Spirit was in such tangible manifestation that the sick were healed when Peter's shadow fell on them, and those who were possessed by demons were set free by the power of the Spirit.

The supernatural manifestations that swept
into that upper room and then exploded out
onto the streets of Jerusalem actually set a *precedent*
and a pattern for the Holy Spirit's divine activity
that would be repeated over and over
in the book of Acts and then throughout the Church Age.

Journeying further into the book of Acts, we come to Acts 6:8. This verse tells us of Stephen preaching the Word of God with the Spirit *moving* to confirm the Word with signs and wonders. It says, "And Stephen, full of faith and power, did great wonders and miracles among the people."

Then in Acts 8:5-8, evidence of the Holy Spirit's movement is on full display once again. We are told that "Philip went down to the city of Samaria, and preached Christ unto them. And the people with one accord gave heed unto those things which Philip spake, hearing and seeing the miracles which he did. For unclean spirits, crying with loud voice, came out of many that were possessed *with them*: and many taken with palsies, and that were lame, were healed. And there was great joy in that city." Again we see that when the Spirit was allowed to move, the power of God was unleashed and the supernatural took place!

This ongoing pattern of the Holy Spirit's *movement* and *action* shows up again in Acts 10:44 and 45, where we read of the first time that the Spirit of God *moved* upon Gentile hearts: "While Peter yet spake these words [the Gospel], the Holy Ghost fell on all them which heard the word. And they of the circumcision which believed were astonished, as many as came with Peter, because that on the Gentiles also was poured out the gift of the Holy Ghost." Once again, when the Holy Spirit moved, the results were vocal, outward, and visible.

In Acts 11:28-30, we read of a prophet named Agabus who was moved by the Holy Spirit to prophesy of a famine that would come to the Roman Empire. This divine prophetic word was so strong — so saturated with the Spirit's power — that it moved believers of that time to rally and give generously into a common offering for the purpose of caring for fellow Christians who would be in need as a result of the coming famine. Because the Holy Spirit was allowed to freely move and to speak through the gift of prophecy, Christians were empowered to act and take preventative measures to prepare for the challenges of an upcoming difficult season.

As the book of Acts continues, we come to Acts 13:2, where we read that leaders in the church at Antioch "…ministered to the Lord, and fasted, the Holy Ghost said, 'Separate me Barnabas and Saul for the work whereunto I have called them." Once again, where the Spirit was allowed freedom to *move*, He *acted* among God's people and spoke through the gift of prophecy. And as a result of the Holy Spirit's movement among them, Barnabas and Paul were launched into their apostolic ministries.

When Paul ventured into new lands to preach the Gospel, he came to the city of Lystra where he encountered a man who had been crippled from birth. The power and gifts of the Holy Spirit moved through Paul's ministry there, and as a result, Acts 14:10 tells us that Paul "…said with a loud voice, 'stand upright on thy feet….'" And at Paul's word, the crippled man "leaped and walked"! The power of God was released, and like a divine advancing army, that explosion of divine power acted to drive back the forces of darkness and to conquer the sickness in this lame man's body.

In Acts 19, it is recorded that Paul arrived in Ephesus and encountered 12 disciples of John the Baptist who lived in the upper district of Ephesus. After Paul led these disciples of John to faith in Christ, he prayed for them to be filled with the Holy Spirit's power. Acts 19:6 tells us that as Paul prayed, the Holy Spirit moved and the 12 were gloriously filled with the Spirit. The verse says that when Paul laid his hands on them, "…the Holy Spirit came on them, and they spoke in other tongues and prophesied."

I want to say something very important at this juncture. This event in Acts 19 occurred 23 years after the first movement of the Holy Spirit in the upper room on the Day of Pentecost! This is significant to understand. The same types of supernatural events were occurring 23 years later — which shows that the earlier experiences were not anomalies, nor were they events only associated with the original 12 apostles of Jesus. Rather, these miraculous occurrences were *precedents* revealing a divine *pattern* that would continue to the very end of the book of Acts and on to the end of the Church Age.

But we're still not done! In Acts 19:11 and 12, we read that when Paul was preaching in Ephesus, "God wrought special miracles by the hands of Paul: so that from his body were brought unto the sick handkerchiefs or aprons, and the diseases departed from them, and the evil spirts went out of them." This event occurred *years* after the first event in Jerusalem, yet the Holy Spirit was still moving and the powerful results were continuing unabated!

These miraculous occurrences were *precedents* revealing a divine *pattern* that would continue to the very end of the book of Acts and on to the end of the Church Age.

Again and again and again, we see that whenever the Holy Spirit *moves*, believers are visited with *supernatural acts* as various gifts of the Holy Spirit manifest. The writer of Hebrews testified that this was the normal evidence that occurred when the Spirit moved through those who preached the Gospel. It says, "God also bearing them witness, both with signs and wonders, and with divers miracles, and gifts of the Holy Ghost..." (Hebrews 2:4).

It's so important to grasp this truth — that for early believers, the demonstrated evidence of the Holy Spirit's supernatural movement was the expected and even inevitable result of the preaching of the Word!

You see, this was not an exception — this was the *norm* for what occurred in the Early Church when the Holy Spirit moved among the people. It was the pattern of the Holy Spirit's power given by God from the outset of the Church Age, and it is the pattern that God longs for *us* to experience firsthand in this day as well. At a bare minimum, we should experience the basic signs and wonders that Jesus vividly described in Mark 16:15-18 in the Great Commission and that He said should follow *all* who believe!

HERE ARE THE SIGNS THAT SHOULD FOLLOW YOU!

When the Holy Spirit is given liberty to move as He wishes, He comes with all kinds of signs, wonders, and powerful spiritual gifts. When these spiritual manifestations are loosed among God's people, it literally ignites a *fire* that exposes sin, drives out darkness, brings answers to seeking hearts, and liberates people from all types of captivity.

Just moments before Jesus ascended to the Father, He told the disciples, "And these signs shall follow them that believe; In my name shall they cast out devils; they shall speak with new tongues; They shall take up serpents; and if they drink any deadly thing, it shall not hurt them; they shall lay hands on the sick, and they shall recover" (Mark 16:17,18).

According to Jesus, these supernatural signs are supposed to follow those who believe. Since you and I believe, that means these signs are supposed to follow you and me! Unfortunately, these signs listed in Mark 16 are rarely mentioned today. Yet the Early Church believed these words of Jesus and, as a result, regularly experienced these supernatural signs.

When these spiritual manifestations are loosed among God's people, it literally ignites a *fire* that exposes sin, drives out darkness, brings answers to seeking hearts, and liberates people from all types of captivity.

So let's look carefully at this list of divine enablements to see precisely what Jesus said should follow us as we live for Him and share the Gospel with others.

First of all, the word "signs" comes from the Greek word *semeion*, which in ancient history described *the official written notice that announced the final verdict of a court*. It also described *the signature or seal applied to a document to guarantee its authenticity* — or *a sign that marked key locations in a city*.

Jesus was sending His disciples into the world to preach the Gospel. As He sent them forth, He said in essence that *God's signature* would be upon their ministry. These "signs" were to be God's official declaration that His people were sent by Heaven and that the Gospel message was true. For unbelievers, these "signs" would authenticate the fact that this was no manmade message but a message straight from God Himself. And just as street signs point a traveler in the right direction, these signs would point the unbeliever to the Lord Jesus Christ if he or she would only heed them.

The specific signs that Jesus mentioned are as follows:

- They will cast out devils.
- They will speak with new tongues.
- They will take up serpents.
- If they drink any deadly poison, it will not hurt them.
- They will lay hands on the sick, and the sick will recover.

The Lord said that these signs would "follow" those who believe. The word "follow" is the Greek word *parakoloutheo*, from the words *para* and *akoloutheo*. The word *para* means *alongside*; *to be near*; or *to be in close proximity*. The word *akoloutheo* means *to follow* or *to go somewhere with a person, as to accompany him on a trip*. When the word *para* and *akoloutheo* are joined to form one word, as in this verse, the new word means *to tirelessly accompany someone*; *to constantly be at the side of an individual*; *to always be in close proximity with a person, like a faithful companion who is always at one's side.*

For unbelievers, these "signs" would authenticate the fact
that this was no manmade message but a message straight
from God Himself. And just as street signs point
a traveler in the right direction, these signs
would point the unbeliever to the Lord Jesus Christ
if he or she would only heed them.

Because the word *parakoloutheo* has such a strong sense of *following someone*, it eventually came to convey the idea of *discipleship*. A true disciple faithfully follows his teacher anywhere he goes and is committed to his teacher's instruction.

This picture of commitment to another person — of someone's faithfulness to follow and his determination to never be out of step with his leader — is very significant in the context of this verse. It tells us that signs and wonders are to faithfully follow us and the Gospel message. These signs and wonders are continually to be in step with us and with the message we preach. To preach without these miraculous signs in demonstration should seem very strange to us, for God intended these signs to persistently follow us and the message of the Gospel anywhere and everywhere we go.

These signs are God's signature that the message is true. Hence, every time you preach or share the Gospel — whether at church, on the mission field, in a large crusade, in the bus or subway, at your job, or at the grocery store — you should expect these supernatural signs to be present in some form. These signs should accompany you everywhere you go because they are a part of your spiritual equipment as a faithful partner of the Gospel message!

Since this is true, why don't we see more of these signs following Christians? The answer to this question is found in Jesus' words in Mark 16:17. He said, "And these signs shall follow them *that believe....*"

I want to draw your attention to the word "believe." Because of the tense used with this Greek word, this verse would be better translated, *"These signs shall follow them that are constantly believing...."* In other words, these signs don't come automatically just because a person once walked the aisle and gave his heart to Jesus. These signs follow those who are *constantly believing* for them to occur. If a Christian isn't believing for these signs to be manifested or expecting those supernatural signs to follow him, they probably won't. Like everything else in the Kingdom of God, signs and wonders are activated by faith.

To preach without these miraculous signs
in demonstration should seem very strange to us,
for God intended these signs to persistently follow us
and the message of the Gospel anywhere
and everywhere we go.

Through the years of my ministry, I have observed that people who regularly experience the miraculous are those who regularly expect to see it. Rather than being passive, they are very aggressive about pushing forward in the Spirit to see the miraculous manifested in their lives or ministries. Those who press forward and release their faith to see the supernatural demonstrated are the ones who often experience these divine demonstrations in their lives.

Thus, the number of signs and wonders that follow you will be determined by how intensely you are *constantly believing* for them to be in manifestation. As noted above, *everything* in the Kingdom of God is activated by faith. If you're not releasing faith for the miraculous to occur, very little of the miraculous will be in manifestation in your life. If you want signs and wonders to faithfully follow you, you must be *constantly believing* for them to happen!

So when you preach and share the Gospel, *expect* things to happen!

- When you pray for the sick, *expect* them to be healed.

- When you confront someone who is demonized, *expect* that person to be set free.

- When you are in a situation that requires the miraculous, *expect* the miraculous to occur.

- When you need protection, *expect* God's hand of protection to be upon you.

If you haven't been experiencing the supernatural, it may be a signal that you haven't been allowing the Spirit to move as He wishes to move. If He is moving upon you and through you, you *will* see signs and wonders. Remember, these signs *always* follow wherever the Gospel is preached and believers are believing for them to occur. This was Jesus' promise! He guaranteed that God's supernatural signature would be on anyone who preaches the Gospel and opens the way for the supernatural to come to pass *by believing*.

If these signs aren't regularly following you, ask the Holy Spirit to reignite the flame of passion in your heart to see the supernatural signature of God on your life. He wants to show up when you preach or share the Gospel! He wants to authenticate and guarantee that the life-transforming message you share with those who need to hear it is truly Heaven-sent.

Jesus guaranteed that God's supernatural signature
would be on anyone who preaches the Gospel
and opens the way for the supernatural
to come to pass by believing.

They Shall Cast Out Devils

In Mark 16:17, Jesus told the disciples, "And these signs shall follow them that believe; *in my name shall they cast out devils...*"

I have had to deal with demonic manifestations on several occasions in my ministry. I remember one time when a young Satanist teenager came forward at the end of one of my meetings in a large church. That night this young man had come to realize that Satan's powers had taken his mind captive, so he came forward to receive prayer and to be set free.

As I prayed for this one and then that one, I could visibly see from a distance that this particular young man was sending forth spiritual signals of a very strong, evil presence. As I came nearer to him, I sensed that he had been involved in some type of occult activity.

When I finally reached the young man, he looked up at me through eyes that were so tightly squeezed together that they looked like nothing more than little slits in his face. Looking into his eyes, I sensed that a demon was looking back at me from behind his face. When I saw this young man's condition, I knew he was serious about being helped. It had taken a great deal of determination for him to shove aside that manipulating force long enough to forge his way down to the front of the church auditorium.

I laid my hands on the young man, and his body began to shake violently as it reacted to the power of God. Trembling under the weight of God's power, the man fell to the floor, crumbling right next to my feet. As he lay there under the electrifying power of God that was surging up and down his body, suddenly he cried out as though something was trying to exit his body. As I leaned over to pray for him a second time, the horrible demonic influence that had held him captive immediately released him and fled from the scene.

This is just one instance of dealing with the demonized that I've encountered during our years in the former Soviet Union. We have had so many instances that I couldn't begin to count them. When atheism took over, the people turned to psychic phenomena to satisfy their spiritual hunger. As you can imagine, that opened the floodgates for demonic activity in thousands of people's lives.

In Mark 16:17, Jesus said, "…In my name shall they cast out devils…." The word "cast out" is the Greek word *ekballo*, which is a compound of the words *ek* and *ballo*. The word *ek* means *out*, and the word *ballo* means *to throw*. When compounded into one word, the new word means *to throw out, as to evict someone from a place*; *to drive out*; or *to expel*. Historically, it was used to describe *a nation that forcibly removed its enemies out from its borders*.

The word "devils" is the Greek word *daimonion*, meaning *demons*. In Jesus' time, it was widely believed that demons thickly populated the lower, denser regions of the air and that these demons were the primary cause of most disasters and suffering that occurred in the earth. It was believed that demon spirits came into contact with humans primarily through occult practices, such as magic, spells, and necromancy, or by participation in religious paganism, which centered around such occult activities.

It is worth noting that the world in which Jesus lived generally believed that demon spirits were the chief cause for mental sickness or insanity. The ancients also firmly believed that demon spirits were ordered and arranged in a detailed and entirely intentional hierarchy of power. This agrees completely with the picture that Paul gave us in Ephesians 6:12, where he described the rank and file of the devil's kingdom.

Today we tend to think of casting out demons in terms of ordering a demon spirit to leave a person's body or mind. Certainly this is one aspect of casting out demons, and we need to be quick to take authority over demons in this way when we recognize their activity. We see examples of Jesus expelling demons in various places in the gospels. Examples include:

- Matthew 8:16, where it is written, "...And he cast out the spirits with his word...." The words "cast out" are also from the Greek word *ekballo*, meaning *to forcibly throw out*. It tells us that Jesus literally kicked these demons out of people's lives!

- Matthew 9:34, where even the Pharisees acknowledged Jesus' authority over demon spirits. It says, "But the Pharisees said, He casteth out devils...." These words "casteth out" are also from the word *ekballo*, which means even the Pharisees recognized that Jesus literally tossed demons out of people's lives.

- Matthew 10:1, which says, "And when he had called unto him his twelve disciples, he gave them power against unclean spirits, to cast them out...." Once again, the words "cast them out" are from the Greek word *ekballo*. Not only did Jesus expel demons from people's lives, but He commissioned and anointed His followers to do the same.

- Mark 16:17 makes it very clear that casting out demons is a responsibility that every believer possesses. Jesus never went looking for demons, and neither should we. But when they manifest their influence in people's lives, we are to act as Jesus would act — taking authority over them and kicking them out of people's lives, thus setting the people free from demonic control.

Demons were also considered to be the chief force behind occultism, sorcery, witchcraft, and paganism. Therefore, the removal of these practices was viewed to be another facet of casting out demons. This is why events like the one recorded in Acts 19:18,19 were so serious and significant: "And many that believed came, and confessed, and shewed their deeds. Many of them also which used curious arts brought their books together, and burned them before all men: and they counted the price of them, and found it fifty thousand pieces of silver."

Notice that verse 18 says that these new converts came and showed their "deeds." This word "deeds" is from the Greek word *praksis*, which refers to *magical arts, incantations, spells*, or *any item or activity connected with witchcraft or sorcery*. Verse 19 then speaks of those who had been involved in the "curious arts." This comes from the Greek word *periergos*, which is a broad term depicting *everything connected to the practice of witchcraft or sorcery.*

This verse also tells us that the people "…brought their books together, and burned them before all men…." The word "books" is the Greek word *biblios.* Today our idea of a "book" matches the one you are reading right now. But in ancient times, there were no hardbound books; instead, the word *biblios* referred to *scrolls* or *parchments.*

These scrolls and parchments were extremely expensive because the information contained in them was written by hand. But because these new converts wanted to eliminate all demonic activity from their lives, they took their costly occultic parchments and "…burned them before all men…."

The word "burned" is the Greek word *katakaino,* which means *to completely burn* or *to thoroughly burn.* This was done as the people's *public declaration* that they were permanently removing these objects from their lives. They were kicking evil out from their midst and publicly announcing that they could never turn back the clock and return to these past activities. To the people engaged in the burning of what they once considered "treasures," evil had been cast out of their lives forever.

So when you think of casting out demons, don't think only of taking authority over a yelling, screaming demon and ordering it to leave an individual. Part of casting out demons is also removing any items or activities connected with witchcraft or sorcery, including anything associated with magical arts, incantations, or spells. If you study Church history, you will find that early believers were so convinced that this principle was vital to the removal of evil that they defaced the pagan statues and destroyed places of pagan religious practices.

As you deal with people who have been demonized, take authority over those evil spirits and cast them out. Jesus has anointed you to do this, and you can do it. But don't forget that breaking all ties to occult practices is also a part of the process. *Cleanse the person, and then cleanse the environment!*

THEY SHALL SPEAK WITH NEW TONGUES

In Mark 16:17, Jesus continued to elaborate on the kinds of signs that would follow those who believe. He went on to say, "And these signs shall follow them that believe; in my name shall they cast out devils; *they shall speak with new tongues.*"

Regardless of the denomination to which you belong or what you have been taught to believe, it is an irrefutable fact that Jesus said believers would speak with new tongues. In fact, Jesus affirmed that speaking in new tongues would be one of the supernatural signs that would follow all believers!

Regardless of the denomination to which you belong
or what you have been taught to believe,
it is an irrefutable fact that Jesus said
believers would speak with new tongues.

We have already seen the first example of speaking in tongues is found in Acts 2:1-4. There it says, "And when the day of Pentecost was fully come, they were all with one accord in one place. And suddenly there came a sound from heaven as of a rushing mighty wind, and it filled all the house where they were sitting. And there appeared unto them cloven tongues like as of fire, and it sat upon each of them. *And they were all filled with the Holy*

Ghost, and began to speak with other tongues, as the Spirit gave them utterance."

Of all the instances where people spoke in tongues in the book of Acts, this is the most famous example — perhaps because it was the first time this phenomenon ever occurred and thus set the pattern for believers to be filled with the Spirit and to speak in tongues. But this instance is very unique from any other recorded in the book of Acts, for several miracles occurred that day when believers spoke in tongues for the first time.

According to Paul's words in First Corinthians 14:13-15, speaking in tongues is a spiritual language. It is so supernatural and unknown to man that it cannot be understood, not even by the speaker himself, unless he prays for the ability to interpret what he is saying. Since this is Paul's very clear teaching about speaking in tongues, it emphatically asserts that on the Day of Pentecost, the believers did *not* speak in known human languages, but in a supernatural, unknown prayer language, just as believers speak in tongues today.

It is amazing what happens when God's people open up to let Him work through them! When the believers in the book of Acts were filled with the Holy Spirit and began to speak in tongues as an integral part of their life in Christ, a door to supernatural power was opened. The power unleashed through speaking in tongues is evident throughout the book of Acts and is still in operation today.

It is amazing what happens
when God's people open up to let Him
work through them!

If you have never experienced the baptism in the Holy Spirit with the evidence of speaking in tongues, I remind you again that there is help at the end of this book on pages 429-430 and you can turn there right now to receive that help. There I tell you how to move into this divine experience that will empower and transform your life.

There are several instances in the book of Acts where believers prayed and worshiped God in tongues. This was the norm, not the exception — a common practice that was expected to occur in the life of any person who was filled with the Holy Spirit. And just as the early believers freely and fluently prayed in the Spirit, God has enabled us to do the same — *if* we will but open our hearts, open our mouths, and let our spirits speak to God.

When the believers in the book of Acts were filled
with the Holy Spirit and began to speak in tongues
as an integral part of their life in Christ,
a door to supernatural power was opened.

THEY SHALL TAKE UP SERPENTS

In Mark 16:17 and 18, Jesus continued to say, "And these signs shall follow them that believe; In my name shall they cast out devils; they shall speak with new tongues; *they shall take up serpents....*"

In the remote back hills of some states in America, there are religious groups who literally "take up serpents" as a part of their church services. These groups have taken Jesus' words in Mark 16:18 literally, where He said, "And these signs shall follow them that believe...they shall take up serpents...." Based on this scripture, these people have concluded that Jesus was actually ordering believers to "take up serpents" as a way to demonstrate the strength of their faith!

Back behind the pulpit and next to the wall in these churches are cages that contain rattlesnakes and other poisonous snakes. At an appointed moment in the church service, the cages are popped open, the snakes are brought out, and those who are daring enough pass those serpents from one person to the next. But is this what Jesus was talking about when he said believers would "take up serpents"? *Of course not!*

Let's consider the times in which Jesus uttered these words. Then we can better see how these words of Jesus apply to us today.

The word "serpents" is the Greek word *ophis*, which was simply used to depict *snakes*. Snakes were considered to be dangerous, life-threatening creatures. People were especially afraid of snakes because the road system at this time was very much undeveloped. This meant people often had to blaze their own trails to travel to some cities or remote places. Hiding in the rocks or wild grasses along the way were dangerous, poisonous snakes that frequently bit travelers, causing premature death. These snakes were a concern to all travelers, especially to those traveling by foot.

In Luke 10:19, Jesus said, "Behold, I give unto you power to tread on serpents and scorpions, and over all the power of the enemy: and nothing shall by any means hurt you." When Jesus uttered these words to His disciples, it was right after He had commanded them to go into the harvest fields of the world to reap the souls of men (*see* Luke 10:2-11). This verse was Jesus' supernatural guarantee that when believers went to preach the Good News, they would have divine protection against serpents, scorpions, and anything else the enemy might try to use to stop or hurt them. This is why Jesus concluded by saying, "…Nothing shall *by any means* hurt you."

But notice that in addition to *serpents*, Jesus also mentioned *scorpions*. The scorpions in the Middle East were extremely feared because they were loaded with deadly poison. With one sting from the tail of such a scorpion, a person could be permanently paralyzed or even killed. When people took journeys on foot, the prospect of encountering a scorpion was just as scary as the thought of snakes. Scorpions hid in the rocks and in the ruts of the road. Therefore, sitting on the wrong rock or accidentally stepping on the wrong spot in the road could result in disaster.

Jesus' promise to His disciples that they would "tread upon serpents and scorpions" was therefore very important. The word "tread" is the Greek word *pateo*, which simply means *to walk*. Jesus was telling them that even if they walked right over a scorpion or snake, they didn't need to worry because He was giving them special, supernatural protection against these natural dangers. This was a specific promise of protection for those who would be journeying long distances or through rough terrain to preach the Gospel!

To make sure the concerns of all travelers were completely covered, Jesus added, "…and nothing shall by any means hurt you." The word "hurt" is the Greek word *adikeo*, which means *to suffer injustice* or *to suffer some kind of wrong or wrongdoing*. This was the Lord's promise that we need not fear *injustice* or *wrongdoing* as He sends us into His harvest field. In fact, the Greek uses a triple negative in this phrase. It literally says, "…*and nothing* (first negative), *no* (second negative), *by no means* (third negative) *will injure or harm you*." Jesus said this in the strongest terms available to assure followers that as they obey His leading to go into their part of the world to preach the Gospel, they could exercise their authority in His name to remain divinely protected from all forms of evil and demonic strategies.

Now let's go back to where we began in Mark 16:18. Jesus said, "These signs will follow them that believe...they shall take up serpents...." What did this mean to the disciples, and how does it apply to you and me today?

For the disciples, it meant they were divinely guarded by the power of God. This divine protection was so powerful that even if they were to be bitten by a deadly snake or a highly venomous scorpion, it would have no effect on them. An example of this can be found in Acts 28:3-6 when the apostle Paul was bitten by a deadly viper. Paul simply shook off the snake into the fire and went away unharmed.

You see, Jesus gave His disciples supernatural protection because He was sending them to preach the Gospel to the ends of the earth. Things that would normally injure or kill others would have no effect on them whatsoever. Since they were required to walk by foot through dangerous and rough terrain, this was a very important promise!

What does this have to do with you and me? First, it has *nothing* to do with passing rattlesnakes around a congregation! Although believers who do this may be sincere, they are sincerely wrong. This is foolishness and presumption. Jesus never intended for us to deliberately endanger ourselves!

But it does mean that we can claim God's power to protect us when He calls us to carry the Gospel to parts of the world that are considered to be unsafe. We may not deal with serpents and scorpions like the early believers did, but there may be times when we are required to fly on rickety airplanes, drive on dangerous roads, pass through highly volatile areas, or work in regions that are considered dangerous.

We can claim God's power to protect us
when He calls us to carry the Gospel
to parts of the world that are considered to be unsafe.

But as noted earlier, this divine protection is activated in those of us who *believe* that God's promise of protection will work for us. Whenever we enter dangerous territory in fear, doubt, and unbelief, we are likely to get in trouble. But if we will go believing and claiming that God's protection is ours and that the enemy can't do anything to hurt us, our faith in this promise will activate it and cause it to be manifested in our lives!

IF THEY DRINK ANY DEADLY THING, IT SHALL NOT HURT THEM

As we read further in Mark 16:18, Jesus said, "And these signs shall follow them that believe; In my name shall they cast out devils; they shall speak with new tongues; they shall take up serpents; *and if they drink any deadly thing, it shall not hurt them....*"

Jesus went on to say, "...And if they drink any deadly thing, it shall not hurt them...." Based on these words, some sincerely misled groups also deliberately drink deadly poisons, such as strychnine and arsenic. Just as they take up venomous snakes to prove the strength of their faith, these groups intentionally subject themselves to deadly poisons for the same purpose. They actually believe Jesus intended for Christians to consume lethal chemicals to prove that when their faith is strong, such substances will have no effect on them. *But is this really what Jesus meant?* Let's look at this verse to see what He was talking about!

The word "drink" is actually the Greek word *pino,* which means *to drink* or *to consume.* Although this word usually refers to *drinking,* it can also picture *a person who is consuming something,* such as meat or some other kind of food. The word "deadly" comes from the Greek word *thanasimos,* a derivative of the word *thanatos,* which is the Greek word for *death.* However, the word used here in Mark 16:18 describes *something that is deadly or fatal.* The word "any" is the small word *ti,* which means *anything.* This means that Jesus wasn't referring only to liquid chemicals, but to *anything* that is deadly or fatal, including chemicals *or* foods. Hence, this part of the verse could be translated, "*…and if they consume anything that would normally be fatal.…*"

Jesus continued by saying that if believers consume something fatal while they are on a God-sent trip, this fatal substance "shall not hurt them." The word "hurt" is the Greek word *blapto,* which means *to weaken, to disable, to hurt, to harm,* or *to injure.* It depicts *something that is probably not powerful enough to kill, but strong enough to make one sick or ill.* Because the word *thanasimos* ("deadly thing") is also used in this verse, it tells us that Jesus meant the following: "*…And if they consume anything that would normally be fatal or anything that would usually make a person sick, it will have no effect upon them.…*"

Remember that Jesus was speaking to His followers, whom He was going to send to the farthest ends of the world. To fulfill this assignment, they would be required to eat foods they had never seen before. In fact, their journeys to pagan lands would no doubt necessitate that they eat foods they previously considered to be dirty or unclean. For them to take the Gospel to new places meant they would have to eat "mystery food" — not knowing where it came from, who killed it, how long it had been dead, who cooked it, how clean or dirty the kitchen was in which it was cooked, or what effect the food was going to have on their stomachs.

Remember, the Lord had previously told His disciples, "And in the same house remain, eating and drinking such things as they give...eat such things as are set before you" (Luke 10:7,8). If the disciples had rejected what their hosts had prepared for them, they could have greatly insulted or hurt them. Therefore, Jesus said in effect, *"If your hosts have prepared the best they can give you, eat it with joy!"*

As one who travels worldwide, I can personally tell you that sometimes it is difficult to eat what is set before you. But when you look into a plate of food that looks scary, you must shut your eyes, bless it in Jesus' name, lift your fork from the plate, open your mouth, insert that bite, and eat the "mystery food" by faith!

I've seen people come on mission trips expecting to eat the identical kinds of food they eat at home. When they discover they can't have the same food, the same restaurants, the same blend of coffee, and so on, I've seen them get very upset. *But they're not at home.* They are on the other side of the world where those kinds of foods either don't exist or are difficult to come by. If a person is going to take the Gospel to the ends of the earth, he must be willing to eat food that is prepared at the ends of the earth!

This is precisely the reason Jesus told His soon-to-be world travelers that if they consumed anything deadly or sickening, it would have no effect on them. Jesus wasn't encouraging His disciples to deliberately consume poison. Rather, He was assuring them of the divine protection that is available for those who take the Gospel to the ends of the earth.

But as noted earlier, this promise belongs to "those who believe." If you want this promise of supernatural protection from bad foods or fatal substances to be a reality in your own life, you must release your faith and activate this promise. So before you sit down to eat, take a few minutes to bless that food. Call it sanctified, and speak health, wholeness, and freedom into your body. Then eat the food, believing that it will only bless you and that nothing negative can happen to you as a result of eating it!

If a person is going to take the Gospel to the ends of the earth, he must be willing to eat food that is prepared at the ends of the earth!

Jesus provided everything needed for those of us who would follow His call to the ends of the earth. He supplied us with supernatural protection from disasters, calamities, snakes, scorpions, and all the works of the enemy. He also promised traveling mercies and protection from acts of injustice. He even guaranteed that if we accidentally consume bad foods or deadly substances, they wouldn't weaken us physically or injure our health. He covered the gamut of protection, provision, and prosperity as we obey His calling and do His will! (For more on this subject, *see* my book *Will of God — The Key To Your Success*.)

It's time for you to quit worrying and start believing that Jesus meant what He said. If God is giving you an assignment that takes you to a foreign state, a distant country, or an unfamiliar culture, just keep your eyes fixed on Jesus and start moving forward in that assignment.

God isn't going to send you somewhere so you can eat something deadly and die. Rebuke that spirit of fear and release your faith! Don't let the devil keep you trapped at home because you're afraid you won't like the food. The Gospel and the power of God are so much stronger than any meat or drink!

It's time for you to quit worrying and
start believing that Jesus meant what He said.

THEY SHALL LAY HANDS ON THE SICK, AND THEY SHALL RECOVER

Jesus added one last supernatural sign that will accompany those who are believing. In Mark 16:18, He said, "And these signs shall follow them that believe; in my name shall they cast out devils; they shall speak with new tongues; they shall take up serpents; and if they drink any deadly thing, it shall not hurt them; *they shall lay hands on the sick, and they shall recover.*"

Jesus said that believers would lay hands on the sick, and the sick would recover. What category of sick people was Jesus talking about? What did He mean when He said they would recover? Are there examples of this in Jesus' own ministry that we can read and learn from? Let's look deeply into this verse today to see how it applies to you and me!

First, let's look at the word "sick," because this describes the category of sick people Jesus was talking about. This is the Greek word *arroustos*, which comes from the word *arunnumi*. The word *runnumi* normally means *to be well, to be strong, to be in good health,* or *to possess a strong physical condition.* When an *a* is placed in front of this word, it reverses the condition, and instead the new word means *to be in bad health* or *to possess a weak and broken condition*. It is the image of *a person so weak and sick that he has become critically ill*. He is *an invalid*.

The following three scriptures show us examples of times when Jesus healed people who were afflicted with an *arroustos* type of sickness:

- Matthew 14:14 says, "And Jesus went forth, and saw a great multitude, and was moved with compassion toward them, and he healed their sick." The word "sick" in this verse is the Greek word *arroustos*. Matthew informs us that Jesus was especially drawn to those who were so weak that they were without strength. These people whom He healed that day were *invalids*.

- Mark 6:5 tells us, "And he could there do no mighty work, save that he laid his hands upon a few sick folk, and healed them." In Greek, the words "sick folk" also come from the Greek word *arroustos*. This lets us know that these were *extremely sick people*. Most readers presume that these were minor ailments, but the word *arroustos* tells us emphatically that these were *critically ill individuals*.

- Mark 6:13 says, "And they cast out many devils, and anointed with oil many that were sick, and healed them." The word "sick" is the Greek word *arroustos*, which means these individuals were *very frail* and *weak in health*.

These examples of the word *arroustos* vividly show that these were not people who were simply feeling poorly because of some small ailment; these were people who were *devastated* by sickness. They were so physically weak, so critically ill, and so lacking of strength that they had become invalids. This is the category of sick people that Jesus said believers would lay hands on, and they would recover. He wasn't talking about headaches and skin abrasions! He was talking about believers laying hands on people who are *critically ill* and who fall into the category of *invalids*.

Notice that Jesus said believers would "lay hands" on the sick. These words come from the Greek word *epitithemi*, a compound of the words *epi* and *tithemi*. The word *epi* means *upon*, and *tithemi* means *to place*. When they are joined to become the word *epitithemi*, it means *to place upon* or *to lay upon*. This word is used in Luke 4:40 to describe an event during which Jesus *placed His hands upon sick people*.

Luke 4:40 says, "Now when the sun was setting, all they that had any sick with divers diseases brought them unto him; and he laid his hands on every one of them, and healed them." That evening the people brought to Jesus "any sick." This word "sick" is different than the other examples we looked at earlier. It is the word *asthenios*, which depicts *a wide range of infirmities*. This is why it is further amplified by the phrase "any sick *with diverse diseases*," which represents a wide range of sicknesses.

However, the word "diseases" lets us know that some of these people were seriously ill. This word "diseases" is the Greek word *nosos*, which always conveys the idea of *a terrible malady* or *an affliction of the most severe nature*. Often the word *nosos* depicted *a terminal illness for which there was no natural cure*. Hence, it could describe people who were *terminally ill*.

What did Jesus do for these people? He laid His hands upon them, and He healed them. In such cases, Jesus was giving the perfect example of how believers would later lay their hands on the sick — *including the terminally ill* — and see them be restored back to health as a result of believers' obedience.

But when you look carefully at Mark 16:18, you'll notice that Jesus promised *recovery*. That recovery could be instantaneous, or it could be a process that takes place over a period of time. The words "they shall" are from the Greek word *echo*, which means *to have* or *to possess*. But the tense that is used in this verse doesn't picture something that is instantaneous; rather, it refers to something that occurs *progressively*. In fact, the word "healed" doesn't speak of an instantaneous event either. It is the word *kalos,* which in this case means *to be well, to be healthy*, or *to be in good shape*. Taken together as one complete phrase, it could be translated, *"… They shall progressively feel themselves getting better and better, until finally they are well and healthy."*

This lets us know that all healings do *not* occur instantly; some of them take place over a period of time. But Jesus' promise is that if we will follow His example and lay our hands on the sick, God's power will be released into the bodies of the afflicted. As we release our faith and believe for His healing power to flow from us to the recipient, that divine flow of healing virtue will be deposited into the sick person's body. And just as medicine gradually works to reverse a medical condition, the power of God that was deposited with the laying on of our hands will begin to attack the work of the devil and progressively restore that sick person to a state of health and well-being.

Jesus laid His hands upon them, and He healed them.
In such cases, He was giving the perfect example
of how believers would later lay their hands
on the sick — *including the terminally ill* —
and see them be restored back to health
as a result of believers' obedience.

This is Jesus' promise! And Jesus promised that *any* believer could do this. Any believer, including *you*, can lay hands on the sick and see the sick get better and better until they are fully restored back to health. All that is required for God to use you in this way are three basic criteria: 1) that you have a desire for God to heal through you; 2) that you have hands to lay on sick people; and 3) that your faith is released to activate the power of God to heal. If you can fulfill these three requirements, you're ready to lay hands on the sick and see them restored to health!

Healing the sick is part of your responsibility as a believer. You cannot do it alone, but the Holy Spirit is actively present to impart His power when you act in Jesus' name. So rather than look at sick people and feel pity for them, why don't you pull your hands out of your pockets and go lay them on those sick people by faith, just as Jesus did when He was ministering on the earth? The Word guarantees that God will work with you to bring healing and health to those who are in need.

Healing the sick is part of your responsibility as a believer.
You cannot do it alone, but the Holy Spirit
is actively present to impart His power
when you act in Jesus' name.

All of these signs that Jesus described in Mark 16:16-18 are supposed to follow all who believe. Are they following you? If not, why not? It's a good question to ask yourself.

But these are just the starting points of supernatural activity in the life of a believer. If a believer really opens up and allows the Holy Spirit to move mightily in his or her life, the Spirit will act with amazing levels of power and supernatural manifestations!

What Are the Gifts of the Holy Spirit?

In First Corinthians chapter 12, Paul unequivocally stated that the gifts of the Holy Spirit are *manifestations of the Holy Spirit* to the Church. He wrote in verse 7, "But the manifestation of the Spirit is given to every man to profit withal." Then Paul proceeded to list those gifts or manifestations.

If these gifts are manifestations of the *Holy Spirit*, they must be good, because the Spirit of God does only what is good and profitable for us. In addition, this verse plainly tells us that the Holy Spirit doesn't want to just be present in the Church; He wants to *manifest* Himself in the Church — and one way He does that is through spiritual gifts.

Paul further stated that the nine gifts of the Spirit are designed by God to operate in "every man." The words "every man" is from the Greek word *hekastos,* which is an all-inclusive term that includes *every single person with no one excluded.* It plainly means that God wants *every* Christian to function in spiritual gifts. And "no one excluded" really does mean that *not one believer* is to miss out on receiving and operating in this vital part of his or her spiritual inheritance.

Yes, that means the Holy Spirit wants to manifest these gifts through *you!*

God wants *every* Christian to function in spiritual gifts. *Not one believer* is to miss out on receiving and operating in this vital part of his or her spiritual inheritance.

Paul continued to say that when these gifts are at work, they cause everyone to "profit." The Greek word for "profit" describes *something that is a benefit* or *an advantage gained.* This means the operation of spiritual gifts brings a true *benefit* to the Church and gives believers a supernatural advantage in their daily walk.

The devil knows that these spiritual gifts are beneficial and that they are instrumental in giving believers the advantage over him. That's the reason Satan has withstood their operation in the Church and has even tried to theologically convince people that the gifts of the Spirit passed away with the death of the apostles.

You see, the enemy knows that when a supernatural element of the Holy Spirit is at work in the Church, it brings a dimension of Christ to the Church that believers otherwise do not know. These manifestations of the Spirit are *essential* if the supernatural power of Christ is going to be demonstrated in the lives of His people.

The devil knows that these spiritual gifts are beneficial and that they are instrumental in giving believers the advantage over him. That's the reason Satan has withstood their operation in the Church.

In First Corinthians 12, Paul wrote about a broad range of spiritual gifts. Among these, he listed the *vocal gifts* and *revelatory gifts.* The vocal gifts include *tongues, the interpretation of tongues,* and *prophecy.* These are spiritual gifts that, when vocalized, supernaturally convey a message from the heart of God to a specific person or congregation. The church at Corinth was overflowing with these gifts of the Holy Spirit.

The revelatory gifts of the Holy Spirit include the *word of wisdom, word of knowledge,* and *discerning of spirits.* These are spiritual gifts that cause a person to supernaturally receive understanding from Heaven of something that could not be naturally obtained — or knowledge that is received *independently* of that which could be revealed naturally. These revelatory gifts were also demonstrated in abundance in the church at Corinth.

Paul's list of spiritual gifts in First Corinthians 12 includes three additional gifts of the Holy Spirit: the gifts of *faith, healings*, and *miracles*. However, we can conclude from Paul's words in First Corinthians chapter 14 that the gifts primarily operating among the Corinthian congregation were the *vocal gifts* and *revelatory gifts.*

Before we go on to discuss the nature of these nine gifts of the Spirit found in First Corinthians 12, it's good to note that there are variations of all these manifestations of the Holy Spirit's power. Paul wrote about this in verses 4-7: "Now there are diversities of gifts, but the same Spirit. And there are differences of administrations, but the same Lord. And there are diversities of operations, but it is the same God which worketh all in all. But the manifestation of the Spirit is given to every man to profit withal."

The manifestations and operations of the Holy Spirit are endless in their variety and diversity, but the end result is always toward one end: *"to profit withal."* These nine gifts with their manifold demonstrations are always for our benefit. And because they originate from the Spirit of God, we can be assured that they are good and perfect gifts, because they come "from above" (*see* James 1:17).

THE NINE GIFTS OF THE HOLY SPIRIT

What you are about to read is not intended to be a thorough study of the gifts of the Spirit, but simply a starting point — with a brief definition for each gift and a scriptural example to illustrate how each gift operates. Let's take a look at each of these gifts one by one.

Word of Wisdom

In First Corinthians 12:8, Paul listed a spiritual gift that he called the "word of wisdom." The Greek word translated "word" in this context really refers to a *fragment* of wisdom. The word "wisdom" refers to *special insight* that is not naturally obtained.

Thus, the "word of wisdom" actually describes a gift that operates in that moment when *a fragment of special insight* is supernaturally revealed to an individual about a specific situation. It is received as "wisdom" because it delivers *an answer* or *a directive* to a pressing need, question, or situation, or it provides insight into future events that could not be known naturally.

Example: In Acts 27, the apostle Paul was on a ship with others that was headed directly for disaster. After the crew's long, futile struggle to bring the ship under control, Paul had a dream during the night in which he was told, "Fear not, Paul; thou must be brought before Caesar: and, lo, God hath given thee all them that sail with thee" (Acts 27:24).

This information did not give Paul a full answer regarding his situation, but it was a "word" from Heaven that gave him direction and insight into the future for his situation. He supernaturally knew, at least in part, that all would be well, because he was destined to stand before Caesar in Rome. This is a wonderful example of a supernatural, fragmentary word of wisdom that both gave an answer to a believer for the pressing need of the moment and provided insight into an aspect of God's future plan and purpose for that believer.

Word of Knowledge

In First Corinthians 12:8, Paul also listed a spiritual gift that he called the "word of knowledge." As we just saw, the Greek word translated "word" really refers to a *fragment* of knowledge in this context. Just as we saw that a word of wisdom describes wisdom not naturally obtained, the "word of knowledge" likewise refers to *a fragment of special knowledge* that one supernaturally receives.

This, then, is the ability to supernaturally know facts and details that would not be known in the natural. When a "word of knowledge" is given to a believer by the Holy Spirit, it is often imparted to illuminate listeners to God's intimate, personal involvement in the facts and details of a specific situation or in a person's life so that His purpose can be fulfilled in that situation or in that individual's life.

Example: When Jesus was at the well in Samaria, a woman came to draw water. When she spoke to Jesus, certain facts and details of her life were instantly revealed to Him as He spoke with her. Jesus didn't see every fact and detail about her life at that moment. But the fragments of personal information about this Samaritan woman that the Holy Spirit imparted to Jesus were precisely correct. And when He shared those supernaturally revealed details with her, the woman was immediately made aware of God's tender care for her (*see* John 4:5-30).

Special Faith or the Gift of Faith

In First Corinthians 12:9, Paul included "faith" in his list of spiritual gifts. This is not natural faith, which every person possesses. (In Romans 12:3, Paul clearly taught that *every person* is given a measure of faith.) In this context, Paul was referring to *special* faith, otherwise known as *the gift of faith.*

This spiritual gift is manifested as a sudden impartation by the Holy Spirit of supernatural, special faith at a critical moment to accomplish God's purpose or desire in a particular situation or event. When this supernatural burst of faith is suddenly released in a believer by the Spirit, that person is empowered to believe that the impossible is doable in order to accomplish what can only be done supernaturally.

Example: In Acts 14, Paul was preaching to a group of pagans when he sensed a sudden release of special faith. In that moment, Paul called upon a lame man to stand and walk. In obedience to Paul's command of special faith, the lame man immediately arose and walked — completely made whole in an instant. Paul recognized the divine moment when the gift of special faith was in operation, and he acted on it. As a result, the impossible was manifested as a reality in the natural realm.

Gifts of Healing

In First Corinthians 12:9, Paul also listed "gifts of healing" as a gift of the Spirit. It is significant that the word "gifts" is plural, because it tells us that there are different aspects of this spiritual manifestation — all of them designed to produce healing, but in sundry ways.

Paul recognized the divine moment when the gift
of special faith was in operation, and he acted on it.
As a result, the impossible was manifested
as a reality in the natural realm.

It is also noteworthy that the word "healing" is the Greek word *iaomai*, which means *to cure*. This word would even describe being *doctored* by a physician. This is important, because a medical doctor doesn't normally produce instantaneous results for his patient; rather, he prescribes medicine or orders some procedure that eventually cures the one needing to be healed.

Likewise, this gift of the Holy Spirit is very often a supernatural cure that begins with a prayer and at times the laying on of hands, but the healing may take full effect over a period of time. Although divine in nature, the word "healing" used here nonetheless refers to a progressive result.

Example: In Luke 17, a group of lepers met Jesus as He entered a certain village to seek His healing touch. As you will see in the following example, the "working of miracles" occurs when the laws of nature are overridden, and what could never occur in the natural *suddenly* and *instantly* takes place. A miracle is not what happened with that group of lepers. Luke 17:14 clearly says these lepers were healed and cleansed "as they went." This was a manifestation of a gift of healing — a supernatural touch of the Holy Spirit that generally occurs over a period of time and that ultimately cures a person from his ailment.

Working of Miracles

In First Corinthians 12:10, Paul went on to list the "working of miracles" as a gift that the Holy Spirit distributes as He wills. The Greek text actually says, "the operation of powers." With this phrase, Paul described a divine operation of supernatural power that overrides natural laws and quickly does what is naturally impossible.

When pertaining to the human body, the "working of miracles" usually occurs in a split second — when, for example, a damaged organ or limb is instantly and supernaturally healed or restored.

God's power suddenly speeds up a healing process that would normally take place over a long period of time or that would perhaps never naturally occur — and in a blink of an eye, the process is miraculously complete.

Examples: One operation of the working of miracles would be a supernatural overriding of the laws of nature that enables one to do what no human could naturally do. An example of this occurred when Jesus walked on the water. In a split second, the atoms in that water solidified for Jesus to walk on a firm path. This was the power of God overriding natural laws.

Another instance when "working of miracles" occurred was the multiplication of the loaves and fishes. This spiritual gift operated through Jesus at a critical moment when the power of God instantly transformed and supernaturally multiplied the small portions of food Jesus held in His hands. Although the instantaneous multiplication of physical matter is impossible in the natural realm, the power of God overrode the laws of nature and enabled the impossible to miraculously come to pass.

When Jesus walked on the water,
in a split second, the atoms in that water
solidified for Him to walk on a firm path.
This was the power of God overriding natural laws.

Prophecy

In First Corinthians 12:10, Paul next listed "prophecy" as a gift of the Spirit that God intends to be actively operative in the Church until Jesus' return for His Church. The word "prophecy" is a Greek word that means *to speak on behalf of God; to speak in advance of a situation; to foretell an event; or to assert the mind of God to others.*

It is important to note that one who speaks a prophetic word to the church is not necessarily called into the full-time ministry of a prophet. In First Corinthians 14:1, Paul encouraged *everyone* to seek this spiritual gift, and in verse 31, he stated that *everyone* can prophesy. Over and over in Scripture, we can see that this simple gift of prophecy manifested to comfort those under duress, bring encouragement to people's hearts, and redirect their attention to God.

According to First Corinthians 14:3, the primary objective of this spiritual gift is to impart *edification, exhortation*, and *comfort* to the listeners. When a person moves in this spiritual gift, he or she is divinely inspired to speak on behalf of God and to deliver a message He wants to convey to His people at a particular time or for a particular situation. This spiritual gift results in an individual or congregation receiving new understanding about a truth, insight, or directive from the heart of God that helps strengthen, encourage, and instruct the listeners so they can walk with Him more accurately.

Example: One instance of the gift of prophecy is found in the event that occurred when the elders of Antioch gathered for a time of fasting and prayer. Acts 13:2 says, "As they ministered to the Lord, and fasted, the Holy Ghost said, Separate me Barnabas and Saul for the work whereunto I have called them."

According to this verse, the gift of prophecy was at work as the Holy Spirit spoke through someone in the group. And when the Spirit spoke, that word from the Lord launched out Paul and Barnabas into their apostolic ministries.

Discerning of Spirits

Paul also listed "discerning of spirits" as a gift of the Spirit in First Corinthians 12:10. The Greek words for "discerning of spirits" actually describe one's supernatural ability to perceive the true nature of a spiritual situation or to discern what spiritual forces are really at work in the life of an individual or in a specific circumstance.

This revelatory gift is a supernatural revealing or discerning of spiritual forces that otherwise cannot be naturally discerned. The manifestation of this gift occurs in an instant. It is as though a curtain has suddenly been pulled apart and one is enabled to see into the realm of the spirit to know what is really happening behind the scenes or to see or perceive the genuine spiritual condition that is otherwise hidden to the eyes.

This gift often manifests in spiritual leaders, since leaders need this grace-given equipment to supernaturally perceive what kind of spiritual influence people are yielding to. The discerning of spirits is a vital piece of spiritual equipment given to leaders as the Holy Spirit wills to aid in the selection of a leadership team, in leading others through difficult situations, and in accurately seeing the true nature of a particular spiritual environment.

Example: In Matthew 9, Jesus was speaking with a group of scribes, and it seemed that they were listening with open hearts. But suddenly Jesus supernaturally knew what He otherwise would not naturally know. He literally "saw" or discerned spiritually what was occurring inside these scribes, and He confronted them. Matthew 9:4 says, "And Jesus knowing their thoughts said, Wherefore think ye evil in your hearts?" Although the people tried to conceal their true thoughts, the gift of discerning of spirits enabled Jesus to supernaturally perceive or see the actual spiritual forces He was dealing with.

Divers Kinds of Tongues

In First Corinthians 12:10, Paul stated that "divers kinds of tongues" is another gift that the Holy Spirit distributes as He wills for the edification of the Church. In this phrase, Paul described the public gift of tongues, which is different from a devotional tongue that one uses in prayer — often referred to in this modern day as a heavenly "prayer language." Also, praying in tongues "publicly," or as a corporate group, is not a manifestation of this gift of "divers kinds of tongues."

Paul was explicitly referring here to that moment when someone is moved supernaturally by the Holy Spirit's inner prompting to deliver a specific message in tongues from the heart of God to an individual or an assembled group.

According to First Corinthians 14:5, Paul taught that when a public message in tongues is interpreted, which we will discuss next, it brings supernatural edification to the Church. Some try to discount this particular gift as a less important gift of the Spirit, but Paul listed it alongside the other spiritual gifts, ranking it equal in importance to the others.

Example: The best scriptural reference to "divers kinds of tongues" is found in Paul's discussion of this gift in First Corinthians 14, where the apostle taught about how to properly flow in the manifestation of this spiritual gift and where he charged that no one forbid its operation. If you want to know more about "divers kinds of tongues," it is imperative that you do a serious and thoughtful study of First Corinthians 14.

Interpretation of Tongues

Finally, in First Corinthians 12:10, Paul mentioned "the interpretation of tongues" as a ninth gift of the Holy Spirit. This gift operates in cooperation with "divers kinds of tongues." When one is inspired to speak a public message in tongues, that vocal gift of the Spirit must be accompanied by a second vocal gift, the gift of interpretation (*see* 1 Corinthians 14:26-28).

It must be pointed out that this particular gift is not the *translation* of tongues; it is the *interpretation* of tongues. One who moves in this spiritual gift supernaturally understands and speaks out the meaning of the message in tongues that has been spoken. The person may not understand what was said in tongues word for word, but he has the supernaturally imparted ability to interpret it — in other words, to give public voice to what God desires to communicate. The length of the interpretation may not necessarily match the length of the message in tongues because this is a Spirit-inspired interpretation rather than a word-for-word translation.

This gift of interpretation of tongues, then, necessarily works in partnership with divers kinds of tongues. Again, this is not a reference to a corporate group publicly praying in tongues together. It refers to the moment when an individual is inspired by the Spirit to deliver a distinct, public message in tongues. Such a message requires public interpretation, and for that to occur, the gift of interpretation must be present and active.

Example: Once again, for a deeper understanding of the interpretation of tongues, it is best to refer to Paul's instructions in First Corinthians 14, which covers the operation of this gift in-depth. The church at Corinth had the gift of "divers kinds of tongues" in regular manifestation. Therefore, Paul wrote to help guide and instruct the Corinthian congregation on how to properly flow in the gift of interpretation as a necessary accompaniment to the gift of "divers kinds of tongues."

I want to add that the gifts of the Spirit often work in pairs or in groupings. For example, where the working of miracles is at work, it is often accompanied by special faith — and these two gifts working together can move mountains of opposition that literally are *impossible* to move in the natural realm. When the word of knowledge is in operation, it is often accompanied by the gifts of healing and the working of miracles. The breadth and variety of how these spiritual-gift combinations can manifest is manifold, but it is helpful to remember that wherever one of these spiritual gifts operates, it often does so in partnership with one of the other gifts.

The church at Corinth was so "enriched" with these spiritual manifestations that Paul felt it necessary to write an entire "chapter" in his first letter to this congregation about how to manage the operation of these spiritual gifts (*see* 1 Corinthians 14). *Imagine that* — so many of these gifts were in operation in a single Corinthian church service that the church had to be instructed on how to properly manage them!

IS IT RIGHT OR WRONG TO SEEK SPIRITUAL GIFTS?

Many who were reared in traditional churches have been taught that it is wrong to *seek* spiritual gifts. But if these spiritual gifts are from God, why would it be wrong to seek them? If they really are God-given manifestations of the Holy Spirit, shouldn't we earnestly desire for them to work among us?

It must be noted that Paul never rebuked or corrected the Corinthian believers for having so many spiritual gifts or for seeking God for their manifestation. In fact, in First Corinthians 14:1, Paul instructed them to "desire" spiritual gifts. In that verse Paul wrote, "Follow after love and *desire* spiritual gifts...."

The first part of the verse contains a command: that we are supposed to ardently follow after love. No one would argue that we are to pursue having loving relationships with others. But if we believe the first part of the verse, we must take the *entire* verse as ours to obey. That means we must also embrace the part that *commands* us to "desire" spiritual gifts.

The Greek word for "desire" means *to be fervently boiling over with zealousness* for the object desired. It depicts *an intense desire that causes one to seek something until it is obtained.*

This is not a mere want or wish. This Greek word emphatically means that Paul wanted the church of Corinth to have *an intense longing* and *a burning zealousness* to experience more and more of these spiritual manifestations in their midst.

Paul knew spiritual gifts were vital to bring the supernatural dimension of Christ to that church. That is why he *intensely* desired the Corinthian Christians to *fervently boil over with desire* in their urgent pursuit of those gifts. In other words, believers are *to consistently and constantly be burning, boiling over, and longing for* the gifts of the Holy Spirit.

So when the apostle Paul taught on the gifts of the Holy Spirit, he was actually saying, "*Desire — constantly and consistently burn with zeal and intensely long for — the gifts of the Holy Spirit.*" This may be contrary to what you have heard or been taught, but it's the Bible. God said it's right for you to want the gifts of the Holy Spirit! In fact, He wants you to *burn* with zeal and intensely long for the working of the Holy Spirit in your midst. The Holy

Spirit is the power that produces transformation in your life and in the lives of the people He wants you to minister to as you go through each day (*see* 2 Corinthians 3:18).

> God said it's right for you to want the gifts
> of the Holy Spirit! In fact, He wants you
> to *burn* with zeal and intensely long for
> the working of the Holy Spirit in your midst.

Staying mindful of the gifts of the Holy Spirit that reside within you is a vital key to your spiritual growth and maturity. The Bible tells us in First Timothy 4:14 (*NLT*), "Do not neglect the spiritual gift you received through the prophecies spoken to you when the elders of the church laid their hands on you."

I have learned that if I'm intentional about moving in the gifts of the Spirit — if I am open to the gifts, fervently desire the gifts, and purposely make room for them in my personal life and in our church — the manifestation of the gifts of the Spirit in our midst and in my life increases.

There are churches that once moved powerfully in the gifts of the Holy Spirit. But somewhere along the way they adopted the mindset, *Well, maybe operating in the Spirit is not the best thing to do. Visitors just don't understand things like prophecy, tongues, and interpretation of tongues.* So little by little, these churches began to neglect or pull back from the gifts of the Spirit — and, as a result, their fire has dwindled.

This is exactly what God *doesn't* want us to do.

I have learned that if I am open to the gifts,
fervently desire the gifts, and purposely make room
for them in my personal life and in our church —
the manifestation of the gifts of the Spirit
in our midst and in my life increases.

What are you to do with your spiritual gifts? Second Timothy 1:6 (*NKJV*) commands you to "…stir up the gift of God which is in you through the laying on of my hands." The words "stir up" are from the Greek word *anadzoopureoo*, a triple compound of three Greek words: *ana*, *zoos*, and *pur*. The word *ana* conveys the idea of *repeating an earlier action* or *doing something again*. The word *zoos* is from the word *zao*, which means *to be enthusiastic*, *to be passionate*, *to be fervent*, or *to be zealous*. And the word *pur* is the Greek word for *fire*.

I must note that in ancient Greece, fire was viewed to be *a life-giving force*. It was used not only to keep people warm in their homes, but also in matters related to the divine and supernatural. In addition, it was a force to defeat enemies. Fire was central to life and considered both practically and spiritually essential for one's existence.

In ancient Greece, fire was viewed
to be *a life-giving force*. Fire was central to life
and considered both practically and spiritually
essential for one's existence.

New Testament believers had a great supply of the fire of the Spirit. In fact, there were so many gifts of the Spirit operating in the church at Corinth when the church came together that the apostle Paul had to give them some guidelines. In First Corinthians 14:26, he wrote, "How is it then brethren? When ye come together, every one of you hath a psalm, hath a doctrine, hath a tongue, hath a revelation, hath an interpretation. Let all things be done unto edifying."

Imagine a church where the Spirit is moving so strongly that it results in every single member operating in the gifts of the Spirit! That's what was happening in Corinth. The word for "every one" is the Greek word *hekastos*, which indicates *every single member of the church*. Every time the people came together, one person had a psalm, one had a tongue, another had an interpretation, another had a revelation — and on and on it went. They had so many gifts that the people were interrupting each other, trying to administer them.

Notice that Paul *didn't* say, "Tone it down! It's too much. You're going to scare people away." Instead, he said in essence, "It's great that every one of you has something of the Spirit to bring. Just be polite and respectful of each other. One at a time, let your gifts be given in a way that they build and strengthen the church." Paul's instructions were effective for the Corinthians then, and they still serve as guidelines for the Church now.

Where Are the Gifts of the Holy Spirit in the Church Today?

One reason the operation of the gifts of the Spirit is rare in the modern Church is that some church leaders are afraid of what might happen — afraid of running visitors away or afraid of excess and error where the supernatural is concerned. They might say, for example, "We don't want to freak out the new people and scare them off, so we're going to tone things down." So these church leaders structure their churches as "seeker-sensitive" — focused primarily on appealing to unbelievers, and they pull back from allowing and encouraging the operation of the gifts of the Spirit. As a result, the church becomes weak and spiritually anemic and ultimately lacks the supernatural presence of God.

But that is not biblical. The Church — which in Greek is the *ekklesia,* meaning *the called-out ones of God* — is not for unbelievers, but for *believers.* Although unbelievers should be very welcome in our churches, we should not design our services for them. Services should be designed for believers.

Another common reason we don't see the Holy Spirit operating today as He did in the Early Church is that pastors and church leaders are not allowing time for Him to move in their services. It's the responsibility of God's undershepherds to keep the fire of the Holy Spirit burning — not only in their own personal walk with the Lord, but also in the hearts of the believers God has put under their charge to lead. Leaders should always purpose to make room for His gifts to manifest whenever He desires.

The gifts of the Holy Spirit often manifest during times of worship. Passionate worship — which I will discuss in Chapter Six — creates an environment for the Holy Spirit to move freely.

Leaders should always purpose
to make room for God's gifts to manifest
whenever He desires.

However, due to the limitations of time and space in many churches, allowing for an open-ended worship time can sometimes be challenging. Let me explain.

At our own church, we have several services on Sunday to help as many people as possible experience an encounter with Christ in a corporate setting. However, we have only so much time because of these space constraints and our need for multiple services. Because real estate is at such a premium in the vast metropolitan city of Moscow, parking is limited. We can only fit so many cars in the parking lot, so many people in each service, and so many children in the children's ministry. As one service ends and the next one is about to begin, we have to courteously help the adults and children exit the building and then the parking lot, while warmly welcoming the next group, allowing them to find a parking place and a seat in the sanctuary or the children's ministry.

Thankfully, the gifts of the Holy Spirit do manifest in our services. But because of our schedule and limitations, we have to keep things moving, and we aren't able to go as long as we want to go. I believe this example describes many modern-day churches that are actively advancing the Kingdom. *So how do we make room for the Holy Spirit to move in our church?*

We have created additional opportunities for Him to move. These include our Friday night prayer meetings and our home groups. During these encounters, the limitations are removed and the gifts of the Spirit are in full operation. Prophecy, the gift of tongues and the interpretation of tongues, words of wisdom, and words of knowledge all manifest in these settings.

The home groups are really the best place for the Holy Spirit to minister, because they provide a smaller, more intimate setting. It is a safe place for believers who are just beginning to operate in the gifts to experiment and learn how to yield to the Spirit's unction as He prompts them to step out and obey Him in blessing others.

I encourage you to do whatever you can do to create an environment that is inviting to the Holy Spirit, especially if you're a spiritual leader. Create spaces and places for Him to work.

Without question, the presence and power of the Holy Spirit is paramount to the health and strength of the Church. There is more instruction in the New Testament on the operation of the gifts of the Spirit than most of the other tenets of the faith. For example, the Holy Spirit moved on the apostle Paul to pen three chapters in First Corinthians, as well as significant portions of Romans chapters 8 and 12, on the subject of spiritual gifts. Since the Holy Spirit took that much time to write about it, it is vital that we develop a hunger for Him and desire His gifts to operate in the Church.

Do whatever you can do to create an environment
that is inviting to the Holy Spirit,
especially if you're a spiritual leader.
Create spaces and places for Him to work.

Remember, the gifts are for the edification of the Body of Christ. The Old Testament, the four gospels, and the book of Acts provides us with a pattern of how the Holy Spirit moves and works. The book of Acts in particular shows us how the Holy Spirit worked among the Early Church believers — a pattern we are to replicate in the Church today.

One thing is sure: When the Holy Spirit is allowed to move, He speaks, He acts, and He unleashes phenomenal amounts of supernatural power that utterly transform what human reasoning, effort, and talent can never touch. I remind you again of the words of the great missionary, Hudson Taylor: "We have given too much attention to methods, and to machinery, and to resources, and too little to the Source of Power, the filling of the Holy Ghost."[45]

When our hearts are open to the work of the Holy Spirit, He will set them ablaze with His passion to fulfill the plans and purposes of God. It will be like throwing one log after another on the fire as that Holy Ghost fire keeps us burning stronger and stronger, year after year, without abatement or diminishing till we finish our race or till Jesus returns!

When the Holy Spirit is allowed to move,
He speaks, He acts, and He unleashes
phenomenal amounts of supernatural power that
utterly transforms what human reasoning,
effort, and talent can never touch.

It was true in the earliest days of the Church, and it's true today: We can stay ablaze with the Holy Spirit's power as we become more and more dependent on and sensitive to Him. The Gospel will be established in the hearts of those we come in contact with who were once gripped by the power of darkness. We will heal the sick, cast out demons, raise the dead, and testify to the living reality of Jesus Christ as the miraculous abounds among us and through us to a dying world!

The Early Church was literally ablaze with the fiery power of the Holy Spirit. And as we allow the Spirit of God the freedom

---

[45] *Tongues of Fire*, ibid.

to move among us, His gifts will also manifest in *our* midst. The Holy Spirit is always ready to do the supernatural work that the human heart craves.

So stay open and allow the Holy Spirit to do all that He desires to do in you and through you. You will see Him using you more and more to display His power in people's lives to heal, restore, set free, and make whole!

The Holy Spirit is always ready to do
the supernatural work that the human heart craves.

Think About It

1. For many churches today, most members wouldn't even notice if the Holy Spirit were to withdraw completely from them. They would still continue "business as usual," because they never gave Him much attention or opportunity to move in their midst.

   Many don't know the power of God on an experiential level because the Person of the Holy Spirit isn't discussed or demonstrated in their services. They tend to dismiss the testimony and validity of those who yield to the Holy Spirit's operations because they have already concluded that His ministry ended when the last apostle died. As a result, they focus on utilizing their own natural talents instead of relying on the powerful working of the Holy Spirit in their lives.

   What about you? Have you become so focused on what you can do that you've failed to acknowledge and possibly even forgotten what only the power of the Holy Spirit can do? Why live in a manner that's limited to what you can figure out on your own? What steps could you take to give greater place to the Holy Spirit in your life so He can reveal to you treasures of wisdom and knowledge that are accessible to you in the mind of Christ?

2. The Holy Spirit is the energizing Agent you release in your life whenever you employ the various sources of fuel being discussed in this book. He is likened to oil — for example, when David wrote, "...I shall be anointed with fresh oil" (Psalm 92:10). Deliberately choosing to access the anointing

of the Holy Spirit prevents you from being ground down by the friction of fearful thoughts or the irritations of life.

During the course of your daily duties and routine, do you find yourself plagued by worry or anxiety from pressures you may face? How do you engage and draw from the supply of the Holy Spirit to lubricate and saturate yourself — spirit, soul, and body — with His fuel to prevent yourself from experiencing burnout?

3. When you give place to allow the Holy Spirit to move, His creative force will always release power that transforms. People are drawn out from spiritual darkness and moved into the Kingdom of light, moved from sickness into health, and delivered from an impoverished soul into a prosperous state of being.

Through it all, the Holy Spirit is moving continually to advance the eternal plan and purpose of God. The question is, are you moving with Him?

Signs will follow you, if you are moving with the Holy Spirit. If you are giving place to allow Him to move through you, your life will continually be ablaze — because our God is a consuming fire. Fire purifies gold until all dross is removed and only the refined brilliance of the metal remains. The fire of the Holy Spirit will consume all that is His and fill it to overflowing with Himself, even as He burns away all that is contrary to Him.

In what areas of your life do you sense the Holy Spirit moving and removing obstacles to His presence? Invite Him to do a deeper work in your thoughts, your desires, and throughout your personality until the fire of His holiness is all that remains.

CHAPTER 5

ABLAZE WITH WORSHIP

So far we have examined three key fuels that are needed to keep the fire in your heart burning. We have seen that God wants you to be *ablaze with God's Word, ablaze with prayer, and ablaze with the supernatural work of the Holy Spirit.* Now we come to the fourth ingredient that fuels spiritual fire in the heart of any believer or body of believers — *praise* and *worship.*

When a person or congregation intentionally focuses on glorifying God in the presence of His Word and in an atmosphere of praise and worship, His manifest presence is released to transform lives wherever change is needed. The power of God's presence that is ushered in when believers worship Him can supernaturally shift mindsets, unlock revelation, bring deliverance to the oppressed, and heal afflicted bodies.

I can personally testify that the concept for every book I've written has come to me during times of worship. When the atmosphere is charged with the presence of God during those times of worship, a door is opened to a spiritual dimension, allowing revelation to flood into our receptive hearts and minds. There is nothing to be compared to those intimate moments during worship when the flame of our spiritual fire is turned up in the presence of God.

> When the atmosphere is charged with the presence
> of God during those times of worship,
> a door is opened to a spiritual dimension,
> allowing revelation to flood
> into our receptive hearts and minds.

Worship leader, singer-songwriter, and author Matt Redmond stated, "So often when my worship has dried up, it's because I haven't been fueling the fire. I haven't set aside any time to soak myself under the showers of God's revelation. Often, time is the key factor. But if we can find space to soak ourselves in God's Word, His presence, His creation and spend time with other believers, then we'll find that the revelation floods back into our lives, and our hearts will respond with a blaze of worship once more."[46]

In fact, a study of the history of the Old and New Testaments shows that when believers have had a strong passion for worship, there was always a strong manifestation of God's supernatural presence. One of the most powerful examples in the Old Testament is seen in the life of Solomon.

Solomon was serious about worshiping God — from carrying out the intricate details of building the temple and crafting its

---

[46] Jeff Deyo, *Awakening Pure Worship: Cultivating a Closer Friendship With God* (Shippensburg, PA: Destiny Image, 2018).

furnishings to overseeing the painstaking preparation of the animal sacrifices. He assembled a huge cast of singers clothed in fine clothes, along with large numbers of skilled musicians of cymbals, trumpets, harps, and stringed instruments. His well-organized and well-planned efforts resulted in God's supernatural presence sweeping in and filling the temple. The heavy presence of His glory was so strong that the priests actually *collapsed* under the weight of it (*see* 2 Chronicles 5:12-14).

We see this strong presence of God manifested during times of worship throughout the Old Testament. But worship was also very important during the time of the New Testament. The gospel of Luke begins with songs of worship. When Mary went to visit her cousin Elizabeth, the Bible tells us that Mary worshiped the Lord for choosing her above all other women to be the one who would birth the long-awaited Messiah (*see* Luke 1:46-56). When Jesus was born, an angelic choir appeared in the night sky immediately afterward, declaring glorious praise to God at the moment of the birth of Christ (*see* Luke 2:13,14).

From the very beginning to the end of the book of Revelation, worship is an integral part of God's plan for His people. A. W. Tozer said, "I can safely say, on the authority of all that is revealed in the Word of God, that any man or woman on this earth who is bored and turned off by worship is not ready for heaven."[47] What an appropriate statement, for as the Bible shows us, we will be worshiping God for all of eternity.

Theologian Albert Barnes noted the importance of praise and worship in the lives of those who know Christ when he said, "Praise is one of the great duties of the redeemed, for it will be

---

[47] A. W. Tozer, compiled by James L. Snyder, *Tozer on Worship and Entertainment* (Camp Hill, PA: Wingspread Publishers, 1997).

their employment forever."[48] And theologian and author Karl Barth said, "...Worship is the most momentous, the most urgent, the most glorious action that can take place in human life. That's because it gets us ready for what's to come."[49]

The eternality of worship was once driven home to Billy Graham during a conversation he had with his crusade worship leader, George Beverly Shea. Graham was discussing the importance of preaching when suddenly George Beverly Shea interrupted and told him jokingly that he would be unemployed in Heaven because preaching eventually won't be needed, but Shea, as a worship leader, would have a job forever leading the redeemed in worshiping the Almighty!

"Worship is the most momentous,
the most urgent, the most glorious action
that can take place in human life.
That's because it gets us ready for what's to come."
— *Karl Barth*

As important as worship is, statistics show most Christians do not comprehend the true nature or value of worship, said George Barna, the founder of The Barna Group, a market research firm specializing in studying the religious beliefs. Barna stated that "when asked to define what worship means, two out of three [Christian adults] are unable to offer an appropriate definition or

---

[48] Steve Arterburn, "A Glimpse of Glory," *New Life Daily Devotion*, (March 11, 2012), https://www.christianity.com/devotionals/daily-new-life-steve-arterburn/new-life-daily-devotion-march-11-2012.html.
[49] *The Daily Devotional Bible, New Living Translation*, "A Daily Dress Rehearsal, 2 Thessalonians 1:1-3:18" (Brentwood, TN: Integrity Publishers, 2003).

description of worship."[50] His studies furthermore found "…that a common obstacle to facilitating real worship is that the church's leaders do not understand what worship is and isn't."[51] Barna stated that "despite seminary education and denominational guidance, a shockingly high number of church leaders have no real understanding or philosophy of worship."[52]

Barna additionally found that "among adults who regularly attend church services, one-half admit that they haven't experienced God's manifested presence at any time during the past year. Remember, this is not among the Easter-and-Christmas-only church attenders, but among people who attended an average of more than two dozen worship services last year."[53] Barna also made this statement: "For most…worship is to satisfy or please them, not to honor or please God. Amazingly, few worship-service regulars argue that worship is something they do primarily for God; a substantially larger percentage of attendees claim that attending worship services is something that they do for personal benefit and pleasure."[54]

Yet the function of worship to actually bring the presence of God to a person or congregation is paramount in importance. Pastor and author David Jeremiah stated it succinctly: "If you don't worship…you'll never experience God." [55]

---

[50] Ralph W. Rowe, MD, *Is 9-11 a Call To Heal America?* (Eugene, OR: Resource Publications, 2009), p. 8.

[51] George Barna quote, "Quotes on Worship From Various Authors," *Renewing Worship*, https://www.renewingworshipnc.org/worship-quotes/.

[52] Ibid.

[53] Doug Hull, "Biblical Worship," *Faithlife Sermons*, https://sermons.faithlife.com/sermons/444348-biblical-worship.

[54] George Barna quote, "Quotes on Worship From Various Authors," *Renewing Worship*, https://www.renewingworshipnc.org/worship-quotes/.

[55] David Jeremiah quote, "Quotes on Worship From Various Authors," *Renewing Worship*, https://www.renewingworshipnc.org/worship-thoughts/.

Worship really is *that* vital, yet there does seem to be a lack of understanding about what worship *is* and what worship *isn't*. There apparently is even confusion about whom worship is designed *for*. Yet worship will be one of our primary occupations for all of eternity, so it is safe to conclude that it is critical for us all to learn the answer to the question: *What is worship?*

WHAT IS WORSHIP?

Let me answer this question by telling you where my wife Denise and I live and what we occasionally do for enjoyment. We live in Moscow, Russia, a city well known for its culture and music. In fact, right in the heart of Moscow is a world-renowned, magnificent theater called the *Bolshoi Theater* — the illustrious stage on which world-acclaimed operas, ballets, and symphonic productions take place.

My longtime friend, Phil Driscoll, who is himself respected worldwide as a distinguished musician, has told me categorically that there are no more qualified musicians in the world than those at the Bolshoi Theater. In addition to opera and music, those familiar with the Bolshoi Theater know that it is also unquestionably one of the finest, most preeminent ballet companies of any in the world.

Because we live in Moscow near this marvelous theater, my wife and I occasionally buy tickets to attend its performances. As we sit in our seats at the Bolshoi, we are enthralled with the mind-boggling performances that are conducted on its stage. The phrase "left speechless" aptly describes how some of those performances impact the audience.

Consequently, the church we founded in Moscow is located in the heart of a city that includes an abundance of these world-class musicians. We are greatly blessed that some of the musicians from the Bolshoi Theater play every week in church for our weekly worship services.

But as wonderful as the music is at the Bolshoi Theater — and as much as the human talent on that stage enthralls their audience — the presence of God is not ushered in through those performances. That stage is a platform for human achievement, which indeed is impressive and noteworthy. The skill with which they sing, dance, and play their instruments is awe-inspiring! But as marvelous as it is, their performances do not form a conduit through which God's amazing presence charges the atmosphere and changes people's lives. Although the natural talent represented in the theater is exceptional, almost beyond description, it doesn't have the same effect as anointed worship.

I am invited to speak around the world in many types of events, and, as a result, I see and experience all types of music in churches and various Christian events. More often than not, I am blessed to experience phenomenal musicians and singers who play and sing in these events. Every song is marvelously sung, and the instrumentalists play with impressive skill. Every movement on stage is flawlessly choreographed. But even though music is executed with excellence in a Christian environment, it does not always qualify as worship.

Sometimes it is professionally produced Christian music that is impressively performed, but this alone does not necessarily qualify as worship. It may just be good music — but good music alone does not charge an atmosphere with the presence of God that has the ability to change lives.

I am thankful for professional musicians who serve in the Church with excellence. I personally find it sad that so often worship in the Church falls short in terms of professionalism. Because we represent Jesus Christ, we should be excellent in everything we do. That means we should have fine musicians who bring the sounds of Heaven to us with both skill *and* anointing during times of worship. What we do should be no less in terms of excellence and professionalism than what secular artists bring to the stage to perform for human applause.

But no matter how professionally music is performed, we must remember that when these things are done *only* from the head — using one's voice or fingers on an instrument — it does not necessarily constitute the kind of worship that charges an atmosphere with the powerful presence of God. It is impressive when a well-trained voice fabulously sings the lyrics of a worship song, when an instrumentalist plays a worship melody with skill, or when a dancer dances to worship music with poise and grace. But if the people who do these things are only performing to impress those who are in the audience, that doesn't qualify as worship. To be true worship, it must come from a different place than mere talent; it must come from *the heart*.

Because we represent Jesus Christ, we should be excellent
in everything we do. That means we should have
fine musicians who bring the sounds of Heaven to us
with both skill *and* anointing during times of worship.

Something happens when Christians are worshipful in their attitude and approach to God — humbly and intimately adoring Him from their hearts as they play their instruments and sing their worship songs. This kind of true worship causes believers to enter into the realm of the Spirit and literally become channels, or conduits, through which the Spirit of God enters their atmosphere. And when His divine presence manifests, everything is open to being changed supernaturally, as I will show you in the pages to come.

True worship causes believers to enter into the realm of the Spirit and literally become channels, or conduits, through which the Spirit of God enters their atmosphere.

In John 4:23 and 24, Jesus spoke of this kind of worship. He said, "The hour cometh, and now is, when the true *worshipers* shall *worship* the Father in spirit and in truth: for the Father seeketh such to *worship* him. God is a Spirit: and they that *worship* him must *worship* him in spirit and in truth."

In these verses, Jesus used the word "worship" five times, and in each usage, it is a translation of the Greek word *proskuneo*, which is a compound of the words *pros* and *kuneo*. The word *pros* means *toward*, and the word *kuneo* means *to kiss*. When these two words are compounded into one, they form the word *proskuneo*, which means *to fall on the ground toward someone and to kiss*. When used to depict a person's worshipful position before the Lord, this word pictures *one who has prostrated himself, either outwardly or inwardly, bowing in his heart before God and worshiping Him with kisses in intimate adoration.*

During the time that the New Testament was being written, the word "worship" — or the Greek word *proskuneo* — was specially used to depict *one who fell on the ground prostrate before a superior to worship* or *to collapse onto one's face or on one's knees in order to worship.* This word *proskuneo* depicted *worshipers who extended their arms toward a god in absolute love, affection, and devotion and even lovingly blew kisses toward that god.* Further, the word "worship" — the Greek word *proskuneo* — pictures *one who uses all available methods necessary to adore and worship a god.* These means may include singing, playing a musical instrument, dancing, or using a sundry of movements, gestures, or words to convey adoration and worship.

In John 4:23-34, the use of this word *proskuneo* tells us that God seeks those who worship Him with the mind, the body, and the spirit. You see, in authentic worship, there's an intellectual dimension, a physical dimension, and a spiritual dimension.

Perhaps no one made this clearer than the apostle Paul in his first letter to the Corinthians. In First Corinthians 14:15 (*AMP*), he wrote, "Then what am I to do? I will pray with the spirit [by the Holy Spirit that is within me] and I will pray with the mind [using words I understand]; I will sing with the spirit [by the Holy Spirit that is within me] and I will sing with the mind [using words I understand]." In this verse, Paul clearly stated that real worship is both spiritual and intellectual. It involves the spirit *and* the mind. And as we discover in First Thessalonians 5:23, God has made us spirit, soul, and body. As three-part beings, every part of us is to be involved in worship.

Furthermore, because God has placed His own Spirit inside us as believers, it means we do not have to find a physical building to enter into worship. We *are* the *temple* of God because He has placed the Holy Spirit in us by virtue of the new birth. In First Corinthians 6:19, Paul stated this truth: "What? know ye not that your body is the *temple* of the Holy Ghost...."

Because God has placed His own Spirit inside us
as believers, it means we do not have to find
a physical building to enter into worship.

When I read the word "temple" in this amazing verse, my mind immediately goes to an immense Orthodox church located in the heart of Moscow — a gigantic, white marble cathedral with golden domes that is called "Christ the Saviour." I've traveled the world and seen many great sights in my life. But when it comes to decorative architecture, this building is by far one of the most splendid I've ever seen anywhere in the world. Its interior is highly adorned with ornamentations of gold, silver, and precious stones.

This cathedral has arched and vaulted ceilings. It is filled with highly decorative marble, granite, gold, silver, precious gems, hand-carved etchings, mosaics, and frescoes. Smoke is continually wafting upward from the incense burned as a part of worship.

When Paul wrote that we are the "temple" of the Holy Spirit, he used the Greek word *naos,* the Greek word for *a temple* or *a highly decorated shrine*, similar to the one I just described. Most believers in New Testament times had grown up in a pagan Greek culture where they had seen highly decorated, ornate pagan temples their entire lives. Highly decorated temples of this sort were built all over the Greek and Roman world, so this image of a *naos* was a common sight for most of those who read Paul's letters.

So when Paul used the word *naos*, an image like the cathedral I described would have flashed through the readers' minds. To them, the word *naos* depicted *a highly decorated shrine* with tall, vaulted ceilings, marble columns, granite floors, hand-carved woodwork overlaid with gold and silver, precious gems, and burning incense billowing into the air around the front of the altar.

So what was Paul saying when he used this word *naos* to describe you and me? He revealed that when you and I came to Christ, the Holy Spirit came into our hearts and gave life to our spirits that had been dead in trespasses and sin. His work in us was glorious — and when it was all finished, He declared you and me to be His own special workmanship (*see* Ephesians 2:10). In fact, the Holy Spirit made us to be a home so fabulous that He was pleased to move in, settle down, and permanently take up residency in our hearts — and we became His temple.

Think about it — at the moment of your new birth, you became *a walking sanctuary* and your spirit became *a temple* containing the very presence of God Himself. If your eyes were opened to see your spiritual interior, you would be shocked to see how marvelously adorned your heart is spiritually!

This is why scholar, apologist, and lecturer Ravi Zacharias aptly stated, "The Christian does not go to a temple to worship. The Christian takes the temple with him or her. Jesus lifts us beyond the building and pays the human body the highest compliment by making it His dwelling place, the place where He meets with us."[56]

Think about it — at the moment of your new birth,
you became *a walking sanctuary*
and your spirit became *a temple*
containing the very presence of God Himself.

[56] Kelly Malone, *Hearing Christ's Voice* (Garland, TX: Hannibal Books, 2006), p. 55.

As temples of the Holy Spirit, we are in position to launch into worship at any time, at any place, and at any time of day — whenever we choose to humbly bow our hearts to God in worshipful adoration. How glorious to realize we don't have to go to a physical location to worship because we are now the very sanctuaries of God on this earth!

Nonetheless, the Bible speaks of a powerful potential we possess as believers when we corporately worship alongside other believers in a church meeting or a Christian gathering. In those moments when authentic worship transpires in a room full of united believers, the portion of Christ each of us carries is released to produce a powerful, combined supply of His holy presence. As wonderful and essential as it is to worship at will when we are alone at any time or at any place, the special sense of God's presence that is ushered in when we are worshiping with other believers is unlike any other experience.

But I want you to understand that worship is not merely about music, talent, or performance. Worship is about *God*. The act of worship occurs when we reach a point of abandonment in His presence — when we focus solely on God and are lost in adoration of Him. As individuals or as a body of believers, we humble ourselves before Him, set our focus wholly upon on Him, and direct our expressions of love and our songs and melodies of praise and thanksgiving toward Him. As we do this, our worship ascends to Him like loving, intimate kisses upon His face.

When God receives such worship, the Scripture shows that it touches Him deeply. In fact, He literally chooses to enter into the midst of it and become a part of what is happening. That is the moment when the atmosphere is divinely charged with power that transforms the worshipers.

Jesus and His Disciples Were Worshipers

The New Testament reveals that Jesus and His followers were worshipers. Matthew 26:30 and Mark 14:26 (*NKJV*) both record a key moment of corporate worship: "And when they had *sung a hymn*, they went out into the mount of Olives."

Think about that — this moment was just after Jesus washed the disciples' feet and served them Communion as an act of covenant. It was also just before Jesus took upon His body the stripes that would bring healing to mankind and just before He endured the public humiliation and horrific death on the Cross for our redemption. In Jesus' last moments with His disciples before these eternally significant events occurred, He paused and took time with them to enter into a time to worship the Father.

This pattern of worship continued through the book of Acts as the Early Church followed Jesus' example to worship. Acts 2:46,47 tells us that the early believers "...*continuing* daily with one accord in the temple, and breaking bread from house to house, did eat their meat with gladness and singleness of heart, *praising God* and having favor with all the people...." Just as the apostles had learned from Jesus to have a passion for souls and to love the Word of God, they had also learned from Jesus to worship the Father — and they transferred this deep desire to worship Him to the entire Early Church.

Although early Christians faced trials and great difficulties, they steadfastly continued to passionately worship God. For instance, Acts 16:25 tells us that Paul and Silas, after being beaten with many stripes and imprisoned for preaching the Gospel, "sang praises unto God" so loudly that other prisoners in the prison could not help but hear them. The two were incarcerated in stocks in the deepest part of a dungeon-like prison. But Paul and Silas knew that even then — *especially* then — it was time to focus on God and to enter into a time of worship.

The worship of these two men in the midst of their suffering so deeply touched God's heart that He joined them in that prison. His presence flooded into that dingy dungeon and produced a supernatural earthquake that *shook* the very foundations of the prison, *broke off* the prisoners' chains, and miraculously caused the prison doors to *swing open wide* (*see* Acts 16:26)!

Think of that! When Paul and Silas entered into worship together, God's presence *exploded* into that prison, producing delivering power that set Paul and Silas free. And as a result of that powerful encounter with God during a time of worship, not only were Paul and Silas delivered, but the jailer and his whole family also came to Christ! It was the act of worship that brought this *delivering, saving power* into that dark moment. All of this was the result of a "worship service"!

When Paul and Silas entered into worship together,
God's presence *exploded* into that prison,
producing delivering power that set Paul and Silas free.

WORSHIP SONGS IN NEW TESTAMENT SCRIPTURE

One day as I was studying, I began to wonder what kind of songs the early believers sang. The answer to this question is easy to determine because the New Testament is filled with something called "hymnic literature." In other words, the actual words of hymns and songs are recorded in the pages of the New Testament.

Some scholars estimate there may be as many as 30 songs recorded in Scripture that early New Testament believers sang!

Most New Testament hymns and songs are recorded in epistles written by the apostle Paul. He frequently quoted the lyrics to these songs in his epistles. I imagine that when Paul was writing a letter to a particular church, he must have thought to himself, *How can I make this point clear to the people I'm writing to? Oh, I know, I'll quote that song that they sing in their church. That will help them get my point!* Then the apostle would add to his letter the lyrics of a well-known song that was sung in that church.

There are four indisputable examples of songs quoted by Paul that I want to share with you. The first is found in Ephesians 5:14, where Paul wrote, "Wherefore he saith, Awake thou that sleepest, and arise from the dead, and Christ shall give thee light." This verse actually represents the words to a song that was apparently sung by the Ephesian believers and was well-known to them. When Paul inserted it into his epistle, it was familiar to the believers in Ephesus.

The second example I want to show you is found in Colossians 1:15-20, which is actually Paul quoting the lyrics to a song that must have been known to the church in Colossae. This is indisputably hymnic literature. In these amazing verses, Paul quoted the words to a well-known song. Exalting the supremacy of Christ, Paul wrote of Him:

> **Who is the image of the invisible God, the first-born of every creature: For by him were all things created, that are in heaven, and that are in earth, visible and invisible, whether they be thrones, or dominions, or principalities, or powers: all things were created by him, and for him: And he is before all things, and by him all things consist. And he**

is the head of the body, the church: who is the beginning, the first-born from the dead; that in all things he might have the pre-eminence. For it pleased the Father that in him should all fullness dwell; And, having made peace through the blood of his cross, by him to reconcile all things unto himself; by him, I say, whether they be things in earth, or things in heaven.

These verses, which are considered by many scholars to be the most important scriptures establishing the supremacy and deity of Christ, were lyrics to a song sung in church in the First Century!

Or how about the famous words attributed to the apostle Paul in Philippians 2:9,10? In these important verses, Paul incorporated the lyrics to a familiar song that believers sang, which described Christ's sacrifice on the Cross and His exaltation. The words to this ancient song are found in these verses: "Wherefore God also hath highly exalted him, and given him a name which is above every name: that at the name of Jesus every knee should bow, of things in heaven, and things in earth, and things under the earth."

The fourth example of a New Testament song is found in Second Timothy 2:11-13. These verses also represent hymnic literature, for it's in these verses that Paul quoted a familiar song to remind believers of the commitment that Christ requires of those who follow Him. It says:

For if we be dead with him, we shall also live with him: if we suffer, we shall also reign with him: if we deny him, he also will deny us; if we believe not, yet he abideth faithful: he cannot deny himself.

Look at the powerful words of that song! These verses reveal that early believers were not just singing worship songs that made them feel good. They were singing songs that called for consecration and commitment.

The songs sung by the Early Church mirrored the messages that were being preached at that time. We therefore know that the early believers were hearing messages that called for utter commitment, regardless of the circumstances they were facing in their personal lives.

Although many people forget the words of a sermon soon after it's preached, they are more prone to remember a message that has been set to music. When a sermon is made into the lyrics of a song, the people can take that song with them wherever they go and sing it in their daily lives. The songwriters of the New Testament understood the power of singing the Word of God, so they would set to music what the church leaders were preaching.

The songs sung by the Early Church mirrored
the messages that were being preached at that time.
We therefore know that the early believers
were hearing messages that called for utter commitment,
regardless of the circumstances
they were facing in their personal lives.

That's why we can look at the hymnic literature that Paul quoted and ascertain the types of sermons that were being preached in the infancy of the Church. Those early Christians were literally singing many of the teachings they were hearing. The examples I just cited reveal to us that these believers were singing divine revelation that would help them build a solid foundation for their lives.

What Is the Difference
Between a Psalm, a Hymn, and a Spiritual Song?

In Ephesians 5:19 and 20, Paul urged the Ephesians believers, "Speaking to yourselves in *psalms* and *hymns* and *spiritual songs*, *singing* and *making melody* in your heart to the Lord; giving thanks always for all things unto God and the Father in the name of our Lord Jesus Christ...."

- The word "psalms" is a translation of the Greek word *psalmos*, which simply means *a song of praise*.

- The word "hymns" is the Greek word *humnos*, which describes *a sacred composition designed to give glory to God*.

- The words "spiritual songs" come from the Greek phrase *odais pneumatikais*, and it signifies *songs in the Spirit, singing in the Spirit*, or *singing in tongues*.

- The word "singing" is a form of the Greek word *ado*, which means *to sing with the voice*. It particularly describes expressive, vocal singing.

- The word "melody" is the Greek word *psallo*, which means *to pluck the strings of a harp or bow; a heartfelt expression of music*. In this passage, the instrument is not a harp or bow; it is the heart of a believer as he or she sings with earnest love to the Lord.

To get a fuller understanding of this verse, we could read it this way: "*You are to be continually speaking songs of praise, hymns, sacred compositions designed to give glory to God, and spiritual songs, which includes singing in the Spirit or singing in tongues, along with heartfelt expressions in songs that are plucked from the strings of your heart....*"

Colossians 3:16 (*NIV*) commands us to sing "…psalms, hymns and songs from the Spirit, singing to God with gratitude in your hearts." Since this is the command of Scripture, we must make it our aim to include every one of these forms of worship in our private and corporate adoration of God.

HOW GOD RESPONDS
TO OUR WORSHIP

What happens *spiritually* when we enter into times of worship?

First, Psalm 22:3 tells us, "But thou art holy, O thou that inhabitest the praises of Israel." The word "inhabits" is actually a Hebrew word that means *to sit enthroned*. It pictures the presence of God *sitting* or *resting on top of* a person or an entire congregation when that individual or that body of believers is truly worshiping Him from the heart. Those expressions of intimate love and adoration create an atmosphere that literally attracts God's supernatural presence and makes Him feel welcome.

Please take note that the throne upon which God sits and rests is our *praise* and *worship*. When we abandon ourselves to Him, humbly prostrate ourselves before Him physically and mentally, and begin to "blow Him kisses" in worship, God is so deeply touched that it is as if He says, *"I want to come down and be a part of what they are doing!"*

That's what happened when Paul and Silas worshiped God from prison — God's manifest presence was magnetically drawn to their sacrifice of praise (*see* Hebrews 13:15). And as He sat enthroned on their worship by His Spirit, He manifested His glory through His delivering and saving power — even shaking the very foundations of the prison.

The throne upon which God sits and rests
is our *praise* and *worship*.

I vividly remember to this day attending the meetings of Kathryn Kuhlman when I was a teenager. Ms. Kuhlman had one of the greatest miracle ministries of the Twentieth Century. When I heard she was coming to our city to hold a miracle crusade, I volunteered to be a part of the choir. I knew that if I was in the choir, I'd be near the stage and would be able to see everything that was happening up close.

Kathryn Kuhlman was mindful of the power of worship and how it brought the supernatural presence of God into a meeting. Because she knew the presence of God charged the atmosphere of worship, she would purposely wait for the moment when the entire congregation was actively involved in worship before she entered the auditorium. Once the people were united with one voice in worship and God's manifested presence could already be felt almost as tangibly as a surge of electricity, Kathryn would take the platform and begin to minister in the power of God that had already filled the atmosphere.

I watched with wide-eyed wonder as people rose out of wheelchairs, the ears of the deaf were opened, and healings of all kinds took place. Many said, "Kathryn Kuhlman is an amazing miracle worker!" But *she* said, "These results are not because of Kathryn Kuhlman. It's the Holy Spirit at work!"[57] She knew the active ingredient to her miracle ministry was what was happening in the crowds who had assembled as they worshiped God. Reverently bowing before Him and lifting hands in adoration, the people

---

[57] Kathryn Kuhlman, *The Greatest Power in the World* (North Brunswick, NJ: Bridge-Logos Publishers, 1997) p. vii.

created an atmosphere in intimate worship that God entered and sat enthroned upon. He simply couldn't resist the invitation to inhabit their praise and release His powerful, glorious presence to meet the needs of those who had gathered for those meetings.

Reverently bowing before Him and lifting hands
in adoration, the people created an atmosphere
in intimate worship that God entered
and sat enthroned upon.

Discernment, Judgment, and Splendor — Experiencing the Glory

Throughout the centuries of the Old Testament times, the word "glory" described something *very weighty* or *very heavy*. When the presence of God came, His presence was *filled with everything good* — treasures, gifts, and power.

In Solomon's day, the glory of God would come into the temple during worship, and as noted earlier in this chapter, the presence of God's glory was so heavy that the priests couldn't even stand in order to carry out their duties. Although they didn't always physically see God's glory, they felt the effects of it.

Have you ever been in a worship service where the atmosphere became heavy with the presence of God? That was evidence that the glory of God came down and was sitting enthroned upon that meeting or congregation.

I find it interesting when we come to the New Testament that the meaning of the word "glory" changes slightly. Although it still describes something that's *heavy* or *weighty*, the word "glory," which is translated from the Greek word *doxa*, also carries the idea of *discernment, judgment*, and *splendor*.

Combining these meanings of the word "glory" from the Old and New Testaments, we find something truly marvelous. It tells us that when a person or a congregation worships God from the heart — when the attitude is one of humility and intimate adoration and not of mere performance — that worship creates an atmosphere so powerful that God responds by basically saying, *"I want to be a part of what is happening!"* Then He manifests His presence and enthrones Himself on top of that person or congregation.

In that moment, the glorious presence of God becomes heavy with *everything* that is needed — His *goodness*, His *miracles*, and His *deliverance*. It is heavy with the *gifts of His Spirit*. It is heavy with *power* to change and transform those who are present.

But there is something else that makes the glory of God unique for New Testament Christians today. When God's glory manifests, the Holy Spirit *discerns* or *judges* what each individual needs and then distributes His glory accordingly.

For those in need of conviction of sin, God's glory brings conviction of sin. For those who need healing or deliverance, His glory brings healing and deliverance. God's glory is present to restore broken relationships and to provide wisdom and direction for those who need it.

When the *glory* is present, it hovers in the atmosphere, heavy with all of God's goodness. And as the Holy Spirit discerns what each person needs, the glory of God then begins to meet those needs.

> When God's glory manifests, the Holy Spirit *discerns*
> or *judges* what each individual needs
> and then distributes His glory accordingly.

The great writer C. S. Lewis said, "In the process of being worshiped…God communicates his presence to men."[58] That is precisely what happens when we enter into moments of meaningful worship unto the Lord from our hearts. In those moments, God indeed communicates His mighty and miraculous presence to us as we worship Him.

If you understand this, then you'll understand why I say that more can be accomplished in times of worship than at any other time. I testify that during personal times of worship, I have received most of the revelations of Scripture that took me to higher realms. As I mentioned earlier, the concept of every book I have written has been downloaded to me during times of worship. It's as if suddenly a barrier is removed and the Spirit of God communicates tasks, assignments, revelations, and truths to my spirit and mind. When God's glory comes, His thoughts fill my mind and illuminate truth to me. Suddenly I see what I was not able to see before!

You see, when believers are in God's glory — His manifest, tangible presence — amazing things happen! It is truly a supernatural moment of splendor like no other. Worship is vital because it brings worshipers into a place where their hearts are open to the Holy Spirit and He can reveal what they otherwise would have difficulty seeing or hearing. In that place of worship, the Holy Spirit can also ignite His people's hearts with fresh fire

[58] C. S. Lewis, "Worship Thoughts From Various Authors," *Renewing Worship*, https://www.renewingworshipnc.org/worship-thoughts/.

so they can carry His presence with them through every aspect of their daily lives.

When believers are in God's glory —
His manifest, tangible presence — amazing things
happen! It is truly a supernatural moment
of splendor like no other.

THE BLESSING OF GOD'S ANOINTING

In Psalm 133:1-3, David described God's glory and His supernatural presence, referring to it as *the anointing*. David explained that when a corporate body of believers comes together in unity, especially during times of worship, God's blessings are supernaturally and powerfully released:

> **Behold, how good and how pleasant it is for brethren to dwell together in unity! It is like the precious ointment upon the head, that ran down upon the beard, even Aaron's beard: that went down to the skirts of his garments; as the dew of Hermon, and as the dew that descended upon the mountains of Zion: for there the Lord commanded the blessing, even life for evermore.**

Notice this verse says that "precious ointment" was placed "upon the head, that ran down the beard" and the priestly garments. This describes the anointing oil used on the Levite priests, including Aaron, to set them apart for God's special purposes. The "precious ointment" represents the manifest presence and power of God that rested upon their lives. For you and me under the New Covenant, this symbolizes the presence and power of God's Spirit upon us when we come into times of corporate unity.

David went on to say that the anointing of God is "as the dew" of Hermon. What does "dew" have to do with God's anointing and His glory?

Dew is the manifestation of moisture that is always in the air, although most of the time, it is invisible. The fact is, there is always moisture in the air, but we can't always see it. But when the atmospheric conditions are right, the moisture that's *invisible* suddenly becomes *visible*. In that instant, at the "dew point" — the point at which water droplets appear on grass and plants — the unseen moisture suddenly becomes *visible* as it manifests on everything that it can touch.

By using this example, David tells us that just as moisture is always in the air even when it is not seen, so, too, God's presence is always with us even if it isn't always visible. But there is a point at which His presence suddenly manifests, and what is invisible suddenly becomes visible.

Most often, this occurs during times of corporate worship when we come together in *unity* and *humility*. Worshiping the Lord from our hearts, the spiritual conditions become right, and God's presence and power suddenly manifest among us. In those moments, the weighty glory of God leaves the invisible realm and enters the visible realm, touching everyone present in tangible ways.

This is precisely what happened when Moses, Aaron, and the Levites dedicated the tabernacle in the wilderness. This is precisely what happened when Solomon and the priests dedicated the temple. And this is precisely what happened when the disciples and followers of Christ gathered together in unity in the upper room on the Day of Pentecost. As each group humbly united in "one accord," the presence and glory of God manifested and the anointing was released in a powerful way.

Worshiping the Lord from our hearts,
the spiritual conditions become right,
and God's presence and power suddenly manifest
among us. In those moments, the weighty glory of God
leaves the invisible realm and enters the visible realm,
touching everyone present in tangible ways.

Likewise, if we will come into a place of united worship and spend more time worshiping the Lord, we will begin to see His glory more regularly manifest among us and a greater display of the miraculous will take place in our midst.

DIFFERENT SOUNDS — DIFFERENT STYLES

The worship of the New Testament Church most likely included musical elements from the Hebrew, Greek, and Roman cultures, depending on where the worship took place. People were being added to the Kingdom of God in various regions throughout the Roman world, such as Asia Minor (modern-day Turkey), Greece, Northern Africa, and the Middle East. Hundreds and even thousands of miles separated these places, and because each was culturally different, it is likely that the actual styles, music, and expressions of worship varied from region to region and from culture to culture.

The worship of Jewish Christians would have had one particular style, the Greeks another style, and the believers in North Africa a completely different style. The point is that there is room for variation in styles of music when it comes to worshiping God. However, what is most important is not that worship conforms to a certain style — only that *it comes from the heart.*

The sounds and styles of worship may vary from group to group or from generation to generation. The worship I experienced and still love is different from what younger people enter into today, and that's fine. One is not right and the other wrong — they're just different. The styles and sounds may change, but what cannot change is the one essential ingredient — a humble heart focused in adoration and worship of the King of kings.

Styles and sounds may change,
but what cannot change is the one essential ingredient —
a humble heart focused in adoration and worship
of the King of kings.

So whatever your age, your culture, or your nation, I encourage you to find what style suits you best and then to worship the Lord with all your heart. What is important, both as an individual and as a local church, is that you enter His presence with humble adoration and worship the King of kings. As you do, He will come and enthrone Himself upon your worship and usher in His manifested glory. The very atmosphere around you will become heavy with all of His goodness, and the Holy Spirit will begin to discern and meet the needs of each hungry heart present.

And beyond all that, in the power of God's manifested glory, the Holy Spirit will light a fire inside you and all those present who will yield to Him. His greatest joy is that all present would come alive with a fresh, fiery passion to pursue His highest purposes for their lives — ignited with a fire that never goes out or fades!

WHAT IS APPROPRIATE
OR INAPPROPRIATE IN WORSHIP?

Let me address a little further the question of what is right and wrong when it comes to the manner in which worship is actually practiced. I have found a good rule to be applied to this question is found in First Corinthians 14:40, where Paul says, "Let all things be done *decently* and in *order*."

Over the years I have learned that "decently and in order" means different things to different people. What is acceptable to one group may be outrageous and offensive to another group. What is deemed holy, sweet, and touching by one group may be viewed as dead and dull to another. Everyone has his or her own opinions about what is appropriate or inappropriate in worship.

The Body of Christ is composed of too many different groups to list them all here, such as Catholics, Orthodox, Baptists, Episcopalians, Methodists, Pentecostals, and Charismatics. It therefore shouldn't surprise us that Christians have differing opinions about the right and the wrong way to worship God. It also shouldn't surprise us that most people assume that *their* form of worship is the most scriptural.

So who is right and who is wrong? Is there only one correct form of worship? Could there possibly be room for a variety of different expressions of worship in the Kingdom of God? And are we ready to honestly ask ourselves, *Are my opinions about worship influenced only by the Bible, or am I also influenced by my culture and upbringing? What are the guidelines set forth in Scripture?*

You may personally believe that praise and worship with instruments, clapping, dancing, and all kinds of celebration is the right approach to worship. Or you may be a person who loves a quieter, more structured form of worship with hymns and organ music. And then you may be one who enjoys *both* types of worship at different times. There may be times you enjoy a lively celebration in God's presence, and then other times your heart is drawn to a quieter, deeper time of worship.

Regardless of your convictions or preferences on this subject, you can likely find a host of scriptures to support your view of what worship ought to be. But when it comes to the New Testament, only one basic rule is given to the Church to follow regarding this question of what is acceptable and appropriate in worship. That rule is found in First Corinthians 14:40, where the apostle Paul wrote, "Let all things be done decently and in order."

The word "decently" is a Greek word that is found only in this verse and in two other instances in the New Testament: in Romans 13:13 and First Thessalonians 4:12. In each of these scriptures, the word used means *to do something honestly* or *to walk honestly.* It carries the notion of something that is done *properly* as opposed to something done *improperly.* It has to do with *intent* and *motivation* more than outward action, although such a good intention usually results in right actions.

The word "order" is the Greek word *taksis.* It carries the idea of *something done in a fitting way* or *something done according to order.* The Jewish historian Josephus used the word *taksis* when he recorded the *orderly way* in which the Roman army erected their camps — indicating their camps were *orderly, organized, and well-planned.* The commanders didn't engage in last-minute planning. Their camps were not hastily thrown together; rather, they were set up in an *organized* and *thoughtful* manner.

Josephus also used the word *taksis* to describe the way the Essene Jews were respectful of others. These Jews would wait until others were finished speaking before they'd take their turn to speak out. In Josephus' depiction of this behavior among the Essenes, he used the word *taksis* to picture people who were *respectful, deferential, courteous, accommodating, well-mannered, and polite.*

Taking these meanings into account, First Corinthians 14:40 could be translated: *"Let everything be done in a fitting and proper manner that is organized, well-planned, respectful, well-mannered, and polite."*

This throws open the door to all kinds of worship! Worship can be quiet, loud, soft, or bold. The important thing is that the time of worship would not be something thrown together at the last minute with no thought or organization. After all, we're talking about believers coming together to worship *the Almighty God.*

Therefore, when we plan corporate worship, it should be well thought out and organized. At the same time, it's important for us to leave room for the Holy Spirit to "change things up" spontaneously if He desires. Our ultimate goal should always be to follow *His* order, whatever that looks like in a given situation. This is all part of worshiping the Lord "in spirit and in truth" (*see* John 4:23).

Of course, whenever believers worship together, all who participate should be well-mannered, respectful, and polite. It's possible for a group of believers to be bold, loud, and yet well-mannered all at the same time. By the same token, a group of believers can also be soft and quiet, yet be rude and offensive. The style, use of instruments, and volume level are not the biggest questions in God's mind. The big question in His mind is this: *What is the intent and heart motivation of My children when they come to worship Me?* If a group's intent and motivation is correct, their worship will be accompanied by an attitude that reflects the character of Jesus Christ.

So don't get upset if others worship a little differently than the way you are accustomed to worshiping. Jesus is discerning their *hearts*. He is watching to see how much energy and forethought they put into the plan before they enter into His presence. Their form of worship may be different than yours, but if they are worshiping God from pure hearts and with their entire being, you can rest assured that their worship is acceptable to Him.

The big question in God's mind is this:
What is the intent and heart motivation of My children when they come to worship Me?

In Conclusion

When this chapter began, I said that if a person or congregation basks in the presence of God's Word and lives in an atmosphere of authentic praise and worship, the power of God's presence is released to transform minds and lives and to even bring deliverance and healing to those in need of it. I went on to show you the fire that can be ignited in your heart or in your church when an atmosphere is charged with the presence of God. During those times of intimate worship of the Father, a door is opened to a spiritual dimension where He dwells, and revelation floods into receptive minds and hearts.

Nothing can be compared to those moments during worship when the spiritual flame in our hearts is reignited with fresh fuel in the presence of God. That's what God is interested in. He's much more interested in the condition of our hearts than in the style of our worship or the format of our church service.

So don't focus on who has the best form of worship. Instead, I encourage you to concentrate on what is most important to God. Ask yourself: *Do I have an open and pure heart before Him?*

Nothing can be compared to those moments during worship when the spiritual flame in our hearts is reignited with fresh fuel in the presence of God.

Never forget what Jesus said in John 4:23,24: "The hour cometh, and now is, when the true *worshipers* shall *worship* the Father in spirit and in truth: for the Father seeketh such to *worship* him. God is a Spirit: and they that *worship* him must *worship* him in spirit and in truth."

The Father is still seeking worshipers who worship Him in spirit and truth — and the hour is still *now* that He is seeking them. Become one of those true worshipers, and you'll enter a dimension of spiritual passion and the supernatural presence of God that will alter everything in your life!

THINK ABOUT IT

1. Music performed only for the purpose of showcasing human talent is not worship — even if it is performed in a religious setting. Worship is focused exclusively on *God,* from the heart. Even in a gathering of many believers, the act of worship is a personal, intimate expression of adoration pouring from a heart postured in humility.

   True worship produces an atmosphere that constructs a habitation, inviting the living God to be enthroned in His temple — the hearts of His people. Worship creates a conduit that gives God's presence access to transform people's lives in a powerful way.

   Have you ever experienced the tangible presence of God either in your private time of worship or in an assembly of believers at church? When was the last time you opened your heart to worship God until His presence manifested around you?

2. Worship offered to God in sincerity for the sole purpose of honoring Him touches Him deeply and brings Him great pleasure. In fact, He literally chooses to enter into the midst of it and to become a part of what is happening. God delights in manifesting the very qualities we celebrate about Him.

   Jehoshaphat sent the worshipers into battle as the first line of defense. And as they extolled God's goodness and proclaimed His mercy, the Lord disoriented the Israelites' enemies until they slew themselves (*see* 2 Chronicles 20:21,22). When Paul and Silas ignored the bruising and discomfort of their imprisonment to sing praises, an earthquake announced that

God had stepped down in the midst of their situation to bring freedom to His servants — and all who heard the songs they sang benefited too (*see* Acts 16:16-34)!

Regardless of your circumstances — pleasant or not — do you deliberately magnify God's mercies and glorify His goodness toward you? You will not find the Lord manifesting Himself in the midst of pity parties or complaints. Perhaps that's why you have not experienced His intervention of late. When you choose to look away from all that would distract and turn your focused attention on Him because of who He is, God Almighty will cause you to know Him and His ways — and He will show you the reality of His salvation.

3. Ephesians 5:10 tells us to sing psalms, hymns, and spiritual songs, making melody in our hearts to the Lord. Does your soul continually boast of the Lord by singing songs of praise to Him — including singing in the Spirit, or singing in tongues?

As you investigate your own practices of praise and adoration to the Lord, do you acknowledge a deficiency? What are some ways you can begin to bring Him the fruit of your lips with greater consistency? Perhaps you can start by discarding habits of verbalizing worry or negativity and begin to consciously give thanks and praise to the Lord for who He is and for all He has already done. As you do, your worship will ascend to Him like loving, intimate kisses upon His face. Your gratitude will release a stream of worship to delight His heart and cause Him to draw near.

CHAPTER 6

ABLAZE FOR SOULS

I learned many years ago (and it is borne out in Scripture) that one key ingredient that really fuels the heart and keeps it blazing is a sustained pursuit of soul-winning. This is the fifth vital fuel we'll discuss. Nothing ignites the heart like being instrumental in seeing someone rescued from darkness, delivered from the power of sin, washed in the blood of Jesus, and saved from an eternity in hell.

The Early Church was like a burning inferno, alight with the fire of the Holy Spirit, and that fire was continually rekindled as believers surrendered to the power of God and carried the Gospel to the ends of their known world. Likewise, if we are going to burn brightly with the fire of the Spirit, *we* must be active carriers of the truth and power of the Gospel of Jesus Christ to those who need to hear it in our own world.

When we as believers do our part to take the Gospel to those who are lost, a blazing flame of the Spirit is ignited that continually releases the power of God. With that fire burning inside us, the Gospel will detonate its divine power and spread like a spiritual flame across our neighborhoods and to the ends of the earth — and we will be doing our part to fulfill the Great Commission that Jesus gave to the Church more than 2,000 years ago.

A study of Church history reveals a pattern regarding this eruptive manifestation of God's power. This power goes hand in hand with the Spirit-led efforts of any person, any church, or any organization committed to proclaiming the Gospel to the lost. This supernatural presence is God's witness that the message is Heaven-sent.

When a believer or a church is committed to the Great Commission and follows the Holy Spirit's strategy to reach the lost, God's power gloriously shows up in that believer's life or in the life of that congregation. On the other hand, when God's people withdraw from Christ's command to reach the lost, the manifestation of His power begins to slowly wane.

When a believer or a church is committed
to the Great Commission and follows
the Holy Spirit's strategy to reach the lost,
God's power gloriously shows up in that believer's life
or in the life of that congregation.

In theory, God's power is always present, but the manifestation of that power begins to diminish more and more as believers begin to neglect their responsibility to carry the Gospel to those who need to be saved. This verifiable pattern is proven throughout the course of Church history. But God's heart remains the same for people to be reached through the sharing of the Gospel. And when the Gospel is preached by His people, His power shows up in a myriad of miraculous ways!

Matthew 28:18-20 records that before Jesus ascended into Heaven, He gathered the disciples together one last time and told them:

> **...All power is given unto me in heaven and in earth. Go ye therefore, and teach all nations, baptizing them in the name of the Father, and of the Son, and of the Holy Ghost: Teaching them to observe all things whatsoever I have commanded you: and, lo, I am with you always, even unto the end of the world. Amen.**

This passage is what is called the Great Commission. In this command from Christ, we find important truths about God's call to every believer and every local church to "go" with the Gospel to the ends of the earth. In Greek, the tense for the word "go" in Matthew 28:19 literally means *to go and to keep on going*. In other words, this was not a command given only to the believers at the beginning of the Church Age, nor was it a special command for those who would occasionally go on a special mission trip. The command to *go* is God's call to *the Church*. It is His directive to every Christian and to every local church for all time.

God expects His children to be committed to taking the saving message of the Gospel to the lost as *a manner of lifestyle*, and He promises that those who obey this command will experience amazing supernatural power to fulfill the appointed task. This is why miracles are more consistently manifested where the Gospel is being preached beyond the four walls of a local church — because the Gospel *is* the very power of God (*see* Romans 1:16).

A local congregation that ignores God's command to reach the lost with the Gospel will experience fewer manifestations of God's power in their midst, because the purpose for those manifestations has been largely neglected. They may have started out with a strong focus on reaching the lost, and they may have experienced great power as a result. However, if they then begin to draw back from this divine directive to share the Gospel with the unsaved, they will inevitably notice God's manifested power begin to recede in their midst.

God expects His children to be committed
to take the saving message of the Gospel
to the lost as *a manner of lifestyle*,
and He promises that those who obey this command
will experience amazing supernatural power
to fulfill the appointed task.

The demonstration of divine power is promised to those who go *and keep on going*, taking the Gospel to the lost. This includes sharing the message with family, friends, and neighbors, as well as to strangers whom believers meet in daily life, on mission trips, and in every arena of life to the ends of the earth.

It's also important to understand that part of "going" is for believers to do their part in funding mission efforts of churches and organizations, evangelization projects, and missionaries themselves who are going to other parts of the world to take the message of Christ to the unsaved. Many churches today are focused on reaching their cities with various outreaches, and this is a correct thing to do. However, too often churches curtail their financial support for those engaged in mission work in other parts of the world in order to focus solely on reaching their local communities.

Yet we have a responsibility to do *both*. We must share the Gospel with the lost in our neighborhoods and surrounding communities while at the same time retaining a firm commitment to financially support those who are reaching the unsaved abroad. Both aspects are essential and doable. Our hearts must burn to see the unsaved brought into the Kingdom of God both near and far. It is our glorious task to rescue the spiritually perishing and to care for the dying as God enables us (*see* Colossians 1:28).

AN ASTONISHING PROMISE

But in the Great Commission found in Matthew 28:18-20, the Lord Jesus made an astonishing promise to any believer, church, or ministry organization that will *go and keep on going* with the Gospel to reach those nearby and those who are abroad. Jesus said, "...And, *lo*, I am with you always, even unto the end of the world. Amen" (v. 20). Those who take this promise to heart and obey it will be ignited and *remain* ignited with the blazing power of the Holy Spirit!

Our hearts must burn to see the unsaved brought into the Kingdom of God both near and far.

The word "lo" in this verse is actually an exclamatory promise that Jesus makes to anyone who will in any fashion "go" with the Gospel to the lost. In other words, the "lo" belongs to those who "go." In Greek, the word "lo" would better be translated, *"And, WOW, will I ever be with you — even to the ends of the earth!"* In essence, Jesus was saying, "If you will go and keep on going — doing all you can in every way possible to preach and teach the

Gospel — *WOW, I promise that you will experience My amazing presence in the doing of it!"*

Christ promises that His powerful presence will be enjoyed and experienced by all believers who are totally committed to discovering their part by the direction of the Holy Spirit and then *going* to the lost with the message of salvation. That means if believers want to experience the power of God, they must act on what triggers its release. Jesus' promise is that His supernatural, powerful presence will accompany all who will do their part to take the Good News of salvation to others!

The supernatural anointing of God's Spirit is available to empower anyone who will take the Gospel to the unsaved. Noted pastor and author Vance Havner said this: "Without the anointing of the Holy Spirit, the preacher may storm, the teacher may strive, the Christian worker may sweat, but all to no avail."

If believers want to experience the power of God,
they must act on what triggers its release.

You see, we *must* have the power of the Holy Spirit to reach the lost. The full measure of empowerment to be God's witnesses is imparted to us when we are baptized in the Holy Spirit (*see* Acts 1:8). But then it is as we *go* with the Gospel that our obedience ignites the Spirit's power to be released mightily *upon* us and *through* us!

Sometimes Christians hear of amazing signs and wonders that occur on the foreign mission field and wonder why they don't see more of those supernatural happenings in their own churches at home. And it's a legitimate question. Why *do* most of the mighty deeds that astonish believers often occur where missionaries or frontline preachers are taking the Gospel to virgin territory where the Gospel has never or rarely been preached?

But manifestations of God's power aren't supposed to happen only on the foreign mission field. The Holy Spirit wants to move right in your own neighborhood! If you'll obey His leading in every situation of your daily life and *go* to share the Gospel whenever He prompts you, God's power will show up *wherever* you are!

Just as Jesus promised, His powerful presence manifests when the Gospel is being taken to those who need to hear it. The purpose of His power showing up in such places is to verify that the message is Heaven-sent.

These miraculous happenings are guaranteed to occur on the mission field or in any area of your own city where the Gospel has rarely been preached as you go in obedience, led and empowered by His Spirit. This is God's promise — that His power will show up when you do your part by His leading and direction to reach the unreached.

How To Fuel a Dying Flame

Very frequently when churches get well established, they fall back from evangelizing the lost. These congregations may have earlier lived through amazing experiences as they were filled with the power of God. But as time passes, if they draw back from their zeal in reaching the lost that they once had, it seems the power begins to dwindle.

When my wife Denise and I were first married, we were on the staff of a large denominational church that had once been an inferno for the Gospel and had experienced legendary power in the life of that church. But over time, it shrank back from its Christ-given duty to reach the lost, and as a result, the fire of God began to diminish until those glorious times were almost only a memory related by people who still remembered the earlier days.

But then the Holy Spirit once again began to rouse those whose hearts were willing to venture beyond the walls of their church building to reach the unsaved. And as those obedient hearts rose up and began to reach their communities with the Good News of Jesus Christ, the church was reignited with fresh spiritual fire.

Just as fuel on a dying flame can cause the embers to be rekindled, this congregation became once again alight with the fervency of God's heart to save the lost. The people no longer had only memories of a past move of God. Once again they began to knock on doors and share the Gospel, pray for the unsaved to be saved, and deliberately use their finances to win the lost as they set their hearts toward developing an evangelism mentality in that church. And as they did these things, the power of God began to explode in their midst in a fresh, new way!

As those obedient hearts rose up and began to reach their communities with the Good News of Jesus Christ, the church was reignited with fresh spiritual fire.

I was a witness when God's power showed up in that denominational church and His fire began to blaze in people's hearts once again. The altars were filled with people coming to Christ, and miraculous events began to occur in the lives of church members. People were healed; others were delivered from demonic influences;

and financial miracles began to occur in the lives of the people and in the church offerings. It was a remarkable series of events I will never forget.

All these miraculous happenings were occurring inside the walls of a denominational church that didn't even theologically embrace the miraculous as a reality for today's world. But it wasn't a matter of what theological positions the people held — it was a matter of Jesus' promise in Matthew 28:20. Jesus stated that His powerful presence would be demonstrated in the life of *any* believer, or *any* church, or *any* ministry organization that would "go" to the lost as a matter of priority!

MY EARLY EXPERIENCE WITH A CHURCH ABLAZE

When my wife and I first met as students at the university we were attending, we were single adults attending a student church that was radically committed to evangelism and that blazed with burning hearts for souls. As a result, a nonstop flow of unsaved people was coming into the Kingdom, and the members of our fellowship were engaged in many types of evangelistic outreaches to bring people to a saving knowledge of Jesus Christ.

The leadership of the church continually exhorted us regarding our responsibility to reach the unsaved, urging us to reach people who did not know Jesus Christ. And just as Jesus promised in the Great Commission found in Matthew 28:18-20, the power of God showed up in that church! It was simply a spiritual powerhouse! The whole church burned with the fire of God, and the gifts of the Holy Spirit flowed nearly uninterrupted in church services.

Denise and I were deeply involved in evangelism teams in that university church. In fact, the first time Denise and I were ever together was the time we were placed on the same evangelistic team going to a nursing home. The very first thing we did together was to form a two-person team and share the Gospel with a man in that nursing home who was dying of cancer. Although Denise and I were only acquaintances at the time, she and I led that man to Christ together. We didn't realize it, but that elderly man's salvation was the first fruits of what Denise and I would be doing together for the rest of our lives!

Oh, how I revel in the memories I carry of that university church. It was simply overflowing with the power of the Holy Spirit! Those who regularly attended that church could hardly wait for the next service to arrive because they knew that they would experience the amazing presence of God and that gifts of the Spirit would manifest with miracles and healings. Decades have passed since then, and many of the people who attended in those early years have since struggled to find a place to worship God to match what they experienced in that university church so many years ago.

Yet God always wants to move us from glory to glory (see 2 Corinthians 3:18). We'd all do well to remember that the demonstrations of God's power we may have experienced in the past are always only a foretaste of the glory He desires to pour out on His Church in this present hour and in the days to come. However, we must follow the pattern Jesus set forth in Matthew 28:18-20 in order for His manifested power to be sustained and to grow in strength in our midst.

A regretful moment came when the leaders of that university church deemed that the great emphasis to reach the lost needed to be put on pause so a shift could be made to discipleship. The truth is, both emphases are right, and discipleship should have gone hand in hand with reaching the lost. But reaching out was shelved so a new focus could be developed on maturing the believers. The leadership's position was that once a greater state of maturity had been achieved, the church would then return to reaching the lost. This was a fatal decision, however, for when a church turns inward, it greatly reduces the need for God's power to be manifested, and that normally produces catastrophic results after a period of time.

In the case of that student body of believers, it was only a short period of time before everything that had made our university church powerful *evaporated* right before our eyes. As the congregation began to focus only on themselves, numbers began to dwindle until it became nothing but a shadow of the glorious place it had once been. Slowly, that church began to lose the life-giving position of influence it had once held in the community.

The leadership of that student church was very sincere about their desire to help the believers under their charge reach greater spiritual maturity and to develop a system of spiritual accountability. The motives behind their decisions were pure, but they had made a grave miscalculation, and their decision to draw back from reaching the lost resulted in painful consequences. A powerful church that had blazed with the fire of the Spirit became a hollowed-out hull of what it had once been at an earlier time.

I am thankful for the indelible mark that early experience made on my life. I witnessed firsthand the regrettable pattern that develops when any believer or any church retreats from Christ's Great Commission to His people to take the Gospel to the ends of the earth to reach the lost. I learned that manifestations of God's power to empower people aren't necessary if they aren't doing the most vital thing that requires supernatural power!

When a church shrinks back from making souls a priority, the people have made a decision that will result in the manifested power of God waning in their midst. The same is true in the life of an individual believer. Although God's power is available to all believers, that divine power will be consistently manifested in signs and miracles only in the life of a believer, a local church, or a ministry organization that is actively "on the go" in obedience to Christ's Great Commission.

When a church shrinks back from making souls a priority, the people have made a decision that will result in the manifested power of God waning in their midst.

The "lo" in Matthew 28:20 — that is, Christ's promise of His powerful presence — is promised to those who "go" with the Gospel message to others. So if you or your church or ministry organization is experiencing powerlessness, it's time to assess whether or not you are doing what you must do to qualify for the "lo" that Christ promises to those who would "go."

Never forget that God's power works like metal attracted to a magnet. When believers make a sustained, earnest effort to reach out to the lost, the heart to share the Gospel in obedience to Jesus' Great Commission works like a magnet to attract the power of God. Study the Word and Church history yourself, and you'll find that God's power always shows up and all kinds of miraculous events begin to take place where the Gospel is being regularly communicated to the lost!

If believers have unintentionally drifted from reaching out to the lost, they can choose to make an adjustment and get back on track again, just as the denominational church did that I told you about earlier. When that happens, what was turned off can be turned on again! The power of God will once again erupt in their midst.

Study the Word and Church history yourself,
and you'll find that God's power always shows up
and all kinds of miraculous events begin
to take place where the Gospel is being
regularly communicated to the lost!

That is a guaranteed outcome when believers who have neglected the Great Commission begin to share the Gospel with the lost again. The act of sharing Christ will put spiritual fuel back on the fire, and God's power will be reignited to produce signs following the preaching of the Word.

THE GOSPEL IS FOR EVERY CREATURE — NO ONE EXCLUDED!

At the close of the gospel of Mark, Jesus shared His parting words with His disciples:

And he said unto them, Go ye into all the world, and preach the gospel to every creature. He that believeth and is baptized shall be saved; but he that believeth not shall be damned. And these signs shall follow them that believe; in my name shall they cast out devils; they shall speak with new tongues; they shall take up serpents; and if they drink

any deadly thing, it shall not hurt them; they shall lay hands on the sick, and they shall recover.

So then after the Lord had spoken unto them, he was received up into heaven, and sat on the right hand of God. And they went forth, and preached everywhere, the Lord working with them, and confirming the word with signs following. Amen.

Mark 16:15-20

Early Christians believed that the Gospel was for *every creature* — that is, for *every human being* on the planet. That is why they ventured into all the known world of their time to tell every person who would listen about the Good News of Jesus' saving and delivering power. And as you carefully examine these verses from Mark 16, you'll see that Jesus promised all types of miraculous manifestations of His power to those who would obey His Great Commission and go with the Gospel to the lost!

That is why Mark 16:20 says that the Lord worked with them and confirmed the message they preached with supernatural signs and wonders. You see, the Early Church experienced the "lo" that is promised to any believer who will "go" to the lost as Christ commands and as His Spirit leads. Early believers knew the power of God experientially — not because they were better than us, but because they obeyed the Great Commission and went into the world with the Gospel that attracted the power of God to them!

Those early Christians had been transformed by Jesus Christ, and they were not ashamed to speak about Him to others. As a result of their willingness to obey the Great Commission, a holy, spiritual fire raged throughout the Early Church. From the beginning to the very end of the book of Acts, we read a fiery account of Christians boldly preaching the Gospel with miraculous results accompanying them. As long as believers opened their mouths to witness and invested their resources to share the Gospel with others, the power of the Holy Spirit was manifested among them.

Those early Christians had been transformed by Jesus Christ, and they were not ashamed to speak about Him to others. As a result of their willingness to obey the Great Commission, a holy, spiritual fire raged throughout the Early Church.

Likewise, if you truly desire to experience the astonishing and awesome power of God in your life, you must do what is required to release the manifestation of that power! And if the power of God is *not* in operation in your daily life, you need to ask why it's not.

Are you fulfilling the divine command that always causes God's power to show up? Are you on the "go," sharing Jesus Christ with family, friends, neighbors, coworkers, and acquaintances? Are you giving financially to fund the Gospel to reach those in foreign lands? If so, then Jesus promises His powerful presence will mark your life!

THE GOSPEL MESSAGE
IS THE TRIGGER TO THE POWER OF GOD

In Romans 1:16 (*NKJV*), Paul said, "For I am not ashamed of the gospel of Christ, for it is the power of God to salvation to everyone who believes...."

In this verse, Paul stated that the Gospel *is* the power of God. The word "power" comes from the Greek word *dunamis*, an old word that described *power*. This is where we get the word "dynamite." This means the Gospel is *the dynamite of God*.

However, the word *dunamis* could also be used to depict *the full force and might of an advancing army*. This means that when you make a concentrated effort to share the Gospel with the lost, that act is the very trigger that releases the power of God *to advance on the scene like a mighty army* to drive away darkness, to bring the light of God, and to deliver His saving and delivering power to those who are bound and lost.

The word "salvation" in Romans 1:16 is translated from the Greek word *sodzo* — a Greek word that depicts *salvation, healing,* and *deliverance*. This means when we are sensitive to the leading of the Holy Spirit to share the Gospel with the lost, the very act of sharing it releases a divine power that supernaturally rips blinders off people's eyes and releases God's power that brings salvation, healing, and deliverance into their lives! You see, the Gospel *is* the power of God unto salvation!

But Paul also said that the Gospel is the power of God to everyone who "believes." The verb tense for "believes" in Romans 1:16 is very important, for it describes those who are *presently believing*. This is not a promise for someone who believed years ago. This is a promise for those who are in the state of believing *right now* or those who have their faith in gear at the present moment. God's power is activated in people's lives like a divine advancing army when faith is *engaged*.

If you examine your own spiritual history, you will find that those moments when God's power erupted in your life coincided with seasons when you were really engaging your faith. Dormant faith produces nothing. It will never know an ongoing experience of God's manifested power. But the moment a person puts his faith into action, *dunamis* power is released. This divine force will be experienced by anyone who is *presently believing*.

The apostle Paul was so sure of this that he declared that he was not ashamed of the Gospel. Paul knew from experience that the very act of believing the Gospel and preaching it to others was *the trigger* that always released the supernatural power of God. And this is God's promise to any believer or body of believers who will unashamedly go forth with the message of Jesus Christ to others, releasing faith in the unchanging promises of God.

Paul knew from experience that the very act
of believing the Gospel and preaching it to others
was *the trigger* that always released
the supernatural power of God.

WHY BELIEVERS DON'T SHARE THE GOSPEL AND WHAT YOU CAN DO ABOUT IT

I understand many Christians are afraid to share the Gospel with other people for a number of reasons. Some don't know how to share the Gospel; others are embarrassed to speak publicly; and still others are afraid of rejection. But the truth is, if you want to experience the power of God regularly in your life, you have to deal with the hindrances that have held you back in the past and make the decision to "go" (*see* Matthew 28:19). As you share the best news in the world to those who are lost, you will find there is absolutely nothing to be ashamed of, just as Paul said in Romans 1:16. The power of God will show up and erupt on the scene to enable you to witness and to remove the blinders from those who are spiritually blind.

Let me be totally honest with you in saying that some people may not be thrilled with you when you share the Gospel with them. In fact, it is probable that some will rebuff and reject you. But that's all right! Jesus, His disciples, and other early believers all burned with the fire of the Holy Spirit, and they also experienced similar times of being rebuffed and rejected. But in spite of those moments, they also encountered and experienced the power of God *because* they spoke up and shared the Good News with people who were unwitting prisoners in spiritual darkness. When God's power showed up, it sustained them, and they moved on *unaffected* by those who were anything *but* elated with them.

In the same way, God's power will sustain you every step along your way, enabling you to overcome everything that opposes your obedience to the Great Commission. I urge you to turn your focus to those who are waiting for you to share the message of Jesus with them. As you "go," Jesus guarantees that you will experience His life-transforming power. Those who believe will receive salvation with all its blessings of deliverance and healing, and you'll never be sorry you opened your mouth or moved your feet or invested your money to get the Gospel to them.

God's power will sustain you every step along your way, enabling you to overcome everything that opposes your obedience to the Great Commission.

Even if some don't initially show interest, don't be disturbed by that because they will never forget what you have told them. And even if it seems that you have nothing in your "net" right now, never forget there are many "fish" out there in your community, your region, and to the ends of the earth who are waiting for you to throw out that net again at the God-appointed time!

THE KEY INGREDIENT
FOR THE POWER TO BE A WITNESS

One reason why some people are fearful to tell others about Jesus is that they have never received the baptism of the Holy Spirit. They therefore lack the full measure of power that God wants to bestow on them to enable them to be bold witnesses fully equipped with the gifts of the Spirit, which we discussed at length in Chapter 4.

In Acts 1:8, Jesus said, "You shall receive power when the Holy Spirit has come upon you; and you shall be witnesses to Me...." In this remarkable verse, Jesus promised that the infilling of the Holy Spirit will empower a believer to be an effective witness to others as he or she yields to and obeys His promptings. Although someone's sharing of the Gospel always brings God's power on the scene, the baptism in the Holy Spirit divinely empowers a believer to boldly witness and to be used in the operation of His supernatural gifts in order to meet every need.

The infilling of the Holy Spirit will empower a believer to be an effective witness to others as he or she yields to and obeys His promptings.

I mentioned earlier in Chapter 4 the wonderful denominational church I grew up in. This church really believed it was our God-given responsibility to share the Gospel with the lost. Because we *really* believed it, we put our conviction into action and knocked on doors, visited prospective church members, and went out on Saturdays to share Christ with the neighborhood that was near our church. Our church was committed, organized, sincere, and very dedicated. If grades were given for effort, we would have gotten an A+.

But because we didn't believe in the baptism of the Holy Spirit, it is my view that we didn't experience sufficient power to do the job as well as we could have if we had received that heavenly gift. Of course, as we have already seen, God's power shows up in a measure for anyone who will share Christ with others. But if we had embraced the baptism in the Holy Spirit and the inward, consistent empowerment that His infilling affords, we would have experienced an entirely different dimension of success in our efforts to share the Gospel and see people's lives transformed.

I can speak from my own experience back in those earlier days. I personally felt powerless and afraid to witness to people about Jesus. When we approached a new home to knock on the front door, I wouldn't be praying for people to be home and to answer the door. Instead, I'd pray that no one would be home or that a big dog would be in the yard to prevent us from getting through the front gate!

But after I received the baptism in the Holy Spirit, everything changed. I literally became ablaze with the power of God! Just as Jesus promised in Acts 1:8, I was supernaturally enabled to boldly tell others about Jesus with no fear or shame. After that, I prayed for people to be home when we visited, and if there were danger-ous dogs in the yard, I was binding the power of those dogs in Jesus' name because I wanted to get to those front doors to share Christ with the people who lived in those homes. The baptism in the Holy Spirit truly empowered me to tell others the greatest news in the world.

WE MUST GET THE MESSAGE STRAIGHT!

A content problem has emerged in the Church today that must be corrected and overcome *if* we are going to be strong believers, have strong churches, and be part of strong ministry organizations in these last days. Before we go further, I want to address this issue, so please stay with me.

God has ordained every Christian to carry the Gospel message to those who are broken and in need of salvation, healing, deliverance, and restoration. Their minds and souls need to be transformed and their feet need to be set on a path to wholeness in every sphere of their lives.

We are privileged to be the vessels God has chosen to do this glorious work. This transforming Gospel is our assignment, and the Bible says that the feet of those who carry this wonderful message are beautiful (*see* Isaiah 52:7). That means *our feet* are blessed feet *if* we are counted among those who take this saving message to those who need it.

Many benefits are made available to a person who believes and responds to the Gospel, and people need to be informed of all those benefits. However, the great bulk of what is being preached today focuses mainly on *self-help, success,* and *prosperity.* These are certainly among God's benefits that are good and necessary. God wants people to be healthy, to enjoy life, to be partakers of success, and to be financially blessed. The truth is, wherever the Gospel is working in people's lives, the power of that life-giving message always produces fruit in each of these categories, whether or not these subjects are emphasized.

All of these blessings are wonderful byproducts of the Gospel's message and will be produced in the life of any believer, any church, or any nation that embraces the Gospel and the teachings of the Bible. Even lost people — if they live by God's principles — can live greatly blessed lives, because God's principles will work for anyone who applies them.

But we must not forget that these types of tangible blessings, as important as they are for living life victoriously, are limited to life on this earth. As people obey scriptural principles, they can receive these benefits that cause them to be healthier and to enjoy prosperity. But what if they feel healthy and enjoy material blessings right now, yet ultimately go to hell because they never understood that they must repent of sin to be saved and go to Heaven?

If that is the case, we have made a grave error. What is the point of it all if people are blessed right now but miss Heaven and spend an eternity separated from God? This is the reason Jesus asked, "For what is a man profited, if he shall gain the whole world, and lose his own soul?" (Matthew 16:26).

What a dreadful realization to come to at the end of our spiritual race — that we helped people in life be healthy, successful, and prosperous, yet they ended up in hell because we didn't help them grasp God's requirement to repent of sin in order to be saved! I understand that many people are uncomfortable discussing or even thinking about the topic of hell, but hell is a reality whether we like it or not. People we know will go there if they don't receive the message of Christ that can save them from it.

What is the point of it all if people are blessed right now
but miss Heaven and spend an eternity
separated from God?

It is certainly good to be carriers of healing, prosperity, and deliverance to those who are broken or sick and in need of deliverance and restoration. But we must always remember that the most important responsibility we have toward people is to deliver the message that Jesus died to save them from an eternity of separation from God.

J. C. Ryle minced no words when it came to this subject. He stated, "Hell, hell fire, the damnation of hell, eternal damnation, the resurrection of the damnation, everlasting fire, the place of torment, destruction, outer darkness, the worm that never dies, the fire that is not quenched, the place of weeping, wailing and gnashing of teeth, everlasting punishment... these are the words which the Lord Jesus Christ Himself employs. Away with the miserable nonsense which people talk in this day who tell us that the ministers of the gospel should never speak of hell."[59]

THE REALITY OF ETERNITY

I'll never forget a conversation that I had with a friend when Princess Diana tragically died in a car accident August 31, 1997, while fleeing paparazzi in Paris. Her sudden death stunned the watching world because she seemed to be an icon of a blossoming young life. Millions of people watched her funeral service, and for a short time, people all over the world were gripped by the abrupt

---

[59] J. C. Ryle, *Holiness: Its Nature, Hindrances, Difficulties, and Roots* (Peabody, MA: Hendrickson Publishers, 2007), p. 222.

loss of a young woman who one day earlier seemed to have the best this life has to offer laid out before her.

While the world was focused on the unexpected death of the princess, I told a friend on the telephone, "Wow, Princess Diana's sudden death really makes me think of how close eternity is to every person. I wonder where she is in eternity right now — *Heaven* or *hell*?" Because her death brought the reality of eternity to my mind, I was simply speaking my thoughts to my friend on the phone. His response therefore took me aback as he said, "How dare you ask such a terrible question. How could you be so judgmental? How dare you even ask such a question about such a kind and good person! Of course she went to Heaven. She did so many good things for people."

We must always remember that
the most important responsibility we have toward people
is to deliver the message that Jesus died to save them
from an eternity of separation from God.

But my friend misjudged my comment. I was simply suddenly aware of eternity because someone famous had just passed into it, and I felt no judgment. It was just a passing thought.

I apologized for asking that question and never discussed eternity with that friend again, because I realized that I had touched a subject that was difficult for him to consider. I have no idea where Princess Diana is in eternity, but my friend's response told me that he thought doing good things for people was enough to qualify a person for eternal life in Heaven. Yet Scripture states that this is *not* enough.

Countless numbers of even good people have died and gone to hell because they didn't die in Christ. It is not about works; it's about the spiritual state people are in when they die. The Scriptures guarantee that if a person dies *in* Christ, he will be *in* Christ for all of eternity. But if a person dies in a lost spiritual state, he or she will spend eternity in hell, apart from God and in an irrecoverable and lost state forever.

But as I reflected on that difficult conversation, I began to also reflect on how often I, as a pastor, have visited people who were mourning the death of an unsaved friend or relative. I recalled that many times those people had earlier told me how deeply concerned they were for the deceased person's salvation while that person was still living. They would tell me they were sure that the person had never committed his or her life to Christ. They'd assert that they *knew* the person was unsaved and facing a lost eternity. But often when these same concerned Christians actually had to confront the death of their friends or relatives, I heard them say, "Well, I realize that we have no evidence that they ever repented and made Jesus the Lord of their lives, but maybe — *just maybe* — in those last seconds before they died, they made their lives right with the Lord."

The fact is that loved ones die and go to hell, but it is very painful to come to terms with that realization. No one wants this to happen to someone he or she loves. The thought of hell is *horrendous*. So often when people face the loss of a friend or relative, they grasp for hope that their loved one somehow, in some way, miraculously got saved at the very end.

Hell is a *horrific* thought. C. S. Lewis discussed how much he loathed the subject of hell, but added, "There is no doctrine which I would more willingly remove from Christianity than the doctrine of hell, if it lay in my power. But it has the full support of Scripture and, especially, of our Lord's own words; it has always been held by the Christian Church, and it has the support of reason."[60]

As difficult as it is to think someone we know or love went to hell, the Scripture clearly teaches that those who die outside of Christ go there. If we embrace this truth, it will shake us to the core and embolden us to compassionately share Christ with people — yes, to make the benefits of salvation available to them for this present earthly life, but most importantly, to ensure that they become a part of God's eternal family.

At the time I am writing this book, there are approximately 150,000 people who die every day. That is approximately 6,400 people every hour or 2 people who die every second. The truth we all must face is that death is inescapable — and after death, people either go to Heaven or hell, depending on whether they were *in* Christ or *outside of* Christ.

There is a funeral in everyone's future if they die before Jesus returns for His Church. With that sobering fact in mind, could there be any question more important than a person's eternal destiny after this earthly life?

This is why we must burn with passion to take the saving message of the Gospel to as many souls as possible. Jesus *died* for this — so we must *live* for it!

Today I hear many church leaders talk about the need to reach the "unchurched." That phrase is accurate if they are trying only to reach Christians who are not in a local church. But unsaved people are not unchurched — they are "unsaved." They are in eternal jeopardy.

---

[60] Stephen Eyre, "C.S. Lewis on Heaven and Hell, "*C.S. Lewis Institute: Discipleship of Heart and Mind*, http://www.cslewisinstitute.org/cs_lewis_on_heaven_and_hell_fullarticle.

When discussing unsaved people, it is important that we remember they are not people who simply need to be modified by good teaching. They are lost people who are going to hell if they do not come to Christ. We must learn to be straight about the fact that unsaved people are going to hell. *Hell is a real place, and people really do go there.*

As I write about the content of the message we preach and promote, I want to say that when a person receives Christ, he is not merely embracing a new philosophy to improve his lifestyle or modify his behavior. When a person comes to Christ, he is snatched from a lost eternity and is immediately infused with a new God-given nature that makes him a member of God's eternal family. In a split second, *eternal life* is imparted into that person that assures him a destiny in Heaven instead of an eternity in an unspeakably terrible place called hell.

We must learn to be straight about the fact
that unsaved people are going to hell.
Hell is a real place, and people really do go there.

Unfortunately, this *eternity* factor is missing from most of what is being preached and taught today. The subject of hell is rarely preached from the pulpit. Think about it — when was the last time you heard a good sermon or series on hell? Have you *ever* heard one?

Greg Laurie, an author and well-known pastor, rightly said this:

Many people have reacted adversely to the "hellfire-and-brimstone preaching," as it's called. They say, "Well, I don't like that kind of preaching." But, frankly, I can't remember the last time I heard a hellfire-and-brimstone preacher. We've swung so far to the other side that we've lost sight of the importance of what the Scripture says — that we need to warn some, and they need to know that there are consequences for their sin. To leave that out is to do them a disservice, and it is to fail to declare the whole counsel of God. We certainly shouldn't do it in a gleeful manner, but with compassion and love, warning them that the last thing God wants is for any person created in His image to end up separated from Him in this place called hell. [61]

Some spiritual leaders say, "I don't want to make people uncomfortable by discussing hell. It really makes people feel uneasy, so I don't address it from the pulpit." By taking this approach, people in the pews have nearly forgotten the painful reality of hell, and, as a result, don't carry a burden for people's eternal status. They just want people to get saved so their lives will be blessed.

It's true that we need to help people get healthy and blessed, but we cannot neglect the truth that those who die in sin will experience dire, irreversible eternal consequences. Billy Graham said, "I am conscious of the fact that the subject of hell is not a very pleasant one. It is very unpopular, controversial, and misunderstood.... As a minister, I must deal with it. I cannot ignore it."[62]

If you and I desire a life that is ablaze for God, we cannot ignore this fact that hell is a reality and people need to hear the saving message that is so central to the Gospel of Christ. It must explode in our hearts with convicting fire! And as we have seen in Matthew 28:20, Jesus promised that if you will go with the

[61] "The Dynamics of an Effective Invitation: An Interview With Greg Laurie" www.sermoncentral.com/content/a-Greg_Laurie_1_22_07.
[62] Billy Graham, *Peace With God: The Secret of Happiness* (Nashville: Thomas Nelson, 1953, 1984), Part One, Chapter 7.

Gospel to those who need it and do your part to make sure others can go, His powerful presence will be yours!

It's true that we need to help people get healthy and blessed, but we cannot neglect the truth that those who die in sin will experience dire, irreversible eternal consequences.

HELL IS A REAL PLACE

One very real problem is that many Christians today don't really believe in hell. Oh, sure, if you ask most Christians if they believe in hell, they will invariably answer, "Yes, of course, I believe in hell. The Bible teaches it." But if you examine their actions, it will lead you to the conclusion that they don't *truly* believe that their unsaved family members, friends, and acquaintances who haven't been born again are going to hell. If they did, wouldn't it affect them so deeply that they would at least do everything within their power to try to stop them from going there?

If a Christian really believes in hell but does nothing to tell unsaved people he or she encounters in life about the saving power of Jesus to keep them from going there, what does this lack of action say about that Christian? It says that the revelation of the reality of hell is still missing from his or her life.

If believers truly believed in hell, the mere thought of a friend, relative, coworker, or acquaintance going there would motivate them to do something to prevent those individuals from that eternal fate. This is why it's so imperative that the doctrine of hell be taught and preached from the pulpit. A revelation of hell puts a fire in believers' hearts to pray for the salvation of the unsaved and to ask God for opportunities to share the Gospel with them.

William Booth, Methodist preacher and founder of the Salvation Army, said, "Most Christian ministries would like to send their recruits to Bible college for five years. I would like to send our recruits to hell for five minutes. That would do more than anything else to prepare them for a lifetime of compassionate ministry."[63] J. Hudson Taylor, the great missionary to China, said, "Would that God would make hell so real to us that we cannot rest..."[64]

People would rather talk about Heaven than hell because thoughts about Heaven are much more pleasant to contemplate. But Jesus was so convinced of the need to convey hell's reality to the people that He spoke about it in the four gospels *three times more* than He spoke about Heaven! And His apostles, after learning about hell from Jesus, passed on this painful truth to others as the Church was being established. As a result, the doctrine of hell is one of the central tenets of the earliest creeds of the Church.

Jesus taught so plainly about hell that this became a driving force motivating early Christians to reach others with the life-changing message of the Gospel. Their belief in hell was deeply embedded in their hearts because *Christ Himself* planted it there. And as a result of Jesus' profound and revelatory teaching on hell, the early believers embraced a responsibility to "go" with the Gospel to rescue the unsaved — to do all they could to keep them from passing into eternity in a lost state. They burned passionately with the desire to see people saved.

---

[63] David Shibley, *A Force in the Earth: The Move of the Holy Spirit in World Evangelism* (Lake Mary, FL: Creation House, 1997), p. 61.
[64] Dr. and Mrs. Howard Taylor, *Hudson Taylor and the China Inland Mission: The Growth of a Work of God* (London: Morgan & Scott, 1919), p. 626.

Since actions speak louder than your words, what do your actions or lack of actions say about your own passion to see people rescued from an eternity in hell? If you are serious about walking with God as a life ablaze, this is an important question for you to ask and to truthfully answer in your own life.

I challenge you to study what the Bible says about hell. When you get a revelation of hell as the place of torment that it is, it will change you forever. That revelation will ignite the blazing power of God within you to reach out to as many souls as possible and to do your part to fund the Gospel to "rescue others by snatching them from the flames of judgment..." (Jude 1:23 *NLT*).

This brings to mind the words spoken about hell by Charles Spurgeon, one of the greatest preachers of all time whose influence endures today. He said, "If sinners be damned, at least let them leap to hell over our bodies. If they will perish, let them perish with our arms about their knees. Let no one go there unwarned and unprayed for."[65]

WHAT THE BIBLE
ACTUALLY TELLS US ABOUT HELL

Jesus vividly taught about hell more than anyone else. In addition to His authoritative teaching on this subject, there are other references to hell in both the Old and New Testaments. Several particularly strong references to hell can be found in Psalms and Proverbs.

Jesus taught that hell was a place of outer darkness, a place of weeping and gnashing of teeth, a place of endless torment, and a place where people are burned forever with fire and brimstone

---

[65] *Pentecostal Evangel, Issues 4495-4521* (Madison, WI: General Council of the Assemblies of God, 2000), p. 70.

(*see* Revelation 21:8). Jesus also said that hell is a place where the worm never died (*see* Mark 9:44), a place where the fire is never quenched (*see* Mark 9:44), and a place of regretful memories (*see* Luke 16:25). Jesus said it is a place from which those who die in sin can never depart once they have gone there (*see* Luke 16:26).

The book of Revelation also teaches that hell is a great furnace (*see* Revelation 9:2) and a place where inhabitants of hell can never find rest (*see* Revelation 14:11). The books of Psalms and Proverbs explicitly tell us that hell is a place full of eternal pain and destruction and that it consumes lost souls like a beast whose hunger is never satisfied (*see* Psalm 116:3; Proverbs 27:20).

Since Jesus spoke so explicitly about hell and since other scriptures throughout the Bible do the same, how is it possible that this vital and eternal subject is so ignored? People need to come to faith in Christ so their names are written in the Book of Life and their eternity is sealed in the precious blood of Jesus Christ. It's essential that we take the message of Jesus' work on the Cross to the unsaved and do our part to fund the Gospel so it can be carried to others who have never heard it. This matter of "Heaven or hell" is of such great consequence that God sent His own Son to die for it.

Theologian and author R. C. Sproul reminded us that God's mercy is extended to those who repent at the hearing of the Gospel. He said, "God just doesn't throw a life-preserver to a drowning person. He goes to the bottom of the sea and pulls a corpse from the bottom of the sea, takes him up on the bank, breathes into him the breath of life, and makes him alive."[66]

Friend, this is part of our task — to take the Gospel to those who are drowning in sin and bring them the only life-saving

---

[66] Charles Lee Bilberry, *What's So Good About the Good News? Eight Essential Elements of the Gospel* (Bloomington, IN: AuthorHouse, 2012), p. 29.

message that will breathe the life of God into them and give them a place in His eternal family.

Matthew 28:20 says that the act of taking the Gospel to others is so important to God that when we "go" with the Gospel to those who need it, it releases a "lo" moment in our lives. The very act of going or funding the preaching of the message releases the power of God to detonate inside us and through us to bring salvation, deliverance, and healing to a lost world. What I am speaking to you about, if you will embrace it and obey it, will put fuel on the fire in your heart and will literally *ignite* the blazing power of God inside you.

This is part of our task — to take the Gospel to those
who are drowning in sin and bring them
the only life-saving message that will breathe
the life of God into them and give them
a place in His eternal family.

A WORD OF WARNING

The Great Commission that Christ gave to every believer is so important that He has asked every Christian to participate to make sure the unsaved hear the message. God is depending on you and me to be willing vessels to get this message to them. *Aren't you thankful that someone was willing to share this message with you?*

This is so important to God that I want you to see the sobering words that God spoke through the prophet Ezekiel concerning the task of taking the message to those who are unsaved:

> **When I say to the wicked, 'You shall surely die,' and you give him no warning, nor speak to warn the wicked from his wicked way, to save his life, that same wicked man shall die in his iniquity; but his blood I will require at your hand. Yet, if you warn the wicked, and he does not turn from his wickedness, nor from his wicked way, he shall die in his iniquity; but you have delivered your soul.**
>
> **Ezekiel 3:18,19 *NKJV***

These verses clearly state that we are responsible to warn the unsaved that they need to get their hearts right with God. If we choose *not* to share the Good News that will save relatives, friends, coworkers, or acquaintances whom we know are unsaved — and then they die in their sin — Ezekiel says God will hold *us* accountable for their souls. God is actually saying to us, "Their blood I will require at your hand." That plainly means that if you or I could have warned those in our lives who are unsaved and we choose to ignore this responsibility, God will hold us accountable for not telling them what they needed to know.

This is sobering.

But in these verses, God in essence also says, "If you *do* warn the wicked and tell them the truth about the consequences of sin and they don't repent, then they will die in their iniquity, but you will *not* be held accountable for their souls."

God respects the right of every person to say yes or no to Jesus Christ. Each person can choose how he or she will respond to His invitation, even if it is an eternally fateful choice.

You and I are not accountable for people's choice in this matter. However, we *are* accountable for making sure the unsaved we encounter in life understand the need to be saved. We are accountable to share the good news of Jesus' saving power with them as the Holy Spirit leads. We will not give account for their choice, but we will give account for whether or not we obeyed the Holy Spirit and shared the Gospel with them. *Ouch!*

Famed British missionary and renowned author, C. T. Studd, felt such deep conviction to win the lost that he wrote, "Some wish to live within the sound of church or chapel bell; I want to run a rescue shop within a yard of hell."[67] This profound revelation of hell drove him to reach as many as he could reach with the Gospel because he understood the urgency to do it.

Many Christians are nonchalant about the subject of soul-winning, but God is *not* nonchalant about this subject. God was so serious about winning souls that He sent His own Son into the world to pay for their salvation with His own precious blood. Remember John 3:16, which says, "For God so loved the world, that He gave His only begotten Son, that whosoever believeth in Him should not perish but have everlasting life."

God made the greatest sacrifice of all by giving His greatest Gift to procure salvation and deliverance for those who believe and to place them into His eternal family. Now He asks you and me to do our part to share this life-saving message with others!

YOUR TESTIMONY IS POWERFUL!

Those who changed the world in the early centuries of the Church were simply people whose lives had been transformed by the power of Jesus Christ and then shared their testimonies with compelling results. They were not theologians; they were normal,

---

[67] Ray Comfort, *God Doesn't Believe in Atheists* (Gainesville, FL: Bridge-Logos, 1993), p. 173.

everyday believers who told their personal stories of what Jesus had done for them.

You, too, don't have to be a theologian to share the Gospel with others. You don't even have to know a lot of Scripture. The truth is, right now you possess the most powerful tool you could ever hope to possess to share Christ with others. That tool is *your testimony.*

- What has Jesus done in *your* life?
- How has He helped you, healed you, and strengthened you?
- From what has He delivered you?
- How has He protected you?
- In what ways has He provided for you?
- What does it feel like to know you are saved for all eternity?
- What has Christ's forgiveness done for you?

All these make up *your testimony.* Your testimony is the most powerful thing you have to share. Unbelievers don't want to hear theology. Their minds are in darkness, so they don't get it, and your sharing religiously will put them off. But they'll listen to your life story!

Very often when I am on an airplane flying somewhere to speak, I search for opportunities to be a witness to the person sitting next to me on the plane. Many times they will ask me, "Where are you going?" or, "What will you do once you get to where you are going?" I've found that if I tell them, "I'm a minister," they usually won't talk with me much for the rest of the journey. Instead, I have learned to say, "I'm an author" or, "I'm a television broadcaster" or, "I live and work in Russia." All of these answers are true. But usually when they hear that I'm an author or on television or that I live in Russia, they perk up and immediately want to talk.

- "What kind of TV program do you have?" they ask.
- "What kind of books do you write?" they want to know.
- "Why do you live in Russia?" they ask with great interest.

Instead of saying that I have a Bible teaching program, I tell them, "I have an educational TV program." This is true because my TV programs are educational. Then they nearly always ask, "What kind of educational programs do you broadcast, and what type of books do you write?" Instead of saying they are Bible-based educational materials or books based in truths of the Bible, I answer, "My specialty is First Century history, and I particularly write about things that happened in the Roman world and in the vicinity of Jerusalem."

Eventually the conversation leads to, "What led you to Russia? What do you do there, and how long have you lived there?" I say, "Well, the truth is that God led me there many years ago at a terrible moment in history." That is the moment I seize to begin sharing my testimony of what God has done in my life. But by that time, my new neighbor in the seat next to me wants to hear my whole story and has a heart that is wide open. That is my opportunity to share my testimony, which the Holy Spirit uses to minister the Gospel to them.

I've watched Denise share her testimony with female flight attendants all over the world. As she boards a plane, she swings into action to look for an opportunity to share Jesus' saving power with anyone who will listen. I usually watch her zero in on a flight attendant. Her conversation usually begins by telling her how lovely they look, which is completely sincere on Denise's part, as she enjoys it when women are dressed beautifully. But the flight attendant normally answers, "Thank you, and by the way, I like what you're wearing too." Soon a conversation has begun and the two of them begin talking like old friends about clothes, cosmetics, personal interests, and other things — and little by little, walls come down and another heart opens.

What will happen next is very predictable because I've seen it happen for decades. Soon the flight attendant begins to open up to Denise on a personal level about issues she is facing. And when Denise hears what she says, she answers, "Let me pray for you." For years Denise has given flight attendants her phone number to be available for them. And guess what? Who do you think that flight attendant calls the next time she feels a need for prayer? *Denise!* But it all started with a compliment about what a flight attendant was wearing!

If you genuinely love people and care about their eternal status, God will teach you how to build bridges to reach into hearts with His love and truth. That bridge may be your profession, your children, your clothes, even a cup of coffee. God can practically use anything to build a bridge to another person. If you'll ask the Holy Spirit to help, He will show you how to be intentional about what you're doing when you speak to people you meet who need the Gospel. *Never forget that every person you meet is an eternal life and an opportunity for you to make an eternal difference for them.*

I want to tell you again that you don't have to be a theologian or even know a lot of Bible verses to tell others about Jesus. You possess the most powerful weapon you could wish to have — *your testimony.* And you know your own story so well that you don't have to prepare or study for hours to tell it! It's your testimony and you already know it! It's your story — *the story of what Jesus has done in your life.*

If you genuinely love people
and care about their eternal status,
God will teach you how to build bridges
to reach into hearts with His love and truth.

BE READY, BE STRONG

I'm sure that you are thankful someone loved you enough to share Christ with you. What if that person who shared with you had taken a different route? What if he or she had said, "I know this person needs to hear about Jesus, but I'm too busy and too shy to share it." What if that person walked away and left you in your spiritual mess when he or she could have given you a testimony to bring you to Christ? God is so faithful that He would have sent someone else to reach you, but aren't you genuinely thankful for the very person who took a risk to make an eternal difference in your life?

First Peter 3:15 says, "…Be ready always to give an answer to every man that asketh you a reason of the hope that is in you with meekness and fear." This means you and I must always be ready for God to use us as His instruments to reach unsaved people. We are not inconsequential people — we are mighty weapons that God wants to wield! But if we are to be used for God to the greatest measure possible, we must do it His way. As we receive the baptism in the Holy Spirit and stay sensitive to His leading throughout each day, He will turn every one of us into an inferno of effective, spiritual power that yields a harvest of souls!

How do you sustain that power? You keep stoking the flame in your heart with the right kind of fuel to keep it burning. For one thing, as you pray for the lost, you will tap into God's love for those who are unsaved more and more. His love within you will motivate you to share the Gospel with those who need to hear and will absolutely keep that fire blazing inside you. If you are ready and willing to embrace your God-given responsibility to reach unsaved people with the Good News of Jesus Christ, then get ready — because you are about to detonate spiritually!

If we are to be used for God
to the greatest measure possible,
we must do it His way.

Of course, it is imperative that you genuinely believe the Gospel is the answer to all human need. If you'll "go" with the Gospel, you will experience the "lo" of Christ's power in your life. Then as you move your feet to go to the lost, open your mouth to speak to those who need to hear, and do your part to fund the outreach of the Gospel to those in need, your obedience will pull the trigger that releases the power of God that always accompanies the proclaiming of the Gospel of Christ (*see* Romans 1:16).

Remember, Jesus said we are to *go* and *keep on going* to reach the lost in our nearby world and to the ends of the earth. This divine mandate is to become our way of life. If we'll embrace and actually act on Christ's Great Commission in Matthew 28:18-20, Jesus' promise is ours to claim: "*Wow, will I ever be with you — even to the end of the world!*"

Think About It

1. Each time you share the Gospel, you pull the trigger to release supernatural power to ransom the souls of men. The infilling of the Holy Spirit will empower you with boldness to be effective and to be used in the operation of His supernatural gifts. The Holy Spirit's power enables you to experience an entirely different dimension of success in seeing people's lives transformed.

   Have you embraced the power that comes with the infilling of the Holy Spirit and the inward, consistent empowerment that His infilling affords? Every time you invest time, prayer, or finances into winning souls to Christ, you are seeking to fulfill the desire of God's heart.

   Do you set yourself daily to respond to His promptings either to pray for the lost or to share the Gospel with others? Are you specifically involved in helping others in their efforts to win the lost?

2. Soul-winning fuels the fire of God in your heart! It is impossible to actively pursue spreading the Gospel, reaching the lost, and building the Kingdom of God without having the love and power of God surge through your life to the world around you. God is passionate about souls. Are you?

   Are you intentionally reaching out to win the lost by also intentionally supporting those who go? When you fuel the efforts of others for souls, you will fan your own flame into an inferno!

3. There is a funeral in everyone's future if they die before Jesus
   returns for His Church. With that sobering fact in mind,
   how often do you testify to others of the power of salvation
   through the Gospel?

When a person comes to Christ, he is snatched from a lost
eternity and is immediately infused with a new God-given
nature that makes him a member of God's eternal family.
Immediately eternal life is imparted into that person to assure
him or her a destiny in Heaven instead of an eternity in an
unspeakably terrible place called hell.

Do you genuinely love people enough to let them know that
both Heaven and hell are real? If you are not concerned about
another person's eternal destination and status, most likely
you are not truly mindful about your own. How often do you
consider the reality that one day you will look into the eyes of
Jesus and give an account for how you lived your life? If you
have not lived to proclaim the salvation for which He died,
do you believe your life's efforts will warrant the words "well
done" when you stand before the Master? That's something
for you to think about.

CHAPTER 7

ABLAZE WITH
GENEROSITY

In this chapter, we are going to look at the fuel of *generosity* — another key fuel that enables us to stay on fire in our walk with the Lord.

It is important to note that "generosity" spans the gamut of stewardship over our *entire* lives — including the resources of our time, our money, and our energies. But in this chapter, I'm focusing primarily on generosity in *financial giving* because of the sheer abundance of commands in Scripture concerning the Lord's requirements in this area of our lives.

I realize that some people cringe at the mention of money, but what we do with our money is a great revealer of our spiritual condition. A heart that is ablaze with passion for God and His purposes is a generous heart.

In fact, it would be accurate to say that how generous we are with our finances in the furtherance of God's Kingdom is a revealer of how on fire we are *for* Him and how in love we are *with* Him. As the great songwriter Amy Carmichael said, "You can give without loving, but you cannot love without giving."[68]

Martin Luther said, "A religion that gives nothing, costs nothing, and suffers nothing is worth nothing."[69] What a true statement! Nonetheless, the mere mention of money often stirs anger in people. In fact, there may not be a subject more touchy or divisive than the subject of giving. This explains why British preacher and author Stephen Olford wrote, "I am convinced that the devil has caused the subject of giving to stir up resistance and resentment among God's people...."[70]

"A religion that gives nothing,
costs nothing, and suffers nothing
is worth nothing."
— *Martin Luther*

I find it interesting that many people only get upset about the mention of money when it comes to generous giving in the Church or in a Christian context. Yet the truth is that everywhere you go, someone is going to talk to you about money. For example:

- When you go to the grocery store to fill your cart with the items you need to take home, the cashier asks you for *money*.

---

[68] "Amy Carmichael," https://www.goodreads.com/author/show/3935881.Amy_Carmichael.
[69] David Platt, *Christ-Centered Exposition Commentary: Exalting Jesus in James* (Nashville: Holman Bible Publishers, 1999), p. 27.
[70] Stephen Olford quote, "Christian Quotes on Stewardship," https://www.viralbeliever.com/christian-quotes-on-stewardship/.

- When you go to the symphony, to a musical performance, or to the theater to see an exciting new movie, before you are issued a ticket, the cashier asks you for *money*.

- When you go to your favorite restaurant to enjoy a great meal, the server always ends the experience by asking you for *money* to pay for what you have eaten.

- Money, money, money — everywhere you go, people are asking you for money!

So why would we find it strange that God would speak to us about money in the Scriptures? Actually, God talks about money throughout the Bible. In fact, it was one of the topics Jesus most regularly addressed. What we do with our money — how we spend it, save it, and give it — reveals a great deal about our priorities in life and tells the real story of how much we are in love with God and His Church.

Jesus said, "For where your treasure is, there will your heart be also" (Matthew 6:21). His teaching about this subject is very clear: What a person does with his money reveals what is inside his heart. For example, someone may say he loves the Lord — but if he doesn't give as the Lord commands, what does it say about him? That person is either ignorant about giving, is living in disobedience, or doesn't truly love the Lord with all his heart, soul, and strength. You see, words are cheap and easily spoken. If a person really loves the Lord, what he does with his money would reflect that deep love for Him. When a person sacrificially gives as the Lord asks of him, that person demonstrates that his words of love for God are authentic.

Of course, a person who has little money may find it difficult to give substantial offerings, even though when he gives much in proportion to his means, God still sees that as generous. But if a person does have money and doesn't give, his words and actions don't match. His expression of love for the Lord doesn't match his financial giving. When he spends his extra money on all kinds of material things and then drops a few dollars into the offering, his actions reveal the truth that he loves his possessions and his personal pursuits more than he loves the Lord and His Church. That might sound harsh, but when people's words and actions consistently don't line up, their behavior is telling you the truth.

Someone may say he loves the Lord —
but if he doesn't give as the Lord commands,
what does it say about him?
That person is either ignorant about giving,
is living in disobedience, or doesn't truly love the Lord
with all his heart, soul, and strength.

Consider a man who says he loves his wife but never gives her any money or special gifts to demonstrate that love. Yet somehow that same man is able to find the money to go fishing, buy a sports-game ticket, go work out at the gym with the guys, and so on. Then he tells his wife that there just isn't any money available to do what she wants to do. This husband's actions reveal without a word spoken that he loves himself more than he loves his wife.

How does it make that wife feel when her husband acts like this toward her time after time? He can say, "I love you" all he wants, but she knows he really loves himself. What he does with his money tells the real story.

When people's words and actions consistently
don't line up, their behavior is telling you the truth.

Jesus made it clear in Matthew 6:21 that where a person's treasure is — that is, the value he places on his money in his heart and what he does with his money — is the great revealer that truthfully reveals where his heart is. So if you want to know where *your* heart is, follow your money and you'll find out — because money really does tell the truth.

This may sound simplistic, but years of experience have proven to me again and again that the words of Jesus are true. If you follow a person's money, you'll discover what is or isn't important to that person's life.

If you want to know where *your* heart is,
follow your money and you'll find out — because
money really does tell the truth.

GENEROSITY FLOWED IN JESUS' MINISTRY

When writing about every Christian's responsibility to give, D. L. Moody said, "When God gave Christ to this world, He gave the best He had, and He wants us to do the same."[71] And not only did God the Father sacrificially give, but Jesus was a massive giver as well. Jesus taught giving to His disciples, who then passed the spirit of generosity directly to the first believers in the Early Church.

Because of the words recorded in Acts 10:38, we categorically know that Jesus was a sacrificial giver. It says, "How God anointed Jesus of Nazareth with the Holy Ghost and with power: who went about doing good, and healing all that were oppressed of the devil; for God was with him."

---

[71] *D. L. Moody on Spiritual Leadership*, p. 21.

Most people focus on the part of this verse that describes the healing and deliverance ministry of Jesus — both of which are, of course, true and so very important. But there's something else in this verse that's also very significant, and I overlooked it for many years. I'm talking about the phrase that says Jesus "went about *doing good.*"

Not only did God the Father sacrificially give, but Jesus was a massive giver as well. Jesus taught giving to His disciples, who then passed the spirit of generosity directly to the first believers in the Early Church.

The words "doing good" are a translation of the Greek word *euergeteo*, an old word that denotes *a benefactor, a philanthropist, one who financially supports charitable works,* or *a person who uses his financial resources to meet the needs of disadvantaged people.* This word was used only to portray the provision of food, clothes, or some other commodity to meet a physical or material need. Thus, the use of this word in Acts 10:38 emphatically means that a part of Jesus' ministry was comprised of meeting the physical and tangible needs of people who were disadvantaged in some way.

Of course, we know that Jesus performed *supernatural miracles* of provision — such as the time He multiplied five barley loaves and two fish to feed a large crowd of thousands of people (*see* John 6:1-13). However, the word *euergeteo* in Acts 10:38 tells us that His ministry also provided *natural, material* help to people who were in need.

By reading the four gospels, it becomes evident that Jesus' ministry possessed enormous financial resources that came from various places. Besides offerings that were received, Luke 8:2,3 reveals that there was a group of very wealthy women who supported Jesus' work. Another indication of Jesus' significant resources is the fact that He had a treasurer — His disciple, Judas Iscariot — who was responsible for handling the ministry finances.

In John 12:3, it is recorded that Mary used a pound of expensive spikenard — a rare scented oil — to anoint Jesus' feet. Judas asked Jesus, "Why was not this ointment sold for three hundred pence, and given to the poor?" (v. 5). We can infer from Judas' words that Jesus' ministry had a philanthropic outreach to the poor, over which Judas had been placed in charge as treasurer.

Acts 10:38 makes it even more clear that a significant outreach of Jesus' ministry was to provide physical and material assistance to people in need. The use of the word *euergeteo* explicitly tells us that Jesus used His resources to do *good works*, such as caring for the poor and helping feed the needy. Thus, He set an example for us today to be generous in our giving.

In Acts 10:38, Luke mentioned this philanthropic aspect of Jesus' ministry in connection with His healing ministry — in the very same sentence. The Holy Spirit was conveying the message that God is just as interested in being financially generous to grant relief to people and reverse the conditions of lack and poverty as He is in supernaturally healing or restoring wholeness to people's bodies. Thus, we can know that being generous is just as much a part of Jesus' ministry — and His will for people — today as it was when He "went about doing good" in His earthly ministry almost 2,000 years ago.

Hebrews 13:8 says that Jesus is the same yesterday, today, and forever. What He did is what He is still doing. If Jesus longed to physically heal sick bodies, deliver those who are spiritually oppressed, and abound in the grace of giving when He walked the earth, that is what He still longs to do. The fact is, no one was ever more generous than Jesus — and He is still generous today!

From the beginning of the Old Testament to this present moment, God has demonstrated generosity as He has cared for the needs of His people and made provision for those who come to Him in faith — including you and me. Since Jesus is the same yesterday, today, and forever, doesn't it make perfect sense that He would want us to demonstrate His caring, generous nature through our present-day walk with Him?

If Jesus longed to physically heal sick bodies,
deliver those who are spiritually oppressed,
and abound in the grace of giving
when He walked the earth,
that is what He still longs to do.

GENEROSITY FLOWED IN THE EARLY CHURCH

God is a generous, giving God, and wherever He is working in people's hearts, their hearts burn with a desire to give. Every person who truly desires to be like Him begins to flow in a spirit of generosity. This is exactly what happened among the First Century believers. They had learned to be generous givers from the apostles, who had learned it directly from Jesus.

As we return to our pattern book — the book of Acts — we read that early Christians were ablaze with the Spirit and, as a result, were generous in their giving. In Acts 2:42 and 43, we read, "…They continued stedfastly in the apostles' doctrine and fellowship, and in breaking of bread, and in prayers. And fear came upon every soul: and many wonders and signs were done by the apostles."

But then look what follows in Acts 2:44,45: "And all that believed were together, and had all things common; and sold their possessions and goods, and parted them to all men, as every man had need." This powerful text shows us one of the most amazing miracles that occurs when God's power and fire ignites our hearts — an innate desire *to give* is birthed within us.

God is a generous, giving God,
and wherever He is working in people's hearts,
their hearts burn with a desire to give.
Every person who truly desires to be like Him
begins to flow in a spirit of generosity.

When hearts come alive with the fire of God, one manifestation of that divine fire is the desire to open wallets and purses and allow an outflow of His generous heart to pour through us. Stingy hearts are closed hearts; open hearts are generous. It is the latter kind of heart — the heart that God's Spirit flows through freely — that we see demonstrated in the Early Church.

The attitude of generosity wasn't a one-time event either. Look at what took place in Acts 4:31 when God's Spirit was moving mightily among believers: "And when they had prayed, the place was shaken where they were assembled together; and they were all filled with the Holy Ghost, and they spake the word of God with boldness.'

We would all long to see God's Spirit move so powerfully that the building we are meeting in literally shakes from His presence!

But something else very powerful was also seen happening in Acts 4:32. It goes on to say, "And the multitude of them that believed were of one heart and of one soul: neither said any of them that aught of the things which he possessed was his own; but they had all things common."

Here we see another powerful effect that the presence of God has on people — *that of generosity.* As the Holy Spirit moved powerfully in the midst of the early believers, a demonstration of God's love began to occur among them. Instead of being stingy and selfish and hoarding their possessions to themselves, the people began to say to the Lord, "What I have is yours!"

But there's more to see in the following verses. It goes on to say in Acts 4:33-35, "And with great power gave the apostles witness of the resurrection of the Lord Jesus: and great grace was upon them all. Neither was there any among them that lacked: for as many as were possessors of lands or houses sold them, and brought the prices of the things that were sold, and laid them down at the apostles' feet: and distribution was made unto every man according as he had need."

When the people began to be generous with God and with each other, God became generous with *them*, and signs and wonders erupted in their midst! In other words, the early Christians' generosity ignited a dynamic cycle of blessing and power as a synergistic "snowball effect" began to take place in the Spirit. God moved; the people gave; and then God generously distributed demonstrations of His power to confirm the truth of Christ's resurrection through great signs and wonders.

This was a clear message from Heaven during the days of the Early Church that God is generous with those who are generous. When His people freely give of their substance from their hearts,

He responds by giving from the fullness of who He is and by moving mightily in their midst.

The Early Church was so on fire for God that they held nothing back — not even their personal possessions. The new community of Christians literally came ablaze with a passion for giving! And the more they gave, the more logs they threw upon their spiritual fire, causing that flame to grow into a spiritual inferno that would eventually spread throughout the known world!

When His people freely give of their substance
from their hearts, He responds by giving
from the fullness of who He is
and moving mightily in their midst.

FROM STINGY TO GENEROUS — A TESTIMONY OF GOD'S RESPONSE TO SACRIFICIAL GIVING

When Denise and I first began in ministry, we were part of a large denominational church that was more than 100 years old. The pastor began to teach and preach about the need to become generous in giving. Initially the people didn't like it, but the pastor continued steadfastly teaching, "If you really love the Lord, it will show up in your giving, for where you put your treasure is the great revealer of what you really love."

God began to pour out His grace on that congregation as they grew in understanding that if they would become generous, God would respond by becoming generous with them as well, and they would move into a cycle of His blessing.

The church members began to give sacrificially. It was remarkable to see people give offerings larger than they had ever dreamed possible. Then something miraculous happened! God showed up in that church as they had never experienced — and with God's generous presence also came a mighty anointing along with joy. The power of God spilled into that church as never before!

The altars began to fill up when an invitation was given for the lost to come to Christ. As time passed, people kept walking down the aisle to commit their lives to Jesus. Week after week, the altar was filled with people getting saved and rededicating their lives.

The church literally came alive and moved into perpetual revival. Looking back over my entire Christian life, I'd have to say that what transpired in that church while Denise and I were there was one of the most miraculous occurrences I've ever witnessed — and I have seen a lot of miracles in my life and ministry!

When people opened their pocketbooks and became generous with God, it was as if God said, "I like that so much that now I'm going to show you how generous I can be!" And He responded by pouring out the Holy Spirit mightily upon that 100-year-old congregation and flooding it with divine life again!

Never forget that God is generous with the generous!

God will be *merciful* toward those who have been tightfisted in their finances. But He is *generous* and manifests His liberality in grand and glorious ways toward those who open their hearts and hands — *including their wallets!* — to the Lord.

St. Francis of Assisi is recorded to have said, "For it is in giving that we receive."[72] It is true that when we open our hearts and

---

[72] "Francis of Assisi Quotes," *BrainyQuote*, https://www.brainyquote.com/quotes/francis_of_assisi_121465.

pocketbooks to give to God, it puts us in a position for God to pour out His own generosity on us. Christian author Randy Alcorn stated, "The more you give, the more comes back to you, because God is the greatest giver in the universe, and He won't let you outgive Him. Go ahead and try. See what happens."[73]

Jesus Himself taught this in Luke 6:38 (*NLT*), where He said, "…Your gift will return to you in full — pressed down, shaken together to make room for more, running over, and poured into your lap. The amount you give will determine the amount you get back."

Never forget that God is generous
with the generous!

That means if you have a generous heart and give accordingly, God will be generous with you. But wait — it also means if you are stingy in your heart and your giving is stingy as a result, what you receive will be dramatically less. *Whew*, that may sound abrupt, but that is exactly what Jesus meant when He said, "Whatever measure you use in giving — large or small — it will be used to measure what is given back to you."

In Second Corinthians 9:6, the apostle Paul repeated this same truth when he wrote, "He which soweth sparingly shall reap also sparingly; and he which soweth bountifully shall reap also bountifully."

Could it be any clearer?

---

[73] Randy Alcorn, *The Treasure Principle: Unlocking the Secret of Joyful Giving* (Colorado Springs, CO: Multnomah, 2017), p. 76.

If we are stingy, we will experience "stingy" results. But if we are generous and bountiful, we will experience the generous and bountiful supply of Heaven.

This means if an individual or a church is stingy with God, that person or congregation is going to reap a stingy harvest, but those who are generous with God will reap generously. We have His promise on this (*see* Luke 6:38). He has established it as a spiritual law that we can count as absolutely true!

If we are stingy, we will experience "stingy" results. But if we are generous and bountiful, we will experience the generous and bountiful supply of Heaven.

Let me use the example of the Dead Sea for a moment. It is dead because life flows into it, but there is no outlet for water to flow out of it. It is the *Dead* Sea because it continually receives and never gives. Scientists say if an outlet was formed for the Dead Sea to flow through, its waters could teem with life — but because this body of water has no outlet for water to flow through, it has become the Dead Sea.

The Dead Sea is like many Christians — they receive, but they're not conduits through whom generosity flows to others. They invest in themselves; they spend on themselves or on their families. But because they don't allow the same generosity to flow through their lives to bless others or the work of the ministry, they eventually lose their spiritual vitality.

Friend, this is not how God fashioned Christians to exist. Never forget that a lack of generosity is detrimental to the life of a believer. In fact, this type of selfishness and stinginess will eventually cause any Christian to experience the loss of spiritual fire and divine passion. On the other hand, those who are generous in their giving will become like burning infernos, perpetually emitting the fiery heat of God's life and goodness to ignite hearts for Him wherever they go!

The great preacher Charles Spurgeon noted, "In all of my years of service to my Lord, I have discovered a truth that has never failed and has never been compromised. That truth is that it is beyond the realm of possibilities that one has the ability to outgive God. Even if I give the whole of my worth to Him, He will find a way to give back to me much more than I gave."[74]

"It is beyond the realm of possibilities that one has the ability to outgive God."
— Charles Spurgeon

SACRIFICIAL SURRENDER REQUIRED

From the very beginning of time, God has asked His people to give with serious and thoughtful intent. For example, in the Old Testament, if people were going to offer a sacrifice to God, they sometimes had to prepare for days or weeks to do it. There were specific requirements regarding how the altar was to be built and how they were to bring their gift to God. In some instances, altars had to be built before an offering could be offered. To build an altar meant stones had to be carefully collected, measured, and prepared before they could become a part of the altar.

---

[74] Robin Bertram, *No Regrets* (Lake Mary, FL: Charisma House, 2014), p. 143.

Once the altar was built, wood for the fire had to be gathered, and last but not least, an animal had to be selected for the sacrifice. It could not be just any animal; it had to be one without a spot, blemish, or defect of any kind.

All of these details involved time, care, thoughtfulness, effort, and planning. None of it was last-minute or happenstance. Great preparation went into the act of giving an offering to God.

I suppose people could have given spontaneously, on a whim, but God wanted His people to take their giving seriously. He didn't want people to come to an altar casually or to carelessly select just any ol' animal for a sacrifice. God required His people's giving to be a serious moment in their lives — a moment that they thought about and put effort into — so that their giving cost them something of their time, effort, and resources.

Once a person had gathered the stones to build an altar and prepared their offering — their sacrificial gift — they then offered it and simultaneously called on the name of the Lord. They used that moment to call upon God and to ask Him to respond by getting involved in their lives and helping with anything they were facing at the moment. If they wanted a generous response from God, they would be extra generous in their gifts because they understood that God answered generously to those who had generously given.

For these reasons, I can testify that giving is not what my wife and I normally do in the spur of the moment. Of course, if we are impressed suddenly to give a gift, we do it immediately and without delay. But most often, we take giving so seriously that we consecrate our gifts through prayer and take time to prepare our offerings.

God required His people's giving to be
a serious moment in their lives — a moment
that they thought about and put effort into —
so that their giving cost them something
of their time, effort, and resources.

When Denise and I come to church or to a Christian gathering, we prepare our offering or gift before we get there. We don't wait until the last minute at church to prepare our gift. We consider the act of giving into God's Kingdom far too weighty a matter to deal with at the last moment. We know that when we bring our gifts, we are *building our altar to God.*

Some object to this teaching by accusing its proponents of preaching a "works" mentality instead of "grace through faith." But what I'm saying here has everything to do with cooperating with and receiving the grace of God's generosity — His generous favor toward us — by faith in Him and His Word and in His prescribed way of doing things. Because people believe His Word, they cooperate with it intelligently by following biblical patterns, embracing established truths, and studying the Scripture in order to rightly divide it.

We consider the act of giving into God's Kingdom
far too weighty a matter to deal with at the last moment.
We know that when we bring our gifts,
we are *building our altar to God.*

THE PATTERN OF THE PATRIARCHS

If you read through the entire Old Testament, you will discover that this pattern of carefully building an altar on which to sacrificially give generous gifts to God is replete throughout its pages.

In the first part of this chapter, we looked at New Testament patterns of generous giving. These acts of giving are an expression of one's open heart to God through which He can flow freely — with His presence, His power, and His financial blessing in return for one's generosity toward Him.

Now let's look at some Old Testament examples to see the pattern that was set for all time regarding the way that sacrificial gifts should be offered to God. We can study Noah, for example, and see how he built an altar to God after the Flood. At that critical juncture in Noah's life, he carefully gathered and arranged the stones to build an altar; then he collected wood for fueling the fire and selected the best animals to offer as his gifts to God. Not only did Noah offer a sacrificial gift, but he was generous in the way he gave. Then he called out to God, and God answered him with reciprocal generosity.

Then there's the example of Abram. In Genesis 12, Abram and his family arrived in the land of promise — but when they arrived, they saw that giants were living throughout Canaan. When he confronted this dilemma, Abram knew he needed God's help, so he built an altar and sacrificed generously to God. Just like Noah, Abram carefully gathered and arranged the stones to build an altar, collected wood for fueling the fire, and then selected the best animals to offer as his gifts to God.

Abram gave the best he had and then called upon the name of the Lord. In response, God protected Abram and generously provided for him. And if you study the life of Abram (later called Abraham), you'll find that he repeated this pattern at major milestones in his life. At each of these significant "markers" in Abram's journey, he would stop, build an altar, and generously offer sacrifices unto God.

When God brought Abram out of Egypt with great possessions, he was so thankful that he returned to the very spot where he had built his first altar and sacrificed to God there again (*see* Genesis 13:1-4). And when God promised Abram and his descendants the land as a permanent possession, Abram built an altar and offered a generous sacrifice again (*see* Genesis 13:14-18).

In Second Samuel 24, King David was so grateful to God for stopping a plague that had killed 70,000 Israelites, he built an altar and sacrificed to the Lord on the very spot where the plague had been stopped. At that time, the land was owned by Araunah the Jebusite. When Araunah heard that David wanted to buy his land on which to build an altar and sacrifice to God, he said to David, "...Let my lord the king take and offer up what seemeth good unto him; behold, here be oxen for burnt sacrifice, and threshing instruments and other instruments of the oxen for wood" (1 Samuel 24:22).

As good as the offer was, David told him, "...Neither will I offer burnt offerings unto the Lord my God of that which doth cost me nothing..." (1 Samuel 24:24). In essence, David said, *"I will not give an offering to the Lord that costs me nothing."* The Bible goes on to inform us that "...David bought the threshing floor and the oxen for fifty shekels of silver. And David built there an altar unto the Lord, and offered burnt offerings and peace offerings..." (2 Samuel 24:24,25).

David fully understood that if he was going to give something to God, it needed to be something that cost him something or it wasn't a good sacrifice. Bishop Fulton J. Sheen, who was a Roman Catholic bishop, orator, and author, stated, "Never measure your generosity by what you give, but rather by what you have left."[75]

So often we give what is comfortable to give, and this frequently means it never truly qualifies as a sacrifice. C. S. Lewis said this: "I do not believe one can settle how much we ought to give. I am afraid the only safe rule is to give more than we can spare. In other words, if our expenditure on comforts, luxuries, amusements, etc., is up to the standard common among those with the same income as our own, we are probably giving away too little. If our charities do not at all pinch or hamper us, I should say they are too small."[76]

In essence, David said, *"I will not give an offering to the Lord that costs me nothing."*

King David gave so hugely that day that God was with him. And later David would learn that the land he bought from Araunah was designed by God as the very spot on which Solomon would later build the temple — the most holy geographical location on earth.

These verses about King David are so very important because they reveal the proper *heart attitude* we are supposed to possess when it comes to our giving a sacrificial offering to God. What we give to Him should come with sacrifice — which means it should cost us something. God doesn't need our money, resources, and

---

[75] Rich Brott and Frank Demazio, *Biblical Principles for Releasing Financial Provision* (Portland, OR: City Bible Publishing, 2005), p. 185.
[76] C. S. Lewis, *Mere Christianity* (New York: HarperCollins, 1952, 1980), p. 86.

gifts — but when we generously give from a heart of worship, it demonstrates our love for God. As Charles Spurgeon said, "Giving is true loving."[77]

King David gave so hugely that day
that God was with him. And later David would learn
that the land he bought from Araunah
was designed by God as the very spot
on which Solomon would later build the temple —
the most holy geographical location on earth.

SACRIFICIAL GIVING AND
GOD'S MAGNIFICENT RESPONSE

When our giving is done gladly and truly costs us something, God's heart is deeply touched and He responds magnificently. Scripture bears out that the greater the sacrifice, the greater the response from God. A brilliant example is Second Chronicles 1:6 where we read of the moment Solomon was made king of Israel to replace his father David.

Solomon was overwhelmed by his new assignment and knew that he needed divine assistance to effectively lead God's people. Because Solomon had watched his father offer sacrifices at pivotal moments during his kingship, he knew what to do. He had learned from his father to put everything on pause and to be very generous with God for a generous response.

Second Chronicles 1:6 says, "And Solomon went up thither to the brazen altar before the Lord, which was at the tabernacle of the congregation, and offered a thousand burnt offerings upon it."

---

[77] Frank R. Shivers, *Christian Basics 101* (Maitland, FL: Xulon Press, 2010), p. 105.

Stop and think about that verse. In a single day, Solomon offered 1,000 burnt offerings to God! To achieve such an undertaking in a single day meant he had to plan for weeks, possibly even months, in advance. Animals had to be selected from the finest animals across the land. Then these animals had to be gathered, transported to the place of sacrifice, and prepared before being offered on the altar of the Lord. To do this would require many extra workers and priests.

Solomon's offering therefore required great organization, effort, and expense. For him to offer so many sacrifices in a single day, he had to invest a great deal of thought, time, and money. All of this was done from a generous heart to honor God and to call upon His name. In every respect, Solomon went overboard that day — but he needed God's generous response, so he gave generously that day.

And how did God respond to all of this? God's response is recorded in Second Chronicles 1:7 (*NIV*): "That night God appeared to Solomon and said to him, 'Ask for whatever you want me to give you.'"

You see, God was so deeply touched by Solomon's thoughtful, well-planned, and generous offering that He wasted no time in responding. That very same night, God appeared to Solomon and offered Solomon *anything* he wanted!

Later in Second Chronicles 7, we find King Solomon and the leaders of Israel gathered for the dedication of the temple. When Solomon finished praying, verse 1 tells us, "…The fire came down from heaven, and consumed the burnt offering and the sacrifices; and the glory of the Lord filled the house."

Solomon once again sensed a deep need for God's help. Recalling God's generous response the previous time when he gave a generous offering, Solomon did it again — only this time, he was even more generous and sacrificial in his giving. Second Chronicles 7:5 says, "King Solomon offered a sacrifice of twenty and two thousand oxen, and a hundred and twenty thousand sheep: so the king and all the people dedicated the house of God."

God was so deeply touched by Solomon's thoughtful, well-planned, and generous offering that He wasted no time in responding.

Solomon's offering is almost unthinkable! How is it even humanly possible to sacrifice 22,000 oxen and 120,000 sheep *all in one day*?

I once shared dinner with the owner of a huge ranch that included a slaughterhouse where cattle were butchered, prepared, and packed for the market. As he and I discussed this sacrifice of Solomon, he said, "Even with all the technology and machinery we have today, it is virtually impossible for us to slaughter that many animals in a single day."

So Solomon's offering that day was *not* a last-minute afterthought! To bring this kind of generous offering to the Lord required careful, preliminary planning and an enormous amount of time, energy, labor, and organization. This was truly an extravagant expression of worship.

And just as Solomon was generous with God, Scripture shows that God responded in like manner by being very generous with him. Second Chronicles 7:12 tells us, "And the Lord appeared to Solomon by night, and said unto him, I have heard thy prayer, and have chosen this place to myself for a house of sacrifice."

Solomon had discovered the principle of giving! He knew that if he was generous with God, God would be generous with him. Solomon would later record this spiritual law in Proverbs 3:9 and 10, which says, "Honor the Lord with thy substance, and with the first fruits of all thine increase. So shall thy barns be filled with plenty, and thy presses shall burst out with new wine."

This was Solomon's experience. He knew that if he really honored God with his substance, God would likewise move mightily on his behalf. Similarly, if we really love God and want Him to generously respond to *us*, we must be generous in what we give to *Him*. You see, when a believer is generous with God, it so deeply touches Him that He is moved to be generous with him or her — and the same is true with an entire body of believers.

Solomon had discovered the principle of giving!
He knew that if he was generous with God,
God would be generous with him.

Never forget that God is generous to the generous!

GOD'S WORDS ON GIVING IN MALACHI

One of the most important texts on right giving is found in the book of Malachi. In this book of the Bible, we discover that God listens to the conversations that take place among His people and even hears what they have been thinking in their minds.

Apparently, the thoughts and actions of the Israelites revealed to God that they were tired of sacrificial giving. The fact that their hearts had drifted from giving was an indication that they themselves were drifting from the Lord — and God called them to account for it:

Ye offer polluted bread upon mine altar; and ye say, Wherein have we polluted thee? In that ye say, The table of the Lord is contemptible. And if ye offer the blind for sacrifice, is it not evil? And if ye offer the lame and sick, is it not evil? Offer it now unto thy governor; will he be pleased with thee, or accept thy person? Saith the Lord of hosts.

In essence, God told them, *"Your offerings are a stench to Me because of the attitude in which you offer them. In fact, by offering your sacrifice with such resentment, you have contaminated My altar. You are giving defective rejects — the blind, lame, and sick animals — when you could bring Me the best. This is detestable to Me! Why, you wouldn't even do this to your governor! You're doing to Me what you wouldn't even do to him!"*

You see, the Israelites were giving God leftovers that they didn't really want and that cost them nothing of consequence to give. In light of Jesus' teaching about treasures in Matthew 6:21, this meant the people actually loved themselves more than they loved God. Again, follow the money or the treasure, because it always tells the truth. God knew that, and He could not be duped by their defective, less-than-best gifts.

In Malachi 1:10, God continued His rebuke to them. He said, "Who is there even among you that would shut the doors for nought? Neither do ye kindle fire on mine altar for nought. I have no pleasure in you, saith the Lord of hosts, neither will I accept an offering at your hand."

God was essentially saying, *"Shut the doors to My house! If you're going to treat Me so disrespectfully, then stay out of My presence. Don't bring inferior offerings that are an insult to Me and that so clearly show the distance in your heart toward Me."*

Follow the money or the treasure,
because it always tells the truth.

God didn't need the Israelites' offerings. God doesn't need your offerings either. What God has always wanted is His people's *hearts*. Remember, Jesus said, "For where your treasure is, there will your heart be also" (Matthew 6:21).

No one has ever stated this spiritual law more clearly than Jesus did in this verse. The way a person handles his or her money and material possessions is a reflection of that person's true heart condition. God knew it would require a right heart of His people for them to generously give of their best. He also knew that the offering of an inferior gift would be evidence of a wrong heart condition.

Finally, in Malachi 1:14, God uttered this sober indictment: "Cursed be the deceiver, which hath in his flock a male, and voweth, and sacrificeth unto the Lord a corrupt thing: for I am a great King, saith the Lord of hosts, and my name is dreadful among the heathen." These are strong words, and they reveal how serious God is about the attitude of His people's hearts when they give their tithes and offerings to Him.

Evidence That You've 'Returned' in Your Heart Toward God

As I write, I can almost hear some reader thinking, *If I have given God my second-best in the past, how can I remedy this?*

God's answer to that question is clearly stated in Malachi 3:7 and 8, where He told offenders what they needed to do to get things right with Him. He knew that some of those listening would want to get things right, so He told them, "Even from the days of your fathers ye are gone away from mine ordinances, and have not kept them. Return unto me, and I will return unto you, saith the Lord of hosts. But ye said, Wherein shall we return? Will a man rob God? Yet ye have robbed me. But ye say, Wherein have we robbed thee? In tithes and offerings."

The people were robbing God of what rightfully belonged to Him. In Malachi 3:9, God declared that because of their wrong hearts and subsequent incorrect actions, they had come under a self-imposed curse: "Ye are cursed with a curse: for ye have robbed me, even this whole nation."

It is important for us to understand that when we rob God of what belongs to Him, it removes us from the realm of His blessings and thrusts us into a realm where we begin to reap negative things. This verse never says God brings a curse, but infers that by refusing to obey God's principles, we remove ourselves from the blessings that otherwise would be ours.

This may be a spiritual principle that applies in your own personal walk with God. If you've been having financial difficulty or other problems in your life, the issue may be that you have unintentionally removed yourself from the sphere of God's blessing and, as a result, you are experiencing the effects of the enemy's access into your life. You need to understand that this kind of difficulty could be self-imposed because of a wrong heart or wrong action. If you have chosen not to give God the tithe, which biblically belongs to Him, you have removed yourself from the place of divine blessing.

When we rob God of what belongs to Him,
it removes us from the realm of His blessings
and thrusts us into a realm
where we begin to reap negative things.

But God lovingly offers the solution to this problem in Malachi 3:10. He says, "Bring ye all the tithes into the storehouse, that there may be meat in mine house, and prove me now herewith, saith the Lord of hosts, if I will not open you the windows of heaven, and pour you out a blessing, that there shall not be room enough to receive it." In other words, God promises every person, *"If you want to make things right, you need to put the money on the table."*

Of course, not every financial difficulty, struggle, or setback means a person's heart is wrong or even that his or her actions are wrong. The enemy will oppose and contend against *any* promised blessing in our lives. We must be willing to get a firm grip on the promise of God for finances and to contend for its manifestation — *as well as* to joyfully obey God's command to be generous and to give.

Again, what we do with our treasure reveals what is in our hearts. We *could* say that, in God's eyes, our heart strings are so connected to our resources that when we give or expend our resources, our hearts actually follow our choices in the way we spend and distribute the wealth that is at our disposal.

Therefore, if you have made a mistake in this area of your life, repent for it. Begin to take action that shows you are serious about being in right relationship with God in the area of your giving. As you begin giving — or return to your previous practice of faithful giving —start with the minimal amount God requests, if needed; then grow in the grace of giving until you become lavish in your giving to God.

Never fear that you might give too much. One person said, "When it comes to giving until it hurts, most people have a very low threshold of pain."[78] But don't let that be you. Start where you are, and learn to grow in this amazing grace!

If you'll get started — and if you'll be generous with God — then He assuredly promises that He will be generous with you. He will bless you immeasurably and beyond your wildest imagination. In Malachi 3:10, God actually says to *prove* Him in this and see "...if I will not open you the windows of heaven, and pour you out a blessing, that there shall not be room enough to receive it."

THE WINDOW OF HEAVEN?

What is "a window of Heaven," and what always happens when it is opened? The window, or "door," of Heaven appears several times in the Bible, particularly in Genesis 7:11, Psalm 78:23, and Malachi 3:10. Every time that window, or that door, of Heaven opens, miraculous things happen and some type of abundance comes pouring through. And when the Bible mentions "windows," plural, it just means *more* abundance!

The first mention of the window of Heaven in Scripture is Genesis 7:11, where the Bible says that "the windows of heaven were opened" and rain started *falling*. In fact, so much rain fell through this portal over the course of 40 days and nights that Genesis 7:19 records, "And the waters prevailed exceedingly upon the earth; and all the high hills, that were under the whole heaven, were covered."

---

[78] George Barna, *How To Increase Giving in Your Church* (Ventura, CA: Regal Books, 1997), p. 78.

Every time that window, or that door, of Heaven opens,
miraculous things happen and some type
of abundance comes pouring through.

For us to further understand the significance of the window of Heaven, it is necessary to recall how manna came through it for the children of Israel. Approximately two months after the Israelites left Egypt, their food stores began to run low and supplies were rationed. As their stomachs ached for food, they dreamt of the food they had left behind in Egypt and began to complain and murmur amongst themselves. In their dissatisfaction, they even accused Moses of leading them into the wilderness to kill the entire assembly with hunger (*see* Exodus 16:3).

Although God had delivered the children of Israel from Egyptian bondage, they demonstrated ingratitude and a lack of faith. Yet in spite of their thankless attitude, God came through for them once again and told Moses, "...Behold, I will rain bread from heaven for you..." (Exodus 16:4).

Theologian John Gill wrote:

They were a murmuring, rebellious, and ungrateful people, but the Lord dealt kindly and bountifully with them; he did not rain fire and brimstone upon them, as on Sodom and Gomorrah, nor snares and an horrible tempest, as on the wicked; but what was desirable by them, and suitable to their present circumstances, even bread, which was what they wanted, and this ready prepared; for though they did dress it in different ways, yet it might be eaten without any preparation at all; and this it was promised should be rained down upon them, there should be great plenty of it; it should come as thick and as fast as a shower of rain, and

**lie around their camp ready at hand to take up; and this
should not spring out of the earth as bread corn does, but
come down from heaven....[79]**

God not only provided manna — He *amply* provided it.
Psalm 78:23-25 records that God "...opened the doors of heaven,
and had rained down manna upon them to eat...and man did
eat angels' food...." The psalmist tells us several important truths
about this supernatural provision.

- The doors [windows] of heaven were opened (v. 23).

- When the doors [windows] were opened, manna *rained*
  upon them (v. 24).

First, the psalmist told us that when the manna fell, the
"doors [windows] of heaven" were opened. This phrase "doors
of heaven" refers to the "window of heaven" — a heavenly portal
that opens at God's command. Second, the psalmist recorded that
when this manna began falling, it "rained down." This shows that
when Heaven's portal opens, whatever comes through does so in
superabundant measures.

Rabbinical literature asserts that manna fell in such abundance each day that it spread over more than 2,000 square cubits
(a cubit being approximately 17 to 20 inches), with a depth of
50 to 60 cubits. If this was the case, then one day's supply of
manna would have been enough to feed the children of Israel
for 2,000 years![80]

It is impossible to know exactly how much "manna" came
pouring through that portal during those 40 years, but one can
make a rough estimate. If the Israelites numbered approximately

---

[79] John Gill, *Exposition of the Whole Bible*, www.studylight.org.
[80] Isi b. Akiba, *Midrash Tehillim*, Ps. 23.

3,000,000 people, as many Bible scholars believe, it is estimated that they would have needed *4,500 tons* of manna every day. If they gathered 4,500 tons a day every day for 40 years, that means an estimated *65,700,000 tons* of manna supernaturally appeared on the ground over that period of time.

If your city woke up tomorrow to find 4,500 tons of beautiful, freshly baked, nourishing manna lying on the ground all over the city — free to anyone who wanted to go out, pick it up, and take it home — it would be a worldwide sensation. Scientists would fly in from around the world to study it; journalists would write about it; and every major news program would cover the story. However, for the children of Israel, this miracle was an everyday event that occurred for 40 years — as long as the window of Heaven remained open over them! An entire generation of young children was born during that time period who grew up thinking it was *normal* for 4,500 tons of manna to appear each morning out of thin air (*see* Exodus 16:35)!

Finally, an open window of Heaven is promised in Malachi 3:10 to those who bring "all the tithes" into God's house. Taking into account the earlier examples of the window, or door, of Heaven and what happens when it is opened, we can see again that God promises to mightily pour His blessings upon those who give.

The earth was covered with rain during the time of the Flood when the window of Heaven opened. And tons of manna later fell through that heavenly portal over a span of 40 years. And just as abundance always poured through those windows when they were opened, God promises to open a window over generous givers today and abundantly pour out immeasurable blessings on those who willingly give Him the tithe, or the tenth, of all their increase. And He promises to do it so much so that they will not even have enough room to accommodate it all!

Then in Malachi 3:11, God promises to do even more than this for those who willingly give of their substance. In addition to pouring out blessings, He promises, "I will rebuke the devourer for your sakes, and he shall not destroy the fruits of your ground; neither shall your vine cast her fruit before the time in the field, saith the Lord of hosts."

In other words, God is saying to His people, *"If you open your hand to give, I'll open My mouth to rebuke the devourer for your sake!"* God's promise is that the moment we open our hand to give the tithe on all the increase God brings, He will open His mouth to rebuke the devil. For those who give, God literally promises that He will tell the devil, "Move off of those people because they are tithers!"

God is saying to His people,
"If you open your hand to give, I'll open My mouth to rebuke the devourer for your sake!"

MORE ON JESUS' ATTITUDE ABOUT MONEY

Somebody may allege, "All the verses you've referred to are from the Old Testament and were spoken to people who were under the Law." But as I mentioned earlier, money was one of the main topics Jesus addressed during His earthly ministry.

For example, in Luke 21:1-4, we find Jesus in the temple watching *how* people gave and *what* people gave. Luke 21:1 says, "He looked up, and saw the rich men casting their gifts into the treasury."

Jesus stood nearby to watch *what* and *how* people gave their offerings to God. He observed rich men casually casting their offerings into the offering container. It seems they did this in a very casual manner, with no faith required on their part. But the story continues in verse 2 as "[Jesus] saw also a certain poor widow casting in thither two mites."

The word "poor" in this verse is the Greek word *penichros*, which depicts a person living in *abject poverty*. The "mite" depicts the smallest, least valuable bronze coin in the currency of that day. To the natural eye, it appeared that this woman gave very little. But as Jesus watched her act of giving, He told His disciples, "Of a truth I say unto you, that this poor widow hath cast in more than they all: for all these have of their abundance cast in unto the offerings of God: but she of her penury hath cast in all the living that she had" (vv. 3,4).

For this widow, two mites was an enormous sum of money because her resources were very small. In fact, Jesus was so impressed with the enormity of her faith and the size of her gift — in light of what she financially had to give — that He stopped and drew their attention to what this little woman had done. Although the widow barely had enough to survive, she gave "more than they all." This phrase indicates that by comparison, all of the wealthy people's gifts that day *combined* did not equal what the poor widow had given to God that day.

Jesus said that the rich had given out of their "abundance" — which is the Greek word *perisseuo*, describing *excess*. In other words, the rich men didn't even scratch the surface of their fortune with the amount they gave, so they were able to give their offering without much personal sacrifice. But the widow gave of her "penury" — which is a translation of the Greek word *husterema*. This is a word that refers to *the last bit of money possessed*. It had taken little or no faith for the rich men to give their large offerings — but it took *great faith* for the widow to give those two mites.

As I have assured you, it's not difficult to figure out where a person's heart is. You just need to follow his or her money, and you'll find the truth of what that individual highly values in life. Whatever a person loves and adores, that is what he invests in.

This little widow loved God and showed it in the great sacrifice she made. Even though the amount she gave was less than what the rich casually contributed, her gift counted as far more because she gave it so sacrificially and with such reverent faith. Jesus knew this because He watched not only *what* was given, but *how* it was given — whether casually and non-sacrificially or with a generous, open heart. And He knows the same about how we give today.

It had taken little or no faith for the rich men
to give their large offerings —
but it took *great faith* for the widow
to give those two mites.

PAUL AND THE MACEDONIANS

Another important principle about giving in the New Testament is found in Paul's letter to the church at Corinth. Corinth was a very rich town, and the believers there had access to ample amounts of money. It appears that the believers in Corinth didn't suffer financially as many other believers were experiencing elsewhere. At one point, the Corinthians pledged to give a significant offering to Paul's ministry — but then forgot to give it.

As time passed, word began to spread throughout the First Century Church about the super-sized promise of finances that the Corinthians had pledged to give. Rumors of a gigantic offering were circulating everywhere. So in Second Corinthians 8:1-5, Paul reminded them of their need to be faithful to follow through on their promise. But he began by telling the Corinthians about the attitude of sacrificial giving that the congregation in Macedonia possessed. This was a body of believers who had been suffering financially, yet who had given joyfully to God in spite of their personal struggles.

In Second Corinthians 8:1 and 2, Paul told the Corinthian congregation: "Moreover, brethren, we do you to wit of the grace of God bestowed on the churches of Macedonia; how that in a great trial of affliction the abundance of their joy and their deep poverty abounded unto the riches of the liberality."

The Christians in Macedonia were suffering persecution, and many had lost their jobs, their homes, and their money on account of their faith in Christ. But because they had such hearts to further God's Gospel, they pooled together resources so they could give a significant offering for Paul's ministry.

In Second Corinthians 8:3 and 4, Paul expounded about the Macedonian (Philippian) believers' sacrificial giving when he wrote, "For to their power, I bear record, yea, and beyond their power they were willing of themselves: praying us with much entreaty that we would receive the gift, and take upon us the fellowship of the ministering to the saints."

Paul was simply stunned that the struggling Macedonian believers gave such an enormous gift. It was later to these same giving Christians that Paul wrote, "...My God shall supply all your need according to his riches in glory by Christ Jesus" (Philippians 4:19).

Many Christians through the years have considered this verse a promise that was theirs to claim just by virtue of being a Christian. However, Philippians 4:19 specifically holds a promise for *givers*. Because the Philippian believers made a decision to generously give, they were promised that God would generously respond by meeting their needs.

In essence, Paul told the believers at Philippi: *"But my God will supply your needs so completely that He will eliminate all your deficiencies. He will meet all your physical and tangible needs until you are so full that you have no more capacity to hold anything else. He will supply all your needs until you are totally filled, packed full and overflowing to the point of bursting at the seams and spilling over!"*

Years ago, when Denise and I were newly married, we didn't have much money coming in. During that season, it seemed that if we tithed, we would have been left with less to try to make ends meet. During those days, I *loathed* it when someone preached on tithing, because I wasn't tithing as I knew God commanded me to do. On the inside, I would privately name all the reasons I couldn't tithe as I tried to convince myself that I was justified for not obeying this clearly biblical command.

Philippians 4:19 specifically holds a promise for *givers*.
Because the Philippian believers made a decision
to generously give, they were promised that
God would generously respond
by meeting their needs.

Thankfully, I eventually came to a point of humbling myself before God and repenting. As difficult as it was, I said to the Lord, "The tithe is *Yours* — and from this point onward, I will honor You generously with my tithes and offerings. Forgive me for withholding what belongs to You, and give me grace to trust You so I can give with a cheerful heart!"

CULTIVATE A PASSION FOR GIVING!

As we've established, one of the signs that a Christian is on fire for God is the way that person gives of his or her finances. History proves that if a person or a church is stingy, there will be little manifestation of the presence and power of God in that person's life or in the midst of that congregation. On the other hand, if a person or church will learn to become financially generous and sacrificial in giving, God will open the window of Heaven above them, rebuke the enemy for their sakes, and demonstrate Himself to them in mighty ways! *In other words, God shows up in the lives of the generous!*

Never forget that generosity ignites a dynamic cycle of blessing and power. As you give generously, God will generously give back to you. He pours out His presence and power, opening the window of Heaven above the lives of those who give freely and sacrificially to His work.

John Chrysostom, an Early Church father, wrote, "Things themselves do not remain, but their effects do. Therefore we should not be mean and calculating with what we have but give with a generous hand."[81] These words are so powerful! Material things are short-lived, but when we use them for eternal purposes,

---

[81] Craig Brian Larson and Phyllis Ten Elshof, eds., *1001 Illustrations That Connect* (Grand Rapids, MI: Zondervan), p. 98.

they last forever. This is why Martin Luther said, "I have held many things in my hand, and have lost them all, but whatever I have placed in God's hands, that I still possess."[82]

Generosity ignites a dynamic cycle
of blessing and power. As you give generously,
God will generously give back to you.

WHAT ABOUT YOU?

So are you generous with God by sowing sacrificially and without reservation into the work of His Kingdom? If you are not, take this as your opportunity to get started.

How about your church? Is it generous in its support of ministries and missions that are taking the Gospel to the ends of the earth? If not, this is your opportunity to begin praying for your church to become willing and joyful givers into the good ground of such ministries. As a result, God will become more and more generous in blessing your church!

William Carey, the famous Baptist missionary to India, made this profound statement: "I was once young and now I am old, but not once have I been witness to God's failure to supply my need when first I had given for the furtherance of His work. He has never failed in His promise…"[83]

Remember, God answers generosity with generosity.

If you serve God with your finances, your obedience will open the door for Him to pour out His blessings upon you. If you're

---

[82] Martin Luther quote, https://www.sermonsearch.com/sermon-illustrations/4434/quote/.
[83] Howard Dayton, "Tried To Outgive God Lately?" Baptist Press, http://www.bpnews.net/24647/.

not a generous giver, your joy in serving God will eventually wane. But when you live a life of generous giving, you are continually throwing another log into the fire of your heart, and it will cause you to burn ever more brightly for the Lord.

If you serve God with your finances,
your obedience will open the door for Him
to pour out His blessings upon you.

If you are generous with God, you can count on God being generous with you. And when you begin to worship Him generously with your finances, you acquire the right to claim Philippians 4:19 (*AMPC*) for yourself: "And my God will liberally supply (fill to the full) your every need according to His riches in glory in Christ Jesus!"

THINK ABOUT IT

1. In Acts 10:38, we read that Jesus "went about doing good" in His earthly ministry almost 2,000 years ago. Generosity is just as much a part of Jesus' ministry today as it was then because Jesus is the same yesterday, today, and forever. What He did is what He is still doing. If Jesus longed to physically heal sick bodies, deliver those who are spiritually oppressed, and abound in the grace of giving when He walked the earth, that is what He still longs to do.

   How are you giving expression in practical ways to the ministry of Jesus in generosity? Are you looking for ways to "do good" to the many lives that cross your path? You will never look into the eyes of a person for whom the blood of Jesus was not shed. So do you deliberately show kindness to those who are unkind, as Jesus did? Are you generous to those who can never pay you for what you've done? The Lord is good to all! Are you good to all, without respect of persons, as you're led by the Lord and by a heart of compassion?

2. When hearts come alive with the fire of God, one manifestation of that divine fire is the desire to allow an outflow of His generous heart to pour through us. God is a generous, giving God, and wherever He is working in people's hearts, their hearts burn with a desire to give.

   From the very beginning of time, God has asked His people to give with serious and thoughtful intent. David refused to bring God an offering that cost him nothing. (*see* 1 Samuel 24:24). For years, David set aside resources for the purpose of building the house of the Lord. When his leaders and the people willingly joined him in bringing their offerings for Solomon to build a temple, the total amount gathered was staggering.

Your love for God will show up in your willing and cheerful giving, for where you put your treasure is the great revealer of what you truly love. Do you systematically set aside offerings and sacrificial gifts for the purpose of building and advancing the work of the Kingdom of God? How much are you presently saving up so you can inquire of the Lord where He wants you to give your gift to bless others and further His purposes?

3. Your generosity is determined not by how much you give, but by how much you have left. Jesus defined the widow who gave her last mite — the smallest currency available in that day — as the one who gave the most. Consistency, sincerity, and generosity touch the heart of God, who is the most generous Giver of all! You can never outgive Him — but you can capture His attention by how you give and why. It's the heart motive behind the gift that determines its truly enduring value.

Do you bring God offerings that reflect the giving of all you are simply to magnify Him for who He is? Does your passionate, joyful generosity and honor for the Lord capture His attention? If not, what can you do to change that?

CHAPTER 8

ABLAZE WITH HOLINESS

In this chapter, we will look at the next key to adding fuel to the flame of your spiritual fire. For you to be spiritually ablaze — burning with the fire of God for years to come — it is imperative to add the fuel of holiness to your life!

But before we delve directly into the subject of holiness, let's journey backward in time to a moment recorded in Exodus 3. There Moses had his encounter with God at the site of a burning bush as he was tending sheep in the wilderness.

The Bible tells us that one day as Moses was tending his sheep on the backside of Mount Horeb, he saw a burning bush that was not consumed by the fire. Moses turned aside to see this astounding phenomenon. Scripture says he saw it as a "great sight" — something that stunned and amazed him, for he had never witnessed anything like it.

When Moses drew near, the voice of God called out from the midst of the burning bush and said, "Draw not nigh hither: put off thy shoes from off thy feet, for the place whereon thou standest is holy ground" (v. 5).

In that hallowed moment, Moses crossed the threshold that separated the natural realm from the realm that God called "holy." The physical location that Moses entered at that moment was so sacred to God that He commanded him to remove his shoes, lest Moses carry the contamination of the dirt on them unto this holy spot of earth that had become God's sanctuary.

The word "holy" in Exodus 3:5 is *hagia* in the Old Testament Greek Septuagint. This is a form of the word *hagios*, which from this point forward throughout the Bible is the word used to denote the holiness of God, the holy presence of God, or anything that God deems to be holy. This spot where Moses stood was a place on this earth where God dwelt — so holy that no worldly contamination was permitted there.

In that hallowed moment, Moses crossed the threshold
that separated the natural realm
from the realm that God called "holy."

WHAT IS HOLINESS?

Both in the Old Testament Greek Septuagint and in the Greek New Testament, the Greek word for "holy" is translated from various forms of this Greek word *hagios*. It is one of the most important words anywhere in the entire Bible, so it is vital for you to understand exactly what the word "holy" means. It can describe something that, even though it was once common, it has now become separated, consecrated, holy, and sacred — never again to be regarded or used in a common way. This means anything "holy" is in a category that is separate and sacred from other things.

Here's a simple illustration to make this word "holy" very understandable for you. The King James translators were some of the earliest to give the Bible's full name as *the Holy Bible*. The word "Bible" is in reality a translation of the Greek word *biblios*, which simply means *book* or *a scroll of writing*.

As mentioned earlier, the word "holy" — the Greek word *hagios* — means *separated, consecrated, holy, sacred*, or *never to be regarded or used in a common way*.

Anything that is "holy" is in a category that is separate and sacred from other things. That means the Holy Bible is a special book that's *consecrated, separated*, and *set apart* from all other books.

The Holy Bible is so different that no other book in the world that has ever been written compares to it. If you walk into a library, you can probably find a copy of the Holy Bible on its shelves. But even though it is located in a library full of books, the word "holy" in the name "Holy Bible" signifies that it is in a category all by itself. And every time you call that precious Book by its name, you are affirming that it is like no other book, that it is *set apart* into *a special, consecrated, holy category*, and that it is *different* from all the other books in the library.

The Holy Bible is so different
that no other book in the world
that has ever been written compares to it.

The Holy Bible is so different that no other book
in the world compares to it.
Although the Holy Bible is indeed a book,
its name reveals its true nature —
that it is in a class all by itself.

Let's return to the example of Moses that day on Mount Horeb. When Moses approached the burning bush, God told him to remove his shoes because he was standing on "holy" ground. Because that word "holy" in this context is also a translation of the Greek word *hagios*, it tells us that God *consecrated* and *sanctified* that particular spot on the mountain.

In reality, if you had been there and looked at that mountain, you would have thought it looked no different from other mountains in the region. Yet although there was nothing particularly unique about that mountain in terms of its appearance compared to other mountains, God's presence had touched it. And in that moment, that divine presence supernaturally *separated* Mount Horeb from all other mountains and *set it apart* into a holy category. In fact, it became so sacred at that moment that it became known as the *holy mount*. Although it was nestled as one mountain in the midst of an entire mountain range of normal mountains, Horeb ceased to be normal from that day onward. *God's presence had changed its status.*

As you consider the word "holy" in light of the rest of this chapter, keep in mind these ideas of *separation, consecration,* and *being placed into a unique category.* We'll see how the apostle Paul used these concepts throughout his epistles in a powerful way.

For instance, when Paul wrote to the Christians in Rome (as well as to all believers everywhere), he began his letter in Romans

1:7 by saying, "To all that be in Rome, beloved of God, called to be *saints*...."

When people see the word "saints," they sometimes imagine people with halos above their heads. But this is not the right idea at all. The word translated "saints" is actually a form of the Greek word *hagios*. This is the same word we have been looking at so far in this chapter, which means *holy* and describes something that has been *separated, consecrated, sanctified,* and *set apart* for special use. Paul used it to describe Christians — which means that before they came to Christ, they were just regular human beings like everyone else. But when the blood of Jesus cleansed them and the Holy Spirit moved into their hearts, that divine presence *set them apart* and made them so *different* that God immediately saw them in a special, holy light that was different from unsaved people.

Although it was nestled as one mountain in the midst of an entire mountain range of normal mountains, Horeb ceased to be normal from that day onward. *God's presence had changed its status.*

So when Paul called the Christians in Rome (and you and me) "saints," he was really saying that *we are called to be holy, called to be different, called to be sanctified,* or *called to be separate from the rest of the world.* The use of *hagios* tells us that the blood of Jesus and the presence of the Holy Spirit inside us has caused us to be *separated* and *consecrated* — and we are now in an entirely new category that is *holy.*

Second Corinthians 5:17,21 teaches that you and I were reconciled to God the moment we received Jesus as Savior and Lord and the Spirit of God came in our hearts. At that moment, God judicially reckoned us to be righteous. In a fraction of a split second, quicker than the mind can comprehend, the Holy Spirit's presence within removed us from the category of unregenerate human beings and moved us over into the special category of set-apart, consecrated, marked-off, holy beings, created in God's own image. *That* is what the word "saints" means.

This means that if you are a believer, you may look like any other human being in society, but you are not like everyone else. Just as the presence of God came down on Mount Horeb and made it holy, the moment the blood of Jesus washed you and the Holy Spirit entered your spirit, God *separated* you, *consecrated* you, and *set you apart* for Himself. Friend, you are the home of the Holy Spirit — and as such, you are *holy*.

God justified us and made us to be righteous by faith — and in that act, we moved over into a new category of human beings! We might look like regular people, but in actual fact, there is *nothing* regular about us.

As new creations who are separated into a higher, holy category, God expects us to adjust our thinking to His holy written Word and behave accordingly. We should no longer think and act as we once did, because we are not who we once were. We are new, different, and holy — and that means we must think differently, talk differently, and act differently.

God justified us and made us to be righteous by faith — and in that act, we moved over into a new category of human beings! We might look like regular people, but in actual fact, there is *nothing* regular about us.

All of this is contained in the word "saint" used in Romans 1:7 and in other places throughout the New Testament.

Now the Spirit of God lives in us. And just as God's holy presence sanctified the physical location of the burning bush on Mount Horeb, His divine presence in our lives has set perimeters around us that separate us from the rest of the world. We are holy ground!

We are declared righteous; we are justified by faith; and we are made *holy*. Now as believers, we must learn to live in a way that reflects who we really are!

Billy Graham once said, "Living the Christian life means striving for holiness."[84] Since we have been made righteous and God has declared us to be holy, we must press forward and adjust our lives upward so we continually reflect who God has graciously made us to be in Christ!

UNHOLY BEHAVIOR IN HOLY PEOPLE

The Early Church had many problems because of the strong pagan influence of the world that surrounded it. The early Christians who had been saved out of the pagan culture carried some residue with them into their new lives in Christ. Although God had made them new creations in Christ, they were still learning to walk in their new God-imparted status. They still needed to be inwardly transformed by the renewing of their minds (*see* Romans 12:2).

In the pagan world, there were rampant problems with alcohol, drugs, and sexual immorality. Let's use the city of Corinth

---

[84] *Billy Graham in Quotes*, p. 178.

as an example and study its effect on the church that was established there.

Corinth was a very wicked and flesh-dominated city. Its long history of being rebellious to authority is the reason the Romans completely destroyed it around 146 BC, leaving it uninhabitable for nearly a century.

In approximately 44 BC, Roman Emperor Julius Caesar saw that Corinth was an ideal site for a city because of its location on an isthmus between two major ports — one on the west and one on the east. Because Corinth was highly accessible, Caesar decided to rebuild and repopulate the ancient municipality once again.

How a city is birthed often determines the future spiritual state of that city, and such was the case with Corinth. Strange as it may sound to our modern minds, Julius Caesar actually believed he was a direct descendant of Aphrodite — the goddess of sex. In the cult of Aphrodite, intermingling with sacred prostitutes was an integral part of worship. This is important to note, because when Julius Caesar decided to rebuild Corinth, he made the decision to dedicate it to Aphrodite, his supposed ancestor. You can guess why this was so devastating morally to the people who came to occupy the city, as we will see in the following paragraphs.

Since Corinth had been utterly destroyed earlier when it rebelled against Rome, the site didn't have much to offer newcomers and no one really wanted to move there to rebuild it. To lure people to the city that was being reconstructed, Julius Caesar offered a special deal to former soldiers, sailors, and legionnaires. He promised that if they would voluntarily move to help rebuild Corinth, he would give them money, land, and a future leadership role in the new city.

The deal Caesar offered was so impressive that huge numbers took advantage of it and began moving to Corinth to assist in its reconstruction. These former soldiers, sailors, and legionnaires were rough, tough, crude people who were looking for position, land, future influence, and the ability to make fast money. This means the city's founding leaders were opportunists. They were followed by others who scrambled to get to Corinth from all over the Roman Empire because word was out that it was going to be a place to make an easy buck.

Because Julius Caesar had dedicated Corinth to Aphrodite, the goddess of sex, the city soon mushroomed with a thriving sex industry. The constant influx of soldiers and sailors into Corinth fueled the prostitution business until eventually it became the largest source of revenue for the city. It would be difficult to exaggerate the sexual immorality that infested every nook and cranny of Corinth every hour of every day.

In addition to the illicit sex that continually filled Corinth's many brothels, such activity also freely transpired in the many temple precincts that were dedicated to the goddess Aphrodite. In addition, the Corinthians had many public bathhouses that also teemed with perverse sexual activities, including widespread homosexuality. A study of sexual practices in the Greek world shows that sex was even offered in bakeries as clients waited for hot bread. This shows how rampant the problem was in the city. Men were the primary clientele of these establishments, so "bakery prostitutes" would peddle their wares, taking willing clients into an annexed room for a sexual escapade before returning home.

Sexual immorality became so widespread in Corinth that sporting events also became venues for sexual activity. When men left their seats in the stadium to walk to the public toilets, they were regularly approached by prostitutes on duty. Those who accepted a prostitute's proposition would be taken under the arches of the stadium to engage in sex — right under the seats where people were watching the games. Once finished, they would return to their seats for the remainder of the game with no sense of guilt or shame. This was just the way it was in the pagan world.

In today's world, we have specific labels for the different types of sex that people engage in, such as "heterosexual" and "homo-sexual." In recent years, the scope of sexual terms has been greatly expanded, which is a sign of the moral degradation of our own times and a return to paganism. But in the First Century, such labels did not exist. People merely saw themselves as *sexual*. In the pagan world, it didn't matter what a person did or with whom they did it. It was literally an "anything goes" pagan paradise.

At one time, this sounded bizarre to modern man. Unfortu-nately, a society that is adrift today is returning to its lawless roots. But when one considers the pagan environment that existed for the Early Church, it is not difficult to understand how extreme the problem of sexual immorality was within the Church, because so many of its new converts had lived in that environment their entire lives before they were born again.

To all of this, you must add the proliferation of alcohol and other mind-altering substances that enjoyed widespread use and were fused into the fabric of culture at that time. Alcohol was used in idol worship as a sacrament and a tool to commune with the spirit realm, and it was commonly used by prostitutes to "loosen up" their customers. In city bathhouses, alcohol was read-ily available to relax people's inhibitions, which also resulted in their more readily engaging in illicit sexual activities. Modern-day excavations have revealed that in Corinth, some buildings had extensive cellars designed to hold vast stores of alcohol. From all the evidence available, we can conclude that the alcohol business was booming in that city.

In short, about every type of vice and sin was available in Corinth that you can imagine. In addition to the sex industry, Corinth became a swindler's paradise, with plenty of gambling and extortion going on to attract shady people who wanted to make a quick buck.

As a result, Corinth had a worldwide reputation as a party town — a city where a person's flesh could "have its fling" without restraint and where one could avail himself to the vilest of human instincts with no concern of others' disapproval. Like animals yielding to base instincts without a conscience, people surrendered themselves to any indulgence they desired, doing whatever they pleased, with almost no restrictions. And if they were visitors to Corinth, they could usually return to their homes with no one aware of what they had done there. People who came to Corinth knew that "what was done in Corinth, stayed in Corinth."

Foul language, gross immorality, abundant alcohol, and pervasive practices of gambling, extortion, and swindling — that's a description of the city of Corinth at the time the apostle Paul came there to establish the church of Corinth in the middle of the First Century. Into this dark and pagan atmosphere, God's power miraculously showed up — and this church was gloriously birthed through the efforts of Paul and the others who worked alongside him.

As Paul and his team preached the Gospel in Corinth, many of those listening responded. And no matter how perverse and sinful their pagan lifestyles had been in the past, the Corinthians who repented and accepted Jesus as their Lord and Savior were instantly made new creatures in Christ. The blood of Jesus cleansed them; the indwelling presence of the Holy Spirit came to reside in them; and God declared them righteous, granting them the status of "saints" (*see* 1 Corinthians 1:2). Thus, in a split second, God deemed these former pagans "holy" — instantaneously transferring them into a category that set them apart, consecrated them, and made them different from everyone else in the city.

Jerry Bridges, author of *The Pursuit of Holiness*, noted, "God has not called us to be like those around us. He has called us to be like Himself. Holiness is nothing less than conformity to the character of God."[85] But for a believer to actually conform his life to the holy status God has given him, he is required to learn to think and act differently. This practical outworking of holiness will be the result of that believer's focused pursuit to know Christ and to become conformed to His image (*see* Romans 8:29).

In this section, I have dealt extensively with Corinth for a reason you will soon understand. However, this status of "saint" was not only true for believers in Corinth. It applies to every person who has ever come to Christ.

In a split second, God deemed these former pagans "holy" — instantaneously transferring them into a category that set them apart, consecrated them, and made them different from everyone else in the city.

As a believer, your status as a saint of God is secure, no matter who you were yesterday or even who you are *not* today. Regardless of your past, and regardless of whether or not your life still holds reminders of the way you used to live before Christ — you are *not* who you used to be!

---

[85] Jerry Bridges, *The Pursuit of Holiness* (Colorado Springs, CO: NavPress, 1978, 2006), p. 9.

'AND SUCH WERE SOME OF YOU'

New Testament believers had been saved from a world of paganism. As you have read, it was a world where sexual immorality and wickedness of all kinds were widespread.

Let's continue with the example of Corinth for our purposes in this chapter. After reading the information on the previous pages about Corinth's history and lurid environment, you can imagine what kinds of problems with sin tried to linger within the Corinthian congregation. It was a church made up of former prostitutes, drunkards, drug addicts, thieves, scammers, swindlers, and sexually immoral people.

When a Corinthian repented and received Christ as Lord and Savior, God instantly declared him righteous — just as He did with you. Yet even though each person had a newly created spirit indwelt by the Holy Spirit, his or her soul still had to be renewed by the Word of God (*see* Romans 12:2). Old feelings, desires, and ways of thinking were still in the process of being changed. Consequently, many of the newly converted Christians carried some of their old behaviors with them into the church.

Isn't that exactly the same situation the Church often faces with people who get saved today?

Even though each person had a newly created spirit
indwelt by the Holy Spirit, his or her soul
still had to be renewed by the Word of God.
Old feelings, desires, and ways of thinking
were still in the process of being changed.

Let me give you an example from Corinth. First Corinthians chapter 5 informs us that there was a man in the church at Corinth who was sleeping with his father's wife. Paul found out about it and was deeply disturbed by the situation — especially because the congregation had minimized this issue of incest and dishonor and wasn't even acting to correct it. Paul took the Corinthian believers to task for their complacency about the situation and gave them specific instructions on how to deal with the sin before it infected the rest of the church.

Paul was actually harsher in his letters to the Corinthian believers than he was in any of his other letters to various churches and believers. It was not necessarily because the Corinthians were worse Christians. It is more likely that Paul's manner of addressing them reflected the nature of the audience. The believers of Corinth were a rough and tough group of people who likely took heed only when someone spoke strongly to them. He had to be stern and straightforward in his communication with them, because that was the only way his Corinthian audience would get the message!

In First Corinthians 6:9-11, Paul described many of these believers before they came to Christ:

Know ye not that the unrighteous shall not inherit the kingdom of God? Be not deceived: neither fornicators, nor idolaters, nor adulterers, nor effeminate, nor abusers of themselves with mankind, nor thieves, nor covetous, nor drunkards, nor revilers, nor extortioners, shall inherit the kingdom of God. And such were some of you....

Paul itemized quite a dirty laundry list of sinful behavior in this verse! Let's take a closer look at each of these and see who the Corinthians were before they repented and came to faith in Christ.

Fornicators

First, Paul wrote that some of the Corinthian believers were once "fornicators." This is from the Greek word *porneia*, and it describes *all sexual activity outside of marriage*, including adultery, sex between two single people, and homosexuality. The word "fornication" — the Greek word *porneia* — could be committed both by someone married and someone single.

It must be pointed out that the word *porneia* comes from the same Greek root for a *prostitute*. This gives us God's view of fornication or any sexual relationship outside of marriage. One may think he or she is having a "sweet" and "innocent" fling with someone. But because the word "fornication" and "prostitute" shares the same root, we can know God's view of the matter. If a person is having sexual relations with anyone outside of a God-ordained marriage, it is an act of prostitution in His eyes.

There is something else that I believe is critical to point out here. The word "pornography" comes from this same Greek word *porneia*. Specifically, the word "pornography" is from a compound of the Greek words *pornos* — meaning *prostitute*, and *grapho* — which refers to that which is *written* or made into a *graphic*. This means when an individual meditates on pornographic writings, graphics, or photos, he or she is committing *mental prostitution*.

If a person is having sexual relations with anyone outside of a God-ordained marriage, it is an act of prostitution in His eyes.

Someone may say, "Well, pornography didn't exist in the First Century, so Paul couldn't have had that in mind." But you are wrong! Pornography has always been around in various forms. Ruins from the First Century show all kinds of pornographic illustrations that were considered lewd even in their time.

Before we go to the next word, take a moment to let that sobering truth sink in regarding this aspect of the word *porneia*. Although pornography may not drag a person into physical participation with another person, in God's view, it is *mental prostitution*.

Idolaters

Next on Paul's list was the word "idolaters." Of course, the word "idolatry" has to do with the worship of idols, which God hates and is most adamantly against.

Let's look at an early example of idolatry found in First Samuel 5. In that chapter, we read that the Philistines captured the Ark of the Covenant, which, of course, contained God's presence. When they carried it home, they placed the Ark of the Covenant in a pagan temple next to an idol of their pagan god "Dagon."

The next morning when the Philistines went into their temple, they saw the Ark of the Covenant unharmed in the place they had put it, but the idol of Dagon had fallen face down on the floor. The Philistines were shocked to see their god fallen on his face, but they rallied together, picked up the idol, and put it back in its place. The following morning, they came into the temple and once again found the statue of their god Dagon face down on the floor — this time with its head and arms severed from its body. God was using a potent visual aid to make a vivid point — that He will *not* tolerate idolatry or be worshiped alongside any other god.

The Western world today does not generally bow and worship physical idols; nonetheless, we still deal with idolatry on a multiplicity of levels. In God's view, anything we give our greatest attention, devotion, and love to above Him is an idol in our lives. Moreover, if anything preoccupies our thoughts more than God does, it is an idol, and we have entered into the sin of idolatry.

In the case of the Corinthians — and a great majority of the early converts to the Christian faith — their lives had been steeped in idolatrous practices before they came to faith in Christ. To understand more of what this entailed, I encourage you to read my book *No Room for Compromise*, where I discuss the lurid and perverse practices, filled with demonic activity, that were connected to idolatry in the ancient world.

Adulterers

Next, Paul wrote that the Corinthian believers had previously been "adulterers." The word "adulterers" is different from "fornication," which refers to any sexual activity outside of marriage. The Greek word for "adultery" specifically refers to *people who violate their marital covenant by having sexual relations outside of marriage.*

Adultery was a common practice in the First Century, because in the Roman world, husbands were allowed — even expected — to engage in sexual activity with slaves, prostitutes, and concubines without penalty. And although sexual infidelity was not socially acceptable for married women, the violation of that particular social norm was common throughout ancient Roman culture.

Keep in mind that the entire city of Corinth was dedicated to the sex industry and designed for sexual encounters. At the bakery, at the games, in the bathhouse — name the place, and sex was available to men in some form. The act of adultery, particularly for men, was so prevalent that most people didn't even think of it as a sin.

This mentality was entrenched in people's lives. Believers who had become new creatures in Christ had regularly violated their marital vows in this way before they were born again. For this reason, Paul had to teach the believers in Corinth that this type of activity no longer matched who they had become in Christ. As saints of God, made holy and set apart for His purposes, they needed to take a firm stand against adultery, regardless of society's stamp of approval on the illicit practice.

Effeminate

The next word Paul included was "effeminate." The Greek word for "effeminate" is *malakos*, a term that specifically describes *male prostitutes*. These were men who were used by other men for sexual services and who often presented themselves as women in their dress and affectations. Corinth would have had a large number of these male prostitutes to serve a steady stream of clients coming into the city.

Corinth was founded by soldiers who during their careers had often traveled only with other men. Since they didn't have any other outlet for sexual relations, it was common among soldiers in ancient times to have sexual relations with each other. Although this sounds horrible to us, the practice seemed normal to them. Furthermore, male prostitution was a common practice in ancient Greek and Roman cities, where homosexual practices were believed to be acceptable.

In a city like Corinth that was overflowing with former soldiers, sailors, and legionnaires who had been accustomed to this activity while warring broad, it is not shocking to discover that the city had a lot of homosexual activity, including male prostitution. In fact, Paul categorically stated that some in the church of Corinth had been professional male prostitutes before they were redeemed and delivered out of that lifestyle.

Abusers of Themselves With Mankind

Next, Paul mentioned the phrase "abusers of themselves with mankind." This is yet another example of how deeply sin had twisted people's thinking and behavior in the ancient world — and, unfortunately, again in our times. The phrase "abusers of themselves with mankind" in the original Greek means *man lovers* and pictures *two men in bed together*.

Because the Greek and Roman world really did not have a concept for heterosexuals or homosexuals as we have today, this wording was used by Paul to describe the homosexuality that was raging in Greek cities like Corinth. In this sense, Corinth was no exception, as this was prevalent throughout the world during New Testament times. But Paul here emphatically stated that some in the church in Corinth had been saved and delivered from a homosexual lifestyle.

Thieves and Covetous

Paul then mentioned "thieves" and "covetous." The word "thieves" is a translation of the Greek word *kleptos*. It's from this word that we derive the word "kleptomaniac." In Greek, this word depicts *a person who habitually steals or takes financial advantage of others*. It is the picture of *a pickpocket* or *one who longs to put his hands into someone else's pocket to take what isn't his*. This person could be either a scammer or an outright thief.

But Paul also identified those who had previously been "covetous." This word comes from the Greek word *pleonektes*, and it describes *insatiable greed*. It doesn't matter how much covetous individuals get, they never seem to have enough. Their insatiable cravings for *more* propel them to be unscrupulous in behaviors to add more to their pockets or to their stomachs.

Remember, many people moved to Corinth to make a fast buck. The city was a magnet for low-level people of questionable character, who converged there from all over the empire because news was on the streets that money could be made easily in Corinth. From Paul's words in this text, we now know that many who repented and came to faith in Christ had previously been a part of this unscrupulous category of people who took financial advantage of others in the city. Many thieves lived in Corinth who were covetous and driven by insatiable greed, and a large number of them had gotten saved and were part of the church.

Drunkards

Next, Paul wrote that former "drunkards" were members in the church of Corinth.

The word "drunkards" in Greek signified *people who consumed alcohol for the sake of intoxication*. These were not people sitting down to drink a simple glass of wine with their dinner. Their premeditated plan was to become totally intoxicated. As noted earlier, the use of alcohol was widespread throughout the Greek and Roman worlds, and Corinth was no exception, especially given its notorious reputation for being a party town.

When people are intoxicated, their ability to think clearly is suppressed, which of course causes them to make careless and often destructive decisions. Those who are inebriated say things they shouldn't say and do things they shouldn't do because they are under the influence of alcohol or other substances. While they are in that inebriated condition, they often say hurtful or perverted words or do destructive things they later wish they could take back — but they can't. Great pain has always been connected with drunkenness.

According to Paul's word, a significant number of people in Corinth who repented and came to faith in Christ had previously been drunkards. One can only imagine the hurt and abuse they had experienced or the havoc they had wreaked in other people's lives as a result. But they had received Christ and become members of the Corinthian church, genuinely saved.

Revilers and Extortioners

Next, Paul added two more categories of sinners that the Corinthians were before coming to Christ. Paul stated before Christ, many of them were "revilers" and "extortioners."

The Greek word for "revilers" describes *individuals who used foul, dirty, uncultured language*. Since many of Corinth's residents were sailors, soldiers, and legionnaires, it is not too surprising to see the word "revilers" included in this list. It is a kind way of saying they used the foulest, dirtiest, most uncultured language that was available. In other words, many members of the church were *dirty-mouthed people* before they got saved.

The word "extortioners" is derived from the Greek word *harpadzo*, a word that means *to seize*. This means that an "extortioner" was a scam artist who did everything imaginable to seize what belonged to other people. This word "extortioners" depicts *sophisticated thievery*.

What a list — *fornicators, idolaters, adulterers, effeminate, abusers of themselves with mankind, thieves, covetous, drunkards, revilers*, and *extortioners*. According to the apostle Paul, these were the kinds of people who filled the city of Corinth. But people who fit in these vile categories had repented and come to faith in Christ. They had become members of the church in Corinth and were sitting in the services! If a person had been allowed to peek into the past of the church members in Corinth, it would have served as a rude awakening to see the kind of people these believers were before God got hold of them.

Immediately after Paul enumerated this dreadful list, he punctuated his words by saying, "And such were some of you..." (1 Corinthians 6:11). In essence, Paul actually told the Corinthian Christians, "Hey, that's what you were before you repented of your sins and surrendered your life to Christ."

But the congregation of the Corinthian church is actually a good sample of the people who attend every church even today.

We live in a world saturated with all kinds of sexual sin and vices that are proliferating all around us. The truth is, before coming to Christ, nearly every one of us was bound by various types of vices and hangups. *Each of us truly needed a Savior to deliver us.*

If a person had been allowed to peek into the past
of the church members in Corinth, it would have served
as a rude awakening to see the kind of people
these believers were before God got hold of them.

Ephesians 2:2-5 (*NLT*) confirms this truth: "All of us used to live that way, following the passions and desires of our evil nature. We were born with an evil nature, and we were under God's anger just like everyone else. But God is so rich in mercy, and he loved us so very much, that even while we were dead because of our sins, he gave us life when he raised Christ from the dead...."

The truth is, before coming to Christ,
nearly every one of us was bound by
various types of vices and hangups.
Each of us truly needed a Savior to deliver us.

HOW DOES GOD SEE US TODAY?

God has lavished His mercy and grace upon us in Christ Jesus. He willingly came to earth to lay down His life to make us righteous and to move us out of our former state into a new category that He calls *holy*. When God looks at us, He does not see who we *were* — He sees who we *are* in Christ.

Paul painted a picture of what God has done for us in First Corinthians 6:11:

...But ye are washed, but ye are sanctified, but ye are justified in the name of the Lord Jesus, and by the Spirit of our God.

This word "washed" means to *wash thoroughly and completely*, and it points back to the specific, concrete point in the past when they were instantaneously cleansed. It was intended to remind the Corinthians — and to remind you and me — of a *definite moment in time* when our conversion took place, when each of us repented and surrendered to Christ. The blood of Jesus was mercifully applied to our lives, and in a split second, we were each *thoroughly* and *completely washed* in the blood of Jesus Christ and declared to be righteous!

But Paul went on to say, "You are sanctified."

This leads us back to the word *hagios,* which is the New Testament word for "holy." You see, the word "sanctified" is the Greek word *hagiadzo,* and it is from the root word *hagios.* As noted earlier, it means *set aside, consecrated, made different, made holy.* By using this word, Paul told the Corinthians (and us): *"You may look just like everyone else around you, but you are emphatically not like everybody else. When God washed you, He separated you from your old life, He set you apart. He marked you off for Himself. As a result, you unequivocally are not who you used to be! God has made you HOLY."*

- God consecrated Mount Horeb in Exodus 3:5 and set it apart from an entire range of similar-looking mountains.

- The Holy Bible may look like any other book on a library shelf, yet God's holy presence infused in its words makes it different from all other books.

- In the same way, you may look like a normal, run-of-the-mill, ordinary human being, but because of God's indwelling Spirit in you, you are most decidedly *not* normal, run-of-the-mill, or ordinary.

- God has set you apart. He has consecrated you. He has elevated you into a brand-new company of new creations about which there is *nothing* common at all!

- You are *holy* because of God's gracious work in your life!

Leonard Ravenhill made a profound statement along this line, saying, "The greatest miracle that God can do today is to take an unholy man out of an unholy world, and make that man holy and put him back into that unholy world and keep him holy in it."[86]

---

[86] Ravenhill Quotes, Goodreads, https://www.goodreads.com/author/quotes/159020 .Leonard_ Ravenhill.

IT'S TIME TO LIVE UP TO OUR NEW STATUS

You and I have been washed and made into completely new creations — separated unto God, consecrated, and made holy. In light of this fact, God calls us to live our lives in a way that reflects who He has recreated us to be. We are called to think, to speak, to act, and to walk in our new reality, which is *holiness*.

It was for this reason that Billy Graham said, "If you belong to Jesus Christ, you are called to live a life of purity and holiness. God wants your mind to be shaped by Him so that your thoughts and goals reflect Christ."[87]

When Paul told the Corinthians about their new status, he immediately followed up in First Corinthians 6:18 by saying, "Flee fornication."

God calls us to live our lives in a way
that reflects who He has recreated us to be.
We are called to think, to speak, to act,
and to walk in our new reality, which is *holiness*.

The word "flee" is the Greek word *phuego*, and it means *to run, to flee*, or even *to take flight*. It means *to move your feet as fast as you can to get away from something*. Making this even stronger is the fact that the tense used conveys the idea of *habitual fleeing* or *a continuous escaping*. Paul was telling those believers (and us) that we need to make a habit of running from sin — especially sexual sin. The word "fornication" is the Greek word *porneia*, which includes all forms of sexual activity outside of marriage.

---

[87] *Billy Graham in Quotes*, p. 177.

Essentially Paul was telling the Corinthians, *"You're washed; you're sanctified; and you're justified — so now let your new status be reflected in your behavior. Don't hang around sin. It's time for you to use your feet and run from it. Develop a habit of fleeing from it!"*

Paul told the Corinthians to "flee" because fornication was part of their old way of living. It was a strong warning not to hang around the sin they used to be involved in. Paul was saying, *"Use your feet and run as quickly as you can! Put space between you and those old activities. You need to run with all your might to get away from those old places and habits!"*

Then in First Corinthians 6:19 and 20, Paul said, "What? Know ye not that your body is the temple of the Holy Ghost which is in you, which ye have of God, and ye are not your own? For ye are bought with a price: therefore glorify God in your body, and in your spirit, which are God's."

The Holy Spirit has chosen to live inside of us! The Third Person of the Trinity, who is fully God and who is utterly holy, has chosen you and me as His permanent residence to live in. That means our bodies are literally His home! If for no other reason, we need to "flee" from sin so we don't drag the Holy Spirit into situations that are contrary to His holiness. This is what Paul communicated to the Corinthians, and this is what God is saying to you and me today through His unchanging Word!

In the book *The Pursuit of Holiness*, Jerry Bridges said, "As we grow in holiness, we grow in hatred of sin; and God, being infinitely holy, has an infinite hatred of sin."[88]

Bridges continued, "The Christian living in disobedience also lives devoid of joy and hope. But when he begins to understand that Christ has delivered him from the reign of sin, when he

---

[88] *The Pursuit of Holiness*, p. 15.

begins to see that he is united to Him who has all power and authority and that it is possible to walk in obedience, he begins to have hope, and as he hopes in Christ, he begins to have joy. In the strength of this joy, he begins to overcome the sins that have so easily entangled him. He then finds that the joy of a holy walk is infinitely more satisfying than the fleeting pleasures of sin. But to experience this joy, we must make some choices. We must choose to forsake sin, not only because it is defeating to us but because it grieves the heart of God."[89]

Since our sin grieves the heart of God, it should grieve our hearts as well. We must flee from sin and pursue that which pleases Him above all else. Only this way of life will result in an ongoing experience of His power and joy that spiritually invigorates our hearts and exponentially increases our influence for His Kingdom!

If our sin grieves the heart of God, it must grieve
our hearts as well. We must flee from sin and pursue
that which pleases Him above all else.

GOD'S WILL FOR YOUR PURITY

J. I. Packer wrote in his book *Rediscovering Holiness*, "Holiness is in fact commanded: God wills it, Christ requires it, and all the Scriptures — the law, the gospel, the prophets, the wisdom writings, the epistles, the history books that tell of judgments past and the book of Revelation that tells of judgment to come — call for it."[90]

---

[89] Ibid., p. 125.
[90] J. I. Packer, *Rediscovering Holiness* (Ventura, CA: Regal Books, 1992, 2009), p. 33.

Yet as clearly as it is laid out in the Word that holy living is important to God, there is one recurring question I am asked frequently from people all over the world: "What is the precise will of God for my life?" I have an answer that I am 100-percent sure is God's will for your life, and it connects to everything I have been saying to you in this chapter. Here is my simple answer:

For this is the will of God, even your sanctification, that ye should abstain from fornication.

—1 Thessalonians 4:3

God's will for you is your *sanctification*.

That word "sanctification" is translated from the same root word from which the word "holy" is translated. It is the Greek word *hagios*.

When Paul wrote that it is God's will for you to be sanctified, he was simply saying that it is His highest will for you to become *holy in practice* — that is, that your behavior reflects your holy status. You are to behave as a way of life in a manner that is *holy*, *separate*, and *different* than the lost, unregenerate world that surrounds you.

Sanctification is unequivocally God's will for your life. But to attain this, you have to be committed to the premise that you will not think like the world, talk like the world, or act like the world — you will think, talk, and act like God Himself.

You may ask, "How can I do this?" Paul answered your question in First Thessalonians 4:3, where he continued, "For this is the will of God, even your sanctification, that ye should *abstain* from fornication." This word "abstain" is the word *apecho*, a very important word that means *to put space between you and something else.* In this verse, Paul urged Christians to put space between themselves and fornication.

It may not be easy for you to comprehend, but fornication was probably the biggest temptation plaguing the Church in the First Century because it was so widespread and was considered acceptable in the pagan world. Therefore, early believers had to constantly renew their minds with the truth that such practices were *not* acceptable to God, that their bodies had become the temple of the Holy Spirit, and that no sexual activity outside of marriage was acceptable.

Sanctification is unequivocally God's will for your life.
But to attain this, you have to be committed
to the premise that you will not think like the world,
talk like the world, or act like the world —
you will think, talk, and act like God Himself.

Paul was saying, *"Put space between you and any kind of temptation you're facing. You must build a barrier between yourself and temptations so that it is impossible for you to cross the barrier and do what is inappropriate for a holy person to do."*

Let me give you an example from many years ago when Denise and I hadn't been married very long and were leading a single-adult ministry in a large denominational church. There was one sincere brother who kept falling into sexual sin with his girlfriend. Each time it happened, he would come see me — weeping and full of remorse for what he did. Again and again, he would tell me how once again he had fallen into the same sexual sin. Each time he was overcome with shame for his actions — yet it kept happening time and time again.

One day I asked him, "Where are you when this sexual sin takes place?"

"Well, I'm usually at my girlfriend's apartment," he answered.

I told him, "I believe it's time for you to put some space between you and the place where this sexual sin happens. Stay away from your girlfriend's apartment."

"What?" he responded with surprise. "Are you inferring that God wants me to run from my problem? It seems to me that I need to stay there and prove that I'm strong enough to overcome it."

Paul was saying, *"Put space between you and any kind of temptation you're facing. You must build a barrier between yourself and temptations so that it is impossible for you to cross the barrier and do what is inappropriate for a holy person to do."*

As you might imagine, this young man didn't listen to my counsel. And because he didn't "abstain" — because he didn't put space between himself and that place of temptation — he didn't gain a victory over that sexual temptation. The man continued to fall into sin and to be plagued with guilt and shame.

Of course, God wants us to pray! Of course, He wants us to do spiritual warfare! Of course, He wants us to take a firm stand against sin! *But God also wants us to use our brains and to exercise common sense.*

God has called you to holiness. That means you must take preventive measures that help you avoid places or people where you have proven in the past to behave in ways that are below the new you — who is *holy*. God wants you to behave according to His holy ways — *differently* than the world. He wants you to put space between yourself and the things that tempt you to behave the way you used to behave.

If you and I want to know with 100-percent surety a key truth that is God's will for our lives, *this is it*. And as we diligently pursue His will in this area, our holy way of living will be a vital key that unlocks further revelation of God's specific plan and purpose for each of us on this earth.

BODY MANAGEMENT

As Paul was writing about abstaining from sexual temptation, he added these important words:

That every one of you should know how to possess his vessel in sanctification and honor.

The word "know" here is a term that described *a student who has learned practical skills to accomplish a task or a goal.* As used here, Paul was specifically stating that a believer must learn *practical skills* about how to "possess his vessel in sanctification and honor."

The word "possess" in this verse indeed means *to manage* or *to control*, and the word "vessel" is the Greek word *skeuos*, referring to *the human body*. In this verse, God is commanding you and me *to manage* and *control* our physical bodies by developing practical skills and steps to keep ourselves from sin and wrong behaviors. Our urges and base instincts should not control us — we must learn to master them!

The word "vessel" in this verse refers to *the human body*. This clearly means God wants all believers to learn how to develop *body management*.

This could apply to the kind of food and how much food we put in our stomachs, what we watch with our eyes, where we go with our feet, how we spend our money — the list goes on and on. In essence, it means we may need to *acquire skills* that we don't presently have to know how to manage our bodies and lives. This may involve reading books and listening to others who can help teach us in areas where we struggle in this area of managing our bodies.

Our urges and base instincts should not control us —
we must learn to master them!

There are many practical things we can learn from God's Word to help us in this area, especially in the book of Proverbs. For example, Proverbs chapter 7 talks about a young man "void of understanding" who foolishly wandered through the neighborhood of a prostitute and eventually found himself right in front of her house. "With her much fair speech she caused him to yield…" (v. 21). The young man became like a sheep being led to the slaughter, and his life was swallowed up in her trap. What had this young man not done? He had not *abstained* from fornication — he had not put space between himself and sin. Instead, he played around with it, and it cost him his life.

What can be learned from this story? The closer we get to sin, especially the sin that so easily entangles *us* (*see* Hebrews 12:1), the more likely that sin will sink its hooks into our flesh, pulling us closer and closer and closer until we are in its clutches and we give into it.

Referring to sexual temptation, Proverbs 5:8 (*AMPC*) says:

Let your way in life be far from her, and come not near the door of her house [avoid the very scenes of temptation].

Indeed, you and I can save ourselves a lot of heartache if we will live by the wisdom of God's Word. And if we will listen to the wisdom of seasoned, godly saints who are older in years or in their walk with the Lord than we are and who have more of life's experience, we can learn some valuable, practical skills to guard our lives and avoid falling into the trap of fornication.

It is wise to remember the sobering words of Charles H. Spurgeon: "If Christ has died for me… I cannot trifle with the evil that killed my best Friend."[91] When we remember what Jesus went through on the Cross because of our sin, it helps us to remember the destructive nature of sin and to flee from the temptation to yield to its toxic allure.

You and I can save ourselves a lot of heartache
if we will live by the wisdom of God's Word.

SANCTIFICATION AND HONOR

Paul said we are to know how to possess our vessel in "sanctification and honor." The word "sanctification" is from the root word *hagios*, which of course is the root word for "holy." But in this case, it is translated *sanctification* — which, as noted earlier, depicts us living differently from the rest of the world and living in a state of *holiness* in our daily lives.

---

[91] Charles H. Spurgeon, *Charles Spurgeon's Autobiography, Vol. 1* (London: Passmore and Alabaster, 1899), p. 99.

But to sanctification, Paul added the word "honor," which is a translation of a Greek word that refers to *doing something in a respectful way*. We must remember that we belong to God, and His Holy Spirit lives inside us. We must learn to be *respectful* of His presence in our lives. We must learn to be *respectful* of who we are in Christ and to control ourselves from committing fornication.

In First Thessalonians 4:5, Paul added, "Not in the lust of concupiscence...." This word "concupiscence" in the Greek actually means *in the passionate grip of lust*. God doesn't want us to live in the grip of the lust of our fallen nature like those who are not saved. He wants us to rise up and "possess our vessel" — to manage and control our body in holiness and respect for His Spirit living in us.

Then in verse 6, Paul warned, "That no man *go beyond* and *defraud* his brother in any matter: because that the Lord is the avenger of all such, as we also have forewarned you and testified." The phrase "go beyond" means *to cross a line* or *to violate*, and the word "defraud" means *to take advantage* of someone. Within the context of the passage, Paul issued a very strong warning about *crossing a line with fellow believers* or *taking advantage of them* — either ethically, morally, financially, or sexually.

God wants us to rise up and "possess our vessel" —
to manage and control our body
in holiness and respect for His Spirit living in us.

What happens to believers who violate other believers, taking something that is not theirs? God Himself steps in to bring correction. The perpetrators may think they are getting away with what they did, but the Scripture says, "The Lord is the *avenger* of all such...." This word "avenger" is a technical term indicating that *a law has been broken, so the court steps in to enact judgment on the offender.*

In this case, if a believer morally violates another fellow believer, especially in a sexual matter, God will carry out the sentence against the guilty party. Even if the perpetrator escapes judgment from his friends, the Higher Judge will see to it that punishment is applied according to His wisdom. Paul was so serious about this principle that he said in essence, "We have warned you in advance."

Paul ended his discussion on this matter in much the same way he began. He stated, "For God hath not called us to uncleanness, but unto holiness" (v. 7). The word "holiness" is from the Greek word *hagiadzo*, which is a form of the root word *hagios*. This means God is telling us plainly that we are to live by a higher standard — we are to be *consecrated*, *separated*, *set apart*, and *holy*. We are to be *different* in how we think, speak, and act.

MAKE A CHOICE!

For you to live a life ablaze for God, it is essential for you to add a full supply of the fuel of holiness to your fire. Never forget that the Holy Spirit is called the *Holy* Spirit — and that He is most comfortable in places where holiness prevails.

But the walk of daily, practical holiness does not happen automatically just because God has chosen you, cleansed you by Jesus' blood, placed His Spirit inside you, and separated you from the rest of the world. To walk in the reality of holiness in your everyday life is going to take a moment-by-moment yielding to God and a dedicated effort to flee all forms of behaviors that are contrary to what He desires for your life. With the Holy Spirit's help and the truth of God's Word, you can learn practical ways to put space between you and all these things!

Friend, God declared you to be righteous the moment you repented of your sins and surrendered your life to the lordship of Jesus. In one split second, you were washed in the blood and justified in His sight. You are no longer like everyone else in the world. You are sanctified — *consecrated, separated, set apart,* and *made holy.* Your sanctification is the will of God. He has called you to think, speak, and act differently than the world.

God calls you to live according to who you are in Christ! So make a choice today — and renew your commitment at the beginning of every new day — to live by the higher standard of holiness God has called you to live by. Strive for the highest and finest; aim for the most spotless reputation you can achieve. As the Bible commands, "…Give yourselves completely to God since you have been given new life. And use your whole body as a tool to do what is right for the glory of God" (Romans 6:13 *NLT*).

To walk in the reality of holiness in your everyday life
is going to take a moment-by-moment yielding to God
and a dedicated effort to flee all forms of behaviors
that are contrary to what He desires for your life.

Billy Graham noted how crucial it is that we gain a greater revelation of God's holiness: "We have largely lost sight of the holiness and purity of God today. This is one reason why we tolerate sin so easily."[92] Oh, that you and I and the Church today would be reawakened to the holiness of God and His mandate on our lives to live holy as He is holy (*see* 1 Peter 1:15)! The more we understand God's holiness, the more we are confronted, challenged, and *changed*!

---

[92] Billy Graham, *Hope for Each Day Morning and Evening Devotions* (Nashville: Thomas Nelson, 2002, 2012), p. 345.

THINK ABOUT IT

1. The one way to keep your life truly ablaze for God is to pursue knowing Him and becoming conformed to His ways.

    Holiness is nothing less than conformity to the character of God. But for a believer to actually conform his life to the holy status God has given him, he must learn to think and act differently.

    Are you engaged in a practical pursuit of knowing God to produce the outworking of holiness in your life? Are you consistently setting aside time to seek His face, wait in His presence, absorb His Word, and worship Him? God has not called us to be like the world around us; He has called us to be like Himself. What are some specific ways you can turn away from distractions and make room in your life to focus more intently on Jesus?

2. Paul was very clear in First Corinthians 6:9-11 in his description of sinful lifestyles that will not inherit the Kingdom of God. He then emphasized the power of redemption when he stated, "And such were some of you."

    What you "were" is not who you are now in Christ. Practices that controlled your life may not dominate you now that Christ has made you holy as He is holy. You may look just like everyone else around you, but you are emphatically not like everybody else. When God washed you in His blood, and raised you to newness of life in Christ, He separated you from your old life — He set you apart for Himself. Old thoughts may come to you, and old desires may attempt to rise, but you now have the power to manage your thoughts and manage your own body as a continual, living offering to God.

In what specific ways are you yielding to the Holy Spirit to bring about transformation in your life? How are you exercising control over your appetites and inclinations so that you now reflect a new creation in Christ?

3. Christ has been made your wisdom, your sanctification, and your righteousness (*see* 1 Corinthians 1:30). As you grow in your identity of holiness, aligning yourself with the character of God, you will grow in your disdain of sin. Living a sanctified life — separated from sin to live separate unto God — is important to God. Therefore, it must be of premier importance to you if your genuine desire is to stay ablaze spiritually.

Do you keep space between yourself and situations or locations that could easily lure you into sinful practices? What protective standards have you set in place in your life to flee from lust of wrong things and avoid temptation? What practical steps have you taken to disengage from any associations or activities that easily trip you up?

CHAPTER 9

ABLAZE WITH HUMILITY

So far, we have looked at seven key types of spiritual fuel that will cause you to burn like a spiritual inferno for the duration of your time here on earth as you faithfully sustain your fire. We've seen the need to stay ablaze with a love for the Word of God, with prayer, with the Holy Spirit, with worship, with a love for souls, with generosity, and with holiness. Now we move to the next vital fuel you need to keep your spiritual life ablaze — the character quality of *humility*.

Understanding and staying well supplied with this particular fuel is absolutely essential. It could even save you from disaster in your future. I ask you to read this chapter with an open heart and mind, for if you have pride — the direct opposite of humility — it will inevitably douse your spiritual flames and quench your spiritual passion. Pride is fatal, so every on-fire Christian must learn to identify it and aggressively remove it from his or her life whenever it tries to slither back in through another point of access.

On the other hand, when believers possess and maintain true biblical humility, it will arouse their spiritual fire and put them in a position for God to move mightily in their lives. Such humility attracts the strong presence of God in the same way metal is drawn to a magnet.

What Does Pride Look Like?

To understand what biblical humility is, we need to understand what pride is first. Furthermore, we need to know what God thinks of unhealthy pride. In Proverbs 6:16-19, God lists seven deadly sins He despises, and the very first one listed is *pride*. In fact, pride is so foul that Proverbs 13:10 states, "Only by pride cometh contention...." You will find this to be true if you dig deeply into the struggles, fights, divisions, and wars that have been fought throughout history. Nearly all of them have their roots in some form of unhealthy pride.

The scriptures show over and over again that unhealthy pride is *fatal* to man's spiritual, mental, and emotional well-being — and often even fatal to his physical life. It is the root of rebellion and is always accompanied with catastrophic results. For this reason, God always has been and always will be against pride. As you will see in the following pages, God actually *resists* the proud, but He *gives grace* to the humble.

But the story of pride begins with Lucifer, so let's journey back to the time and place where pride was first conceived.

Pride is the root of rebellion and is always accompanied with catastrophic results. For this reason, God always has been and always will be against pride.

THE STORY OF LUCIFER, WHERE THE ISSUES OF PRIDE FIRST BEGAN

The clearest biblical example of pride — what it is, how it behaves, and how God deals with it — is first found in the story of Lucifer. According to Scripture, Lucifer was created to be one of the greatest angels among the heavenly host. The Bible mentions three archangels that God created. First, there is Michael, who gives oversight to the heavenly armies. Second is the archangel Gabriel, who is the message-bearer of Heaven and served as God's spokesman. The third archangel was Lucifer, who was called "the anointed cherub that covers" (Ezekiel 28:14).

Lucifer's position was to be in the presence of God. His name, Lucifer, actually means *one who reflects light*; hence, it means *a light-bearer*. But the primary meaning of the name "Lucifer" is not one who self-generates light, but one who *reflects* light from another source.

This insight into Lucifer's name informs us that he was designed to be like a "mirror," specially designed to stand in God's presence and *reflect* His glory. In other words, if God did not shine upon Lucifer, he could not shine. This is a key pivotal truth to understand as we consider the ghastly story of what happened to him.

God described Lucifer in Ezekiel 28:13, saying, "Thou hast been in Eden the garden of God; every precious stone was thy covering, the sardius, topaz, and the diamond, the beryl, the onyx, and the jasper, the sapphire, the emerald, and the carbuncle, and gold: the workmanship of thy tabrets and of thy pipes was prepared in thee in the day that thou wast created."

If God did not shine upon Lucifer, he could not shine.

Imagine what it might have been like if you and I had been able to gaze upon Lucifer before his fall. I speculate that it would have had the same effect we might feel when looking at a spectacular piece of shimmering jewelry, for he was literally *covered* with every precious stone.

As Lucifer stood in God's presence, God's glory streamed over and beamed upon him. And when that divine light hit all those precious stones that covered Lucifer as his outward adornment, it reflected off the stones' varied angles in the same way that light falls upon a diamond, causing Lucifer to brilliantly refract and reflect God's glory. And like a mirror that you look into each morning to see yourself, Lucifer became a special mirror to *reflect* God's glory and enable Him to enjoy His own splendor.

So God is the One who gave Lucifer his vocation and stationed him in His presence, where he could serve as a *reflector* of His glory. This was Lucifer's function. He was *not* a generator of glory, nor did he have any inherent ability to produce glory on his own merits. He was a *reflector*, which is important to understand in a discussion about the deceptive pride that eventually developed in his heart.

Although Lucifer was covered with all of those precious stones, those stones had no inherent ability to shine by themselves. Any jeweler will tell you that jewels only sparkle in the light and are invisible in the dark. When even the finest gems remain in darkness, one is not even aware that they exist. Emeralds, sapphires, rubies, and even diamonds don't dazzle until light shines upon them. It is only *in the light* that the luster of gems come alive.

This was also true of Lucifer — he had no self-generating splendor of his own. The only time he shone was when God's glorious presence was shining upon him. And when God's glory struck him, those gems lit up and refracted dazzling rays of glory in every direction. What an amazing sight Lucifer must have been to see! Yet he had no visibility at all unless God's glory was streaming and falling upon him.

Try to envision Lucifer in the very presence of God — the "anointed cherub that covers." Imagine him stationed near God's throne, assigned to reflect the Almighty's glory for His own enjoyment. Then try to imagine the enormous implications of what God described in Ezekiel 28:14 and 15, when He said, "I have set thee so: thou wast upon the holy mountain of God; thou hast walked up and down in the midst of the stones of fire. Thou wast perfect in thy ways from the day thou wast created, *till iniquity was found in thee.*"

PRIDE WAS LUCIFER'S DOWNFALL

According to the last part of Ezekiel 28:15, something transpired inside Lucifer that was devastating to his God-assigned status as God's mirror. Somewhere along the way, he lost sight of the fact that he was only a mirror and began to nurse the notion that he was generating that radiance from himself. Ezekiel 28:15 says "iniquity" was found in Lucifer when he became self-focused and self-impressed — and he forgot that he was *designed* to be God's mirror.

In Ezekiel 28:16, God described what eventually happened to Lucifer as a result of this deception. It says, "By the multitude of thy merchandise they have filled the midst of thee with violence, and thou hast sinned...." This verse informs us that Lucifer did not keep his pride and rebellion to himself. As rebels always do, he spread his poison around — whispering words of insurrection and revolt into the ears of other angels with whom he had influence. Lucifer's arrogant claims were so seductive that some angels were swept up into the toxic whirlwind of his seditious words. With their support affirming Lucifer's claim of supremacy, the intensity of the rebellion that swirled within him grew stronger.

Lucifer did not keep his pride and rebellion to himself.
As rebels always do, he spread his poison around.

Ezekiel 28:17 continues the retelling of this event with God's words to Lucifer: "Thine heart was lifted up because of thy beauty, thou hast corrupted thy wisdom *by reason of thy brightness....*" In this statement, God lets us know that Lucifer became so enamored with himself that he lost sight of the fact that he was only a mirror and he began to believe that he was self-generating his own radiance. At that point, Lucifer actually began to merchandise himself to other angels — trying to sell them on the idea of joining him in an insurrection against God.

Imagine Lucifer telling any angel who would listen, "Why are we worshiping God? Look at my beauty and brilliance! If I were your leader and not God, I would be better to you than He will ever be." Slowly and steadily over a long period of time, with one accusing insinuation after another, Lucifer began to plant the idea of insurrection in the minds of some of the angels. On and on the rebel angel spun his web of deception — creating what would become from then on the progenitive root of all pride and insurrection against authority spawned in the hearts of mankind.

God knew what Lucifer was doing because He is all-knowing; yet God was patient with the archangel, giving Lucifer opportunity to repent and to change. But when the iniquity in Lucifer's heart was fully formed, God saw that he had become so full of pride that he would not repent. Lucifer had made his choice, refusing to recognize God's preeminence over him and the other angels. That is when God's patience came to a grinding halt, and He acted to severely deal with the issue.

On and on the rebel angel spun his web of deception —
creating what would become from then on
the progenitive root of all pride and insurrection
against authority spawned in the hearts of mankind.

A CANDID CONVERSATION BETWEEN GOD AND LUCIFER

Lucifer had forgotten that he was a "reflector" by function and had become fixated on his own self-deluded thoughts that he was the one generating the radiant glory that clothed him. It had all gone to Lucifer's head, and he had become obsessed with himself. He was no longer satisfied with his God-assigned position or who God had created him to be. Blinded by his own beauty, Lucifer could no longer see that without God's glory shining upon him, he would become like an invisible diamond in a darkened room. Removed from the Almighty's glorious presence, Lucifer's celestial luster would cease to exist.

Lucifer owed his exalted position in God's presence entirely to the One who had created him. If Lucifer had never been graciously given that position near God, the other angels in Heaven would not have been drawn into his deception through his influence. But once Lucifer became fully self-enamored and in pursuit of his own advantage, he lost all true perspective on the original source of his position. He became convinced that he deserved more power and authority — even the position of God Himself. Ultimately, this ill-fated archangel gathered a force of angels — those who had been drawn into deception and convinced by his lies — and attempted an insurrection to dethrone God and seize His position.

It had all gone to Lucifer's head,
and he had become obsessed with himself.
He was no longer satisfied
with his God-assigned position
or who God had created him to be.

Isaiah 14:12-14 records a conversation that took place between God and Lucifer on the day that God's patience with the situation ended and judgment fell upon Lucifer:

> **How art thou fallen from heaven, O Lucifer, son of the morning! How art thou cut down to the ground, which didst weaken the nations! For thou hast said in thine heart, *I will* ascend into heaven, *I will* exalt my throne above the stars of God: *I will* sit also upon the mount of the congregation, in the sides of the north: *I will* ascend above the heights of the clouds; *I will* be like the most High.**

I can hear the arrogance of Lucifer's words ringing through Heaven as *five times* he uttered the words *"I will."* These statements reveal that *self* was at the center of the pride that had come to consume Lucifer's heart, driving his thoughts and propelling him to ruinous action. Lucifer was full of self-will, selfish ambition, and self-exaltation. His lamentable history shows the evil of this deadly poison called pride.

The moment finally came when God said *enough* and put a stop to Lucifer's rebellion, because He would not allow it to pollute Heaven. Responding to Lucifer's blasphemous vows, God issued His prophetic decree of Lucifer's end: "Yet thou shalt be brought down to hell, to the sides of the pit. They that see thee shall narrowly look upon thee, and consider thee, saying, Is this the man that made the earth to tremble, that did shake kingdoms; that made the world as a wilderness, and destroyed the cities thereof; that opened not the house of his prisoners?" (Isaiah 14:15-17).

Self was at the center of the pride that had come to consume Lucifer's heart, driving his thoughts and propelling him to ruinous action.

The pride that had been festering inside Lucifer's heart was squashed in one moment when God had had His fill of Lucifer's evil attitude. As a result, God cast Lucifer from His presence and all the angelic forces that rebelled with him from His presence. And when Lucifer was suddenly evicted from God's glorious presence, the light went out and Lucifer moved into darkness — where he ceased to shine and where he mutated into Satan, a creature of darkness. Satan has ever since been a doomed creature that functions in spiritual darkness — the ultimate punishment for an angel created to live in the light of God's glory.

LUCIFER WAS ELIMINATED BECAUSE OF PRIDE

In Luke 10:18, Jesus told His disciples, "...I beheld Satan as lightning fall from heaven." Jesus well remembered the moment when God dealt with the pride of Lucifer and used the visual image of lightning to depict the instantaneous nature of the archangel's fall. Just as a flash of lightning occurs in the blink of an eye, so, too, did God's dealings with Lucifer at the time of the archangel's judgment.

Ezekiel 28:16 also records the event. God said, "...Therefore I will cast thee as profane out of the mountain of God: and I will destroy thee, O covering cherub, from the midst of the stones of fire." When God stated, "I will destroy thee, O covering cherub" — He was in effect decreeing, *"I'm going to remove you, O mirror. And when you are removed, the light will go out on you and you will move to the realm of darkness from this point forward."*

The Bible does not say how long God waited before He took action against Lucifer. However, we do know that God is patient to give time to repent. We also know that if one continues to refuse to repent and change his ways, a moment finally comes when God says, *"Enough! I'm finished."* This is precisely what happened with Lucifer.

How long God allowed Lucifer's scheming to play out is not clear. My personal view is that it was probably a process that was strung out over a vast length of time. It seems likely that it required a great deal of Lucifer's cunning wiles over a long period in order to sway such a large number of the heavenly host. Nevertheless, Lucifer kept relentlessly pounding away at their power of reasoning with his seductive words until a significant number of angels joined him in an insurrection against the Most High (*see* Revelation 12:3,4).

You see, the devil has always been a master of mind manipulation. He learned early how to penetrate minds with doubts, questionings, or thoughts of perceived wrongs until everything is distorted and blown out of proportion and his targeted victims become fully ensnared in bitterness, resentment, and unforgiveness.

Heaven is as perfect as an environment can be. Yet in that perfect environment, Lucifer employed enough manipulative cunning to convince huge numbers of heavenly angels to believe his totally slanderous allegations against God. Angels who had worshiped together for eons of time eventually stood *opposed* to each other over nonexistent issues the devil had conjured up in their minds. Satan was so adept at distorting truth that he was able to lure one-third of them into siding with him and rebelling against Almighty God!

Satan learned early how to penetrate minds with doubts,
questionings, or thoughts of perceived wrongs
until everything is distorted and blown out of proportion
and his targeted victims become fully ensnared
in bitterness, resentment, and unforgiveness.

If the devil is persuasive enough to deceive brilliant, mighty, powerful angels, how much easier do you think it is for him to deceive fallen humans? The emotional makeup of people — who live in a far-from-perfect environment and wrestle daily with their own imperfections *and* the imperfections of others — makes them even more susceptible to the devil's masterful skills of lying, deception, and manipulation.

But God had finally had enough of His archangel's prideful attitude and subversive activity to undermine His authority.

Ezekiel 28:17-19 reveals the Almighty's declaration of judgment on Lucifer:

> **...I will cast thee to the ground, I will lay thee before kings, that they may behold thee. Thou hast defiled thy sanctuaries by the multitude of thine iniquities, by the iniquity of thy traffic; therefore will I bring forth a fire from the midst of thee, it shall devour thee, and I will bring thee to ashes upon the earth in the sight of all them that behold thee. All they that know thee among the people shall be astonished at thee: thou shalt be a terror, and never shalt thou be anymore.**

Both Isaiah and Ezekiel recorded what Lucifer would look like after he was cast out of Heaven. This once-dazzling archangel — created to be a reflector of God's resplendent glory — was reduced to an evil, monstrous figure that would eventually be laughed at by the nations of the world. The moment Lucifer was cast out, the light went out that once shone so brilliantly upon him, and his name was changed to Satan. With the same speed that a flash of lightning strikes, he was changed from *the reflector of God's glory* to *the accuser* or *the adversary*.

Lucifer had allowed pride to develop in his heart, and that pride caused him to rebel against authority. As a result, he was eliminated from the glorious position that had been assigned to him by God.

From the time he was kicked out of Heaven until the present day, Satan has been operating in darkness in a vain attempt to regain the glory he lost. Working through society, culture, and entertainment, he strives to get people to worship him. Preying on the hearts and minds of selfish men and women whose hearts are bent toward evil, Satan continues to attempt to steal God's glory.

But it always was and always will be a vain attempt. Satan will forever be eliminated from his exalted position because of his pride.

ABSALOM WAS ELIMINATED BECAUSE OF HIS PRIDE

It is imperative to understand that an unhealthy pride will always lead to a person's elimination, or his permanent removal, from a position of responsibility, favor, or trust. We can find examples of individuals in the Bible who fell into the same trap of pride as Lucifer did. In the Old Testament, we can go to Absalom, the son of David — a clear example of one with a bright future who was eliminated as a result of his pride.

When David was king of Israel, his throne shone gloriously for decades. He had a son named Absalom, who was very beloved by David. Because David loved Absalom, he drew his son into his personal orbit — and the light of David's glory as king then shone on Absalom. The Bible tells us that Absalom became well-known in the kingdom because of his close position to his father. In a certain way, Absalom became a "mirror" that reflected his father's glory.

If David had never brought Absalom into his orbit and given him the attention he received, it is likely that no one would have ever paid attention to him. But because his father's glory shone on him, Absalom became known and shone in the sight of Israel. Absalom's future was very bright — but in reality, if he had not been David's son, it is likely that he would have remained virtually unknown.

As time passed and Absalom basked in and reflected the glory of his father, he became a celebrity in Israel, and admiration was heaped upon him continually from the people. A study of his story shows that as time passed — just as happened with Lucifer — Absalom forgot that he was well-known only because he was close to his father's exalted position. He forgot that it was his position alongside his father that caused him to begin to mirror his father's glory, just as Lucifer had once mirrored the glory of God. Gradually Absalom began to follow the same path that Lucifer had taken, as the son forgot he was a mirror and began to wrongly think he was shining on his own. As a result, Absalom became more self-impressed, deluded, and deceived. It was exactly the same scenario that happened to Lucifer.

In essence, Absalom's ultimate actions reveal that a moment must have come when he said to himself, *Look at me! I am the great Absalom everyone knows and loves. I have a glorious reputation among others in Israel. In fact, I am as loved by the people as my father David, so why should I not be king instead of him?*

Being overly impressed with himself, Absalom began to merchandise himself to the people of Israel just as Lucifer had done to the angels. Every day, Absalom took his position at the city gate, where people would come from far and wide to bring their cases to the king for judgment. Even Absalom's position in the gate of the city was a result of the attention and privilege given to him by his father. But Absalom used his position to intercept the disgruntled people and listen sympathetically to all their grievances against the king, apparently offering expressions of contrived compassion and insinuating that he himself would do something to help them — if only he were king. Second Samuel 15:6 (*NLT*) tells us, "In this way, Absalom stole the hearts of all the people of Israel."

Gradually Absalom began to follow the same path
that Lucifer had taken, as the son forgot he was a mirror
and began to wrongly think he was shining on his own.

Absalom was disgruntled with his father regarding family problems that he thought David had not dealt with correctly (*see* 2 Samuel 13). Whether David was right or wrong in his decision regarding the matter is irrelevant to Absalom's wrong choice concerning his response. Hardening his heart against his father, Absalom began to bond with other disgruntled people who also had something against the king.

Bitter people have a knack for gravitating to other bitter people, and this was what occurred in this case. The disgruntled people of Israel gravitated to Absalom, and he gravitated toward them. And as they came together as a group, each sharing their complaints and offenses against the king with one another, somehow this common airing of grievances gave the group the illusion that they were right and justified in their shared bitter feelings.

Bitter people have a knack for gravitating
to other bitter people.

In the end, Absalom was so impressed with his own glory that he, like Lucifer, tried to exalt his throne above the throne of his father. And in the end, Absalom, like Lucifer, was eliminated as a result of his pride and rebellion. While leading an insurrection against his father's throne, he was riding his horse and became caught by his long hair in the branches of an oak tree. He was then tragically stabbed to death by one of David's men.

This disastrous end of his son was never David's intent. In fact, even though David knew that Absalom was rising against him, he nonetheless had instructed his armed men to "deal gently" with Absalom (*see* 2 Samuel 18:5). But regardless of the king's wishes, Absalom was permanently removed from the scene — the consequence of the pride in his heart that initiated the attempted insurrection.

Absalom forgot he was a mirror of his father's glory. Like Lucifer before him, he came to the dangerous conclusion that he was glorious on his own merits.

Absalom should have been grateful for the privileged position that had been granted to him, allowing him to be near his father. Absalom should have been content to live in his father's orbit of influence, reflecting the glory of the king's royal light. Absalom should have rested in the rich financial provision to which he'd been granted access, as well as in all the other privileges that were his because he was the king's son.

Absalom forgot he was a mirror
of his father's glory. Like Lucifer before him,
he came to the dangerous conclusion
that he was glorious on his own merits.

But this son was *not* grateful, nor did he rest in the provision and privileges that were his. Ingratitude and pride led to his rebellion against the very source of his blessings — and ultimately resulted in his elimination.

JUDAS ISCARIOT WAS ELIMINATED BY HIS OWN PRIDE

When we look at the New Testament, we find a similar situation in the life of Judas Iscariot, who was one of Jesus' closest disciples. No one has ever shone more gloriously than Jesus! Made in the likeness of man, Jesus came as Lord and Savior, bearing the exact image of the Father (*see* Philippians 2:7; Hebrews 1:3).

There is no question that Judas was in the inner orbit of Jesus' smaller circle of disciples because he was in charge of the ministry's finances. This responsibility required a closer relationship with Jesus since Judas and Jesus would have needed to interact regularly about finances and the distribution of food and other resources to help those who were in need.

We can surmise that Judas enjoyed a greater degree of personal attention from Jesus because of his function in the group. Judas' position put him in close relation with Jesus and caused him to be well-known, enjoying a good name in the sight of others. If Judas had never been given this privileged position near Jesus, it is likely his name would never have been known among the people.

Just as Lucifer shone with the reflected glory of God's presence and Absalom reflected the glory of his father King David, so, too, did Judas enjoy the reflected glory that came from his close proximity to Jesus.

But over time, Judas' privileged position went to his head — and like Lucifer and Absalom, he fell into the trap of thinking more highly of himself than he ought to think. Day by day, little by little, Satan pounded Judas' mind with thoughts of his own grandeur until his heart became filled with pride.

Finally, there came a moment of disagreement that arose between Judas and Jesus, and things didn't go the way Judas thought they should go. At that moment, offense entered Judas' heart, and that moment of pride gave birth to betrayal. (*See* my book *You Can Get Over It* to see how Satan wedges his way between relationships.)

Have you ever wondered how it was possible for someone so close to Jesus to become His betrayer? We find the answer in John chapter 12 where we read that Jesus and His disciples were having dinner in the home of Mary, Martha, and their brother Lazarus, whom Jesus had raised from the dead.

Finally, there came a moment of disagreement that arose
between Judas and Jesus, and things didn't go
the way Judas thought they should go.
At that moment, offense entered Judas' heart,
and that moment of pride gave birth to betrayal.

During this time together, Martha showed her love and gratitude for what Jesus had done for them by preparing a large meal for Him and His disciples. Mary showed her love by bringing Jesus an extremely expensive gift. Lazarus showed his love by simply sitting with Jesus at the table to fellowship with Him as a close friend. (I point this out as an interesting demonstration of how different people express their love in different ways.)

MARY'S LAVISHLY EXPENSIVE GIFT OF LOVE

The Bible tells us that the expensive gift Mary brought Jesus was ointment of spikenard — an entire pound of it! Spikenard was one of the most expensive perfumes that existed at that time. Let me tell you a little about spikenard so you can appreciate what Mary did for Jesus that day.

Spikenard was an uncommon perfume extracted from grasses that grew in the country of India. Once the oils were squeezed out of the grass, they were dried into a hard, lardlike substance. Turning that lardlike substance into perfume was a very lengthy and costly process. Add to this the cost of transporting it from

India to other parts of the world, and you can see why this particular perfume cost so much money.

Spikenard was so expensive that few people could purchase it; most had to buy one of the many cheap imitations available. But the word used in John 12:3 tells us that Mary didn't bring Jesus a cheap imitation. She brought Jesus *the real thing* — an ointment so valuable that it was normally reserved and used only as gifts for kings and nobility. *This was the gift Mary brought to Jesus.*

We learn more about the value of Mary's gift in John 12:3, where it says the ointment was "very costly." This phrase "very costly" is from the Greek word *polutimos*, a compound of the words *polus* and *timios*. The word *polus* means *much* or *great*. The word *timios* means *to honor, to respect*, or *to attribute worth to something*. When these two words are compounded, the new word describes *something that is of great worth* or *something that is of considerable financial value.*

As remarkable as it is that Mary even possessed a gift this valuable, it is even more amazing that she brought it to Jesus. And even more phenomenal than that is what Mary did with this perfume once she brought it!

John 12:3 says, "Then took Mary a pound of ointment of spikenard, very costly, and anointed the feet of Jesus...." Everyone must have gasped when they saw Mary take the lid off that bottle, tip it downward, and begin to pour that precious ointment on Jesus' feet. This kind of perfume was not normally used on feet. Mary's action would have been considered a horrible waste in most people's minds, but that's not how she saw it. Mary loved, appreciated, and valued the feet of the Master with all her heart.

Isaiah 52:7 describes why Mary felt this way: "How beautiful upon the mountains are the feet of him that bringeth good tidings, that publisheth peace; that bringeth good tidings of good, that publisheth salvation; that saith unto Zion, Thy God reigneth!" No other feet in the entire world were more beautiful to Mary than the feet of Jesus. Jesus had utterly transformed her life and brought her brother back from the dead (*see* John 11:32-44). For Mary, every step Jesus took was *precious, honored,* and *greatly treasured.*

For three and a half years, Jesus had taught, "For where your treasure is, there will your heart be also" (Matthew 6:21; Luke 12:34). Mary's actions revealed her heart as she poured her *most valuable treasure* onto the feet of Jesus. John 12:3 tells us that she then "...wiped his feet with her hair...." In other words, after Mary poured the spikenard onto Jesus' feet, she reached up to her head, untied her long, beautiful hair, and gathered it in her hands. Then she leaned down and began to wipe Jesus' feet dry with her hair.

In the days of the Early Church, a woman's hair represented her glory and honor. The apostle Paul referred to this in First Corinthians 11:15 when he wrote that a woman's hair was a "glory" to her. For Mary to undo her hair and use it as a towel to wipe the feet of Jesus was probably the greatest act of humility she could have shown. She was demonstrating how deeply she loved and how greatly she valued Jesus.

Mary's actions revealed her heart
as she poured her *most valuable treasure*
onto the feet of Jesus.

We can imagine the tears that streamed down Mary's cheeks as she touched those precious feet. In total humility, she dried Jesus' feet with the glory and honor of her hair, and John 12:3 tells us that "...the house was filled with the odor of the ointment."

OFFENSE BORN OF PRIDE

But the devil used Mary's act of humility and love toward Jesus to create an opportunity for prideful thoughts of bitterness, resentment, and offense to invade Judas' mind. Judas indignantly asked Jesus, "Why was not this ointment sold for three hundred pence, and given to the poor?" (John 12:5).

According to Judas, the spikenard could have been sold for "three hundred pence." The Greek word for a "pence" is *denarius*. In that day, a Roman *denarius* was equivalent to *one day's salary*. So when Judas announced that the spikenard could have been sold for "three hundred pence," he was saying that Mary's perfume was worth *almost a year's worth of a person's salary*! In other words, this was *an extremely expensive* gift!

Then Jesus presented to Judas the right way — in line with God's greater plan — to perceive Mary's gift to Him. It was actually a way of escape offered to Judas from the trap of offense, if Judas had only been willing to accept it.

Jesus explained to Judas that Mary was anointing Him for the day of His burial. He also told Judas to leave Mary alone and not to disturb what she was doing (*see* John 12:7).

Then Jesus continued, saying, "For the poor always ye have with you; but me ye have not always" (John 12:8). These words of Jesus could have easily been misinterpreted. Those who were listening could have thought that Jesus was saying, "Quit talking about poor people! You'll always have the poor, but you won't always have *Me*."

Jesus had continually demonstrated His compassion toward the poor during His three years of ministry. Nevertheless, His words to Judas could have been taken wrongly by those who were listening. *Did Judas misinterpret Jesus' response that evening? Did he perceive Jesus to be arrogant and insensitive to the needs of poor people?*

Jesus presented to Judas the right way —
in line with God's greater plan —
to perceive Mary's gift to Him.
It was actually a way of escape offered
to Judas from the trap of offense,
if Judas had only been willing to accept it.

The disciples watched as this exquisite treasure was poured out on Jesus' feet. To those present who were bereft of a heavenly perspective, it may have looked like superfluous waste and excess. It's obvious that Judas considered it to be exactly that. From his words to Jesus, we can conclude that thoughts of offense were racing through Judas' head as he watched Mary pour out the spikenard on Jesus' feet: *What about all the poor people who could have been helped with the money from the sale of that perfume? Aren't they more important than this expensive demonstration of love?*

As you will see in John 13:2, in that split second, the devil found entrance into Judas' heart during this dinner at the home of Martha, Mary, and Lazarus. The open door could have been offense, pride, or fleshly anger inflamed by Judas' misconstruing what transpired there that night. But whatever it was that allowed the enemy access in that moment — once he had it, he took full advantage of it. Satan began pounding away at Judas' mind, just as he had done with Absalom, until Judas was lured into a plot of insurrection against Jesus — even to the point of betraying Him.

John 13:2 tells us something powerful about the way the devil established a foothold in Judas' heart and mind that night. It says, "And supper being ended, the devil having now put into the heart of Judas Iscariot, Simon's son, to betray him."

Whatever it was that allowed the enemy access
in that moment — once he had it,
he took full advantage of it.

Especially notice the phrase, "...the devil having now *put into* the heart of Judas Iscariot...." The words "put into" come from the Greek word *ballo*, one of the two words that make up the compound word *diabolos*, the name for the "devil" that we discussed earlier. This word *ballo* means *to throw, to cast, to thrust*, or *to inject*. It carries the idea of *a very fast action of throwing, thrusting, or injecting something forward* — such as the throwing of a ball or rock or the forward thrusting of a sharp knife.

In a split second, Judas was penetrated, and it was soon afterward that he began looking for opportunity to hand Jesus over to the Jewish leaders. Perhaps he thought, *I know better than You, Jesus, and I'm going to take charge and orchestrate events the way I think they need to be.* That possibly shouldn't surprise us, since this is exactly the pattern that Lucifer himself fell into. It is the very lure that Satan has used throughout history to seduce others into committing insurrection against those who are their source of blessing.

It wasn't long before the pride that took over Judas' heart and mind propelled him to sell Jesus for 30 pieces of silver. But in the end, pride produced its harvest and Judas was eliminated. In his case, he took his own life because he could not bear to live knowing he had shed innocent blood.

In every case in Scripture where pride is in operation and is not halted by repentance, the person who operates in pride is eventually eliminated or removed from his or her position of responsibility. Lucifer, Absalom, and Judas are just three examples of this spiritual law in action, along with countless others throughout history.

That means you and I have been forewarned. We are *never* to give place to pride in our lives — and if we ever do recognize its evil fruit, we are to halt its operation immediately by the act of repentance. Otherwise, the spiritual law goes into effect: Anyone can be eliminated when pride goes unchecked.

In every case in Scripture where pride is in operation and is not halted by repentance, the person who operates in pride is eventually eliminated or removed from his or her position of responsibility.

A Page From My Own Life

There was a situation of pride in my own life many years ago. It is one of which I am not proud, but I believe it may really be helpful to you if I share it.

When Denise and I first got married, we served in a good church under a great pastor. He was an anointed, strong, solid, leader who was well-known and loved for his rich Bible teaching. At the time, I was only 22 years old. God had given me incredible favor with this man by allowing me into his inner orbit.

The pastor told me, "Rick, you have a special gift of God on your life. I know you don't have experience in full-time ministry, so I'm going to take you into my inner circle and train you, because I want to help you become the best you can possibly be."

I was humbled and honored by this pastor's amazing offer and eagerly accepted it. In my new position, I became like the "anointed cherub that covers" in his life and ministry, shadowing him everywhere he went. Every opportunity that presented itself, I was with him. I regularly and sincerely told people how much I loved and respected him and how great he was as a man of God. And like a mirror that reflects someone else's glory, I began to shine in the eyes of others as I drew closer and closer to my pastor.

Throughout my days of serving that wonderful man, I was provided an environment where my teaching gift could begin to grow and flourish. In fact, the Sunday school class I was teaching grew to a regular attendance of hundreds of people. It was absolutely amazing to see how God's gift in me began to flourish when I was allowed to come alongside that precious man who had taken me into his orbit!

But at one point, pride began to worm its way into my heart, as has happened so often with people who are graciously given opportunity to shine. Like Absalom and Judas Iscariot, I forgot the reason that I was becoming recognized and starting to shine was that I was in my pastor's orbit. Instead of being grateful for the phenomenal opportunity that had been gifted to me, I began to think that the reason I was shining so brightly was that *I* was so amazing!

The truth is, God's anointing on my life to teach the Word of God at that early age was manifesting. But the devil seized that moment to tell me, *"Just look at all you are doing in comparison to everyone else."* Before long, I began to listen, comparing what *I* was doing with what others on the pastoral staff were doing. And when I realized I was being paid much less than the others, I began to nurse resentful thoughts like, *They are making five times more money than I am, and they are touching only a fraction of the people I am touching. Surely I deserve more than I'm making!*

As this pattern of thinking progressed, my initial gratitude for the opportunity to work with this pastor gradually turned to discontent and resentment. The devil took full advantage of the situation and constantly whispered negativity in my ears. He would say, *"You are so abused! You are underpaid and unappreciated. The church keeps talking about its amazing growth, but no one has mentioned the fact that it's because of you!"*

I forgot the reason that I was becoming recognized
and starting to shine was that
I was in my pastor's orbit.

Again and again, I heard the hiss of this serpent inserting its venom into my mind. Eventually Satan began to build a case in my thoughts against my pastor who had graciously taken me into his orbit and given me this privileged position. I didn't recognize the source of those thoughts then, but it was the devil using the open door created by my own pride and wrong attitudes to insert his poisonous way of thinking into my mind: *"Your pastor treats you like a slave. You carry his books, transport his luggage, mow his grass, clean his car — and for what? No appreciation and a meager salary! You are being so abused by this man!"*

More and more I listened to these lying accusations, and agreement began to form in my heart. Before long, I had lost my sense of gratitude for the position I had been given and for the blessings that were being poured out on my life. That pastor — whom I loved and respected — had gradually become a focus of my resentment.

It was the devil using the open door created
by my own pride and wrong attitudes
to insert his poisonous way of thinking into my mind.

My mind and emotions were being inundated by false accusations, until I forgot that the *only reason* I was experiencing success — the only reason my part of the ministry was exponentially growing — was that my pastor had given me the opportunity! He had taken the risk of bringing me under his wings. He had spent hundreds of hours with me, personally discipling me and teaching me what I needed to know in order to excel in the ministry. In fact, the only reason I was beginning to shine in the eyes of others was that I had been allowed into my pastor's orbit and my proximity to him had brought enormous attention to me.

Eventually because of pride, I began to think, *I am more anointed than this man, and I deserve so much more than this. It's time for me to move on — it's time to start my own church.*

It embarrasses me to tell it now, but I believe I need to share this story to demonstrate to you the nature of pride and its destructive path. Soon I was so deceived by my own "brightness" that I proceeded to write that pastor a nine-page, single-spaced letter to document everything I perceived to be wrong about him and why I felt he should be removed as pastor of that church. Because of the pride and deception that had taken root inside me, I couldn't see how terrible my own attitude was. I actually believed I was justified in my behavior — but nothing could have been further from the truth.

"I'm leaving you," I boldly announced to my pastor in the letter. "I'm taking all my people with me, and I'm starting another church."

There I was — a 24-year-old young man with very little experience in the ministry, who had been given a great opportunity by the man I was accusing — and I was reprimanding *him*. This man had been serving as a pastor for 40 years, and I had taken it upon myself to teach him a thing or two! But in that moment of deception, I was clueless that pride was blinding me to the truth regarding my own arrogance.

Because of the pride and deception that had taken root inside me, I couldn't see how terrible my own attitude was. I actually believed I was justified in my behavior — but nothing could have been further from the truth.

I followed through on the declaration I had stated in my letter. I left the church and took a handful of people with me to start my own church. But when I left the pastor's orbit, something amazing happened — the lights went out and I slipped into obscurity. The little church I started flopped; our finances dwindled down to nothing; and I had a serious wake-up call when the realization hit that my own pride had driven me into the wilderness.

Meanwhile, that pastor and his congregation moved on and did wonderfully without me! I had said that *he* needed to be eliminated, but *I* was the one who was eliminated! When I moved out of his orbit, all the brilliance that once shone so brightly faded away — and I found myself pastoring a small group of people in a broken-down building in a poor part of town.

In the midst of my feeling both afraid and extremely embarrassed, God began to deal with me about getting back in line. I heard the Holy Spirit whisper, *"How much time is it going to take before you repent and tell this man you're sorry?"* Time passed. Then one day the Holy Spirit spoke loud and clear to me again and said, *"Your ministry will never move forward until you repent and make things right with your former pastor."*

Finally the day came when I picked up the phone and called this pastor. Overwhelming fear and embarrassment gripped my heart as I dialed his phone number, but I knew making the call was essential if I was going to make things right and move on in God's plan for my life.

I had said that *my pastor* needed to be eliminated,
but *I* was the one who was eliminated!
When I moved out of his orbit, all the brilliance
that once shone so brightly faded away.

When he answered, I said, "Pastor, I have so wronged you. I sinned against you and your entire church, and I'm so sorry. I am repenting for it and asking you to please forgive me."

The pastor answered, "I forgive you, Rick." Then he gently continued, "I forgave you when it happened because I love you so much. But, Rick, I want to tell you, I've never done for anyone what I did for you. I've never given any other person the opportunity I gave you. I treated you like a son, and you paid me back by hurting me more than anyone has ever hurt me. But I forgave you long ago."

What he said was true — he had loved me like a son. Yet I had led an insurrection against this gracious man who had taken the risk and allowed me into his orbit. I did what Absalom did to David, what Judas did to Jesus, and what Lucifer did to God. But by the grace of God, not only was I able to ask the pastor's forgiveness and receive it, but our relationship was also completely restored. We remained precious friends to the end of his long life. I loved him like a father and financially supported him until he breathed his last breath.

I share this experience from my own life because I want you to know that I personally understand the toxic ramifications of pride. I have walked through it and can personally testify that if you have been ensnared by pride, *you* are the one who will be eliminated in the end. However, as in my case, God will forgive you if you acknowledge the wrong you have done, repent, and seek forgiveness from those you have wronged. Even more, He will bring healing and restoration to you and to those you have hurt, which will help you get back on track again with His plan for your life.

ELIMINATION IS THE ENEMY'S PLAN

Pride is a temptation that comes to everyone from time to time — regardless of how long we have walked with God. Pride knows no limitations. It is an "equal-opportunity eliminator."

Pride is fatal — and you should *hate* it. You should also become schooled in how to identify it. For instance:

- Prideful people think too highly of themselves.

- Prideful people get easily offended (because they think they are not recognized properly or treated well enough).

- Prideful people usually come to a place of rebellion against authority.

- Prideful people are ultimately eliminated and then often blame it on others.

When pride is working in us, Satan's ultimate goal is to see that we make destructive choices and behaviors that will lead to our *elimination* from our God-appointed positions. He wants us to be ejected from the game so that we are no longer a threat to his plans and no longer usable in God's Kingdom.

Satan wants to absolutely *quench* the fire of God burning in our hearts. One major way he does it is through pride. This is a major eliminator! Therefore we must be aware of it and guard ourselves against it.

From experience, I would say that the biggest open door to pride is *offense*. An offense may be rooted in a real or a perceived issue. We feel personally insulted, overlooked, taken for granted, or mistreated, or we feel these emotions on behalf of someone else. If we hold on to the hurt rather than surrender it to Jesus, it grows into bitterness and resentment — the perfect breeding ground for pride — and becomes an open door for the devil to gain access and sow seeds of his slanderous accusation into our hearts and minds.

Satan wants us to be ejected from the game
so that we are no longer a threat to his plans
and no longer usable in God's Kingdom.

I say that pride is much like a *handle* that is connected to our heads and hearts. This invisible handle is what the devil grabs hold of and uses to open the door to our thinking and to twist our thoughts.

Let me take this right into the context of your own job and employment. Let's say you are blessed with a job because your employer gave you an opportunity to work. It is likely that someone else out there also applied for your job and that your employer could have given it to someone else — but the opportunity was given to *you*. In fact, let's say your job was a specific answer to your prayers.

Opportunities will eventually arise for you to forget that you were thankful for this job when you first got it. As you get better and better at what you do, the devil will make sure you have a chance to think too highly of yourself. In those moments, you must put your thoughts on pause and remember that your employer is the reason you are shining brightly in what you do. You wouldn't even be shining if your employer hadn't given you the opportunity to be in his orbit and allowed you to flourish!

Don't let pride get you stuck in its poisonous thought pattern that inevitably leads to dissatisfaction. That toxic way of thinking will sour you until you've set yourself up for possible elimination.

Trust me — I've lived it, and I am telling you the truth. If a moment comes when you are tempted to get offended with your boss or employer because you feel that he or she has mistreated you, taken advantage of you, or overlooked you for a promotion — make the decision to give the situation to God and refuse to allow it to fester into offense, resentment, and bitterness. Otherwise, you'll begin to think thoughts like, *I'm not appreciated around here. They really should pay me more for all I do. I make this company look good, and I don't get the appreciation I deserve.*

Don't let pride get you stuck
in its poisonous thought pattern that inevitably leads
to dissatisfaction. That toxic way of thinking
will sour you until you've set yourself up
for possible elimination.

This is the same pattern that led Lucifer, Absalom, and Judas to their downfall. The Bible clearly states that "...God resisteth the proud..." (James 4:6). The word "proud" is the Greek word *huperephanos*, which describes *a person who has an exaggerated opinion of himself and his own importance.*

The word "resisteth" is a form of *antitasso*, a military term that depicts *the orderly arrangement of troops that wage combat against the non-compliant.* It represents *a deliberate, premeditated arrangement of military might to crush an enemy.* It carries the idea of *a well-planned, prepared resistance to stand against, to set oneself against, or to resist a force that is out of order.*

This means God is so against a spirit of pride that He will arrange divine power to stand against its arrogant activity. If an employee in the workplace is operating in pride, for example, it won't be the employer who is eventually eliminated — it will be that employee because he will ensnare himself with his own prideful attitudes. That kind of poisonous thinking lurking beneath the surface always eventually reveals itself and leads to a person's elimination from an appointed position.

God is patient with everyone, and He gives all an opportunity to self-correct, repent, and change their ways. It may be that He is doing that right now with you by allowing you to read this chapter. Regardless, it's important that you take away this key truth from this discussion on pride: If unhealthy pride is not halted and repented of, a moment *will* come when God gets involved to resist it. As the Bible states emphatically, "…God *resisteth* the proud…" (James 4:6). No thinking person wants to be found on the other side of being resisted by God!

If unhealthy pride is not halted
and repented of, a moment *will* come
when God gets involved to resist it.

HUMILITY IS PRIDE'S REMEDY

But wait — the rest of James 4:6 says, "…God resisteth the proud, and *giveth grace to the humble.*"

The word "humble" comes from the Greek word *tapeinos*, which describes *a person who has a modest view of himself.* This pictures a person who was formerly arrogant but has changed his attitude to become humble. Although he previously operated in pride, he has come down from his haughty position to *conform* his behavior to God's commands. This word *tapeinos* means *to make small, to reduce one's self-importance,* or *to humble oneself* from a previous attitude of arrogance. The word "humble" describes a person who has *a modest view of himself* rather than an exaggerated view.

I especially like what Paul wrote about this in Romans 12:3 (*AMPC*):

For by the grace (unmerited favor of God) given to me I warn everyone among you not to estimate and think of himself more highly than he ought [not to have an exaggerated opinion of his own importance], but to rate his ability with sober judgment, each according to the degree of faith apportioned by God to him.

In this verse, Paul wrote that a man ought not "…to estimate and think of himself more highly than he ought [not to have an exaggerated opinion of his own importance]…." This comes from the Greek word *huperphroneo*, which is a compound of the words *huper* and *phroneo*. The word *huper* means *over*, *above*, or *beyond*, and the word *phroneo* means *to think*. But when compounded into one word, the new word carries the meaning as translated in the *Amplified Classic* version — *to think of oneself more highly than one ought to think* or *to have an exaggerated opinion of one's own importance*. When a person fits that description, that is what it means to be proud. This is what Paul said we are *not* to do, and this is the attitude that God always resists.

To be "humble" does not mean that we berate or deprecate ourselves or have a bad opinion of ourselves. It means we don't think too highly of ourselves or have an exaggerated view of who we are, of what we have, or of the accomplishments we've achieved. The word "humble" again describes a person who has *a modest view of himself* — not an exaggerated view.

Let me give you an example from my own life of humility or modesty. I have written numbers of best-selling books, and I'm thankful that the gift of God in my life to teach is evident and a blessing to others. A number of books have been read by vast numbers of people all over the world. Among them are my devotionals entitled *Sparkling Gems 1* and *Sparkling Gems 2*, which are bestsellers in large distribution around the world. For this, I am so thankful. But what if I were audacious enough to say, "I have written the *greatest* devotionals ever written, and no one has written devotionals as rich as mine"? That would be a gross exaggeration and an example of self-exaltation. It would, in fact, be a demonstration of very unhealthy pride.

On the other hand, humility says, "I'm so thankful God chose me and enabled me to be a blessing to others. I'm so grateful for what He has done through my books. There are thousands of wonderful devotionals available, and many of them are better than mine. I'm simply grateful that God has allowed mine to be counted among the others He has so graciously used. And I'm thankful He has allowed me to be included among the writers He is using for His purposes in this hour."

This is an example of humility — *having a modest view of oneself*, not an exaggerated view. You see, humility is never self-exalting, but it sees itself in a balanced way. As I mentioned at the opening of the chapter, humility attracts the presence of God like a magnet attracts metal. When a person has genuine humility, that quality attracts the strong presence of God into his or her life.

Turning our attention again to James 4:6, we see that it goes on to say, "God resists the proud, but He gives *grace* to the humble."

In the Greek language of the New Testament, the word "grace" is *charis*. Pages and pages could be written about the origins and the various nuances of meaning contained in this one word. But one of these historical meanings of *charis* is significant for this discussion. This word *charis* sometimes denoted *special power that was conferred upon an individual or a group of individuals by the gods.*

Humility attracts the presence of God
like a magnet attracts metal.

Once this *charis* was conferred upon a person or group of people, it imparted to them *superhuman abilities*. In other words, it enabled them to do what they could not normally or naturally do. In some secular literature from the early New Testament period, the word *charis* was even used to denote individuals who had been placed under a "magic spell" that transformed their personalities and imparted supernatural abilities to them.

As used in secular Greek literature, *charis* described a specific moment when an individual experienced a supernatural touch of the gods, always resulting in some type of *outward evidence* or *visible manifestation*. In this context, a person or group of people would never experience a supernatural impartation of *charis* without demonstrating *outward evidence*. Experiencing one without the other simply wasn't within the realm of possibility.

In the New Testament, the word "grace" — this same Greek word *charis* — is occasionally translated *favor* because a person who receives *charis* has been *supernaturally enabled* as a result of receiving a manifestation of *favor* from God. So when we read of "grace" in the apostle Paul's writings, we can know that he was referring to God's gracious impartation of a special touch that *enables*, *empowers*, and *strengthens* the recipients.

All of this aptly depicts the word "grace" and its effects on those who receive it. *It is a divine touch that transforms an individual and gives him the ability to do what he could not do before.*

Of course, grace first produces *inward change*, but it also always comes with *outward evidence*. It is never silent; it is never

355

invisible; it always manifests in a visible way. Likewise, when you are touched by God's grace — you should expect His grace to visibly show up in many areas of your life as an outcome. Grace will empower you to have victory over sin. It will enable you to control your tongue. It will transform you as its influence changes your behavior. *Grace is God's supernatural touch of empowerment.*

What we don't want is for God to "resist" us — and that is what He does to those who operate in pride! As already noted, the word "resist" in James 4:6 is the Greek word *antitasso*, which is a military term that depicts *the orderly arrangement of troops to successively wage war against the disobedient.*

In James 4:6, the use of the word *antitasso* signifies that if the arrogant will not willingly bow, God will *arrange* events so that they will bow, regardless of whether it is done willingly or is forced. One way or another, the proud *will* bow. The armed forces of Heaven will see to it. God, however, invites them to humble themselves willingly rather than to be forcibly humiliated.

Grace will empower you to have victory over sin.
It will enable you to control your tongue.
It will transform you as its influence
changes your behavior. *Grace is
God's supernatural touch of empowerment.*

You see, God has no tolerance for pride. If God is resisting you because of pride in your heart, you may as well surrender right now, because you are not going to move any further in your walk with Him until you do. No one can stand against the might of God — *no one.*

WHO IS GOD LOOKING TO USE?

As sons and daughters of God, we are called to stay on fire for Him all the days of our lives so we can be used by Him to do great and mighty things. But who exactly qualifies to be used by God in this way? What qualifies us to be selected by God for His special purposes? What kind of attitude is God looking for in order to use us?

The Bible emphatically states that the number-one qualification God is looking for is *humility*. Listen to the recurring themes in the following verses.

The Lord is nigh unto them that are of a broken heart; and saveth such as be of a contrite spirit.

— Psalm 34:18

The sacrifices of God are a broken spirit: a broken and contrite heart, O God, thou wilt not despise.

— Psalm 51:17

To whom is the Lord "nigh," or near? These verses tell us He is "nigh" unto those who have a "broken heart" and a "contrite spirit." God is looking for a person who does not have an exaggerated opinion of his own importance, but who rates his ability with sober judgment and has a modest view of himself.

In Isaiah 57:15, God declared this:

For thus saith the high and lofty One that inhabiteth eternity, whose name is Holy; I dwell in the high and holy place, with him also that is of a contrite and humble spirit, to revive the spirit of the humble, and to revive the heart of the contrite ones.

With whom does this verse say God chooses to live? Whom does He revive and refresh? This verse answers those questions: those who are humble and have a contrite (repentant) spirit. In other words, God chooses to bless and work with those who do not have an exaggerated opinion of their own importance but rate their abilities with sober judgment and have a modest view of themselves.

Then in Isaiah 66:2, the Lord proclaimed:

For all those things hath mine hand made, and all those things have been, saith the Lord: but to this man will I look, even to him that is poor and of a contrite spirit, and trembleth at my word.

God chooses to bless and work with those who do not have an exaggerated opinion of their own importance, but who rate their abilities with sober judgment and have a modest view of themselves.

Upon whom does God fix His focus? Who captures His attention? This verse declares it is with the person who is empty of pride and who trembles at God's Word. Once again, He looks to those who don't have an exaggerated opinion of their own importance but have a modest view of themselves, recognizing their total reliance upon God.

HUMBLE YOURSELF BEFORE GOD

Having a passion for humility is absolutely essential for stoking the fire in our spiritual lives and for remaining a spiritual inferno that ever burns to see God's will manifested on the earth. Humility is pride's remedy. If we live in a state of humility, it keeps us out of the reach of the devil so he cannot find a handle by which to twist our thoughts and lead us to a place of elimination.

In truth, for us to move forward in the strength and power of God, pride *must* be eliminated from our lives.

Humility is pride's remedy. If we live in a state of humility, it keeps us out of the reach of the devil so he cannot find a handle by which to twist our thoughts and lead us to a place of elimination.

If you are thinking, *Well, I don't have an issue with pride*, that itself may be an indicator that you need to deal with it, because unhealthy pride is a temptation that comes to every single human being — men, women, youth, and children — at one time or another. If you find even a hint of pride in you, believe me when I tell you that it is in your interest to acknowledge it and *eradicate* it from your life!

So today I want to encourage you to take inventory of your relationships — with your spouse, your children, your employer, your parents, your pastor, or with the leaders in your church. Are you dissatisfied, frustrated, and offended with someone? Or are you thankful, appreciative, and at peace with them? Is pride interfering with you in any of these vital relationships?

It would be wise to ask people you respect and trust to tell you if they see that you are acting in pride at any moment in your life. This is such a poisonous trait that you should want them to help you see it before its toxins negatively affect you.

If you find even a hint of pride in you,
believe me when I tell you that it is in your interest
to acknowledge it and *eradicate* it from your life!

And by all means — welcome the Holy Spirit's help. Be willing to hear His voice when He does speak, no matter how uncomfortable His words might be.

I urge you to pray, "Holy Spirit, show me if I have any issues with unhealthy pride that need to be corrected and uprooted from my life. Help me to carry myself with humility and to have a moderate, balanced view of myself, not an exaggerated opinion of my own importance."

Asking the Holy Spirit for His help with this important issue is a safeguard against the devil accomplishing in you what He has successfully waged against so many others. The Holy Spirit's insight — as well as the insight of beloved and trusted friends — could save you from a lot of pain and even elimination from a God-appointed position He has ordained for you to fill.

Again, in James 4:6, it goes on to say, "God *resists* the proud, but He gives *grace* to the humble." This means pride will *eliminate* you, but humility will *promote* you.

The Holy Spirit's insight — as well as the insight
of beloved and trusted friends — could save you
from a lot of pain and even elimination
from a God-appointed position
He has ordained for you to fill.

If you are serious about throwing another log into your spiritual fire, you must come ablaze with humility. This is the fuel that attaches the presence of God to you like metal to a magnet. Humility will help keep His fire burning in you all the way to the finish line of your spiritual race on this earth.

Right now God is looking for people He can promote. Second Chronicles 16:9 (*NASB*) says, "The eyes of the Lord move to and fro throughout the earth that He may strongly support those whose heart is completely His...."

When God finds a person who is ablaze with biblical humility, He says, "This is someone I want to work with! This person is walking in humility and doesn't have an exaggerated opinion of himself. That means he qualifies for Me to pour My grace into him and to undergird what he is doing!"

So if you want God to pour His grace out upon you in an abundant measure and to promote you to your appointed place of purpose in His great plan, here is what you need to do: "*Humble* yourselves in the sight of the Lord, and he shall *lift* you up" (James 4:10).

Don't get into the business of exalting yourself. Let that be God's job. Self-exaltation is the fruit of pride, but God-exaltation is His response to His people's humility.

If you want God to pour His grace out upon you
in an abundant measure and to promote you
to your appointed place of purpose
in His great plan, here is what you need to do:
"*Humble* yourselves in the sight of the Lord,
and he shall *lift* you up" (James 4:10).

Your part is to turn from unhealthy pride with a repentant heart and to throw the fuel of humility onto your fire. Then watch how that powerful fuel causes you stay ablaze day by day as you grow into all God has created you to be — all for *His* glory and honor!

THINK ABOUT IT

1. Offense and frustration are a deadly blend. If left undealt with, they will create an atmosphere that incubates pride. Pride always creates strife — and from strife comes every devilish work to deceive, divide, and ultimately destroy.

   Have you ever acted like Absalom, allowing offense to provoke you into believing that the person in authority over you is ineffective and that you could do better in his or her position? Be careful — that's arrogance speaking. A lack of humility will distort your thinking, causing you to act in ways that can ultimately sabotage your relationships and pull you out of position.

   Has your marriage or another key relationship in your life become endangered because of offenses, insinuations, or perceived wrongs that now have you and the other party opposed to each other? What decisions do you need to make to guard against taking prideful actions that could hurt others and sabotage your own success? Division, slander, offense, and unforgiveness are indicators that pride is seeking access to derail your destiny. Stop it in its tracks with repentance and humility!

2. God resists the proud but gives grace and special empowerment to the humble (*see* James 4:6). All a man's ways are right in his own eyes, but the Lord weighs the hearts and examines the thoughts and motivations (*see* Proverbs 21:2; Jeremiah 17:10).

   If you have embraced ideas motivated by pride or aligned yourself with aspirations that arrogantly defy God's plan for your life, Scripture says He will resist the pride fueling those ideas. Therefore, ask God to shine His light upon your motives. Then refuse to cling to pride in any form. Instead, draw near to Him and embrace humility. Not only will the devil flee from you, but the fire of God will burn brightly in you again. God will empower you with fresh grace because you chose humility.

3. An ungrateful attitude is idolatrous because it is a manifestation of prideful entitlement that serves and enthrones self, not God. Humility will promote you; pride will eliminate you.

   Evaluate your own heart responses. Do you choose to exalt and magnify God with an attitude of gratitude, regardless of your circumstances? Gratitude will keep your heart in the appropriate posture of humility and help ensure that the fire of His Spirit will burn continually on the altar of your heart.

CHAPTER 10

ABLAZE UNDER AUTHORITY

The next life-giving fuel you need to inject into your spiritual fire to stay spiritually ablaze is a healthy dose of respect for *authority*. I am well aware that what you are about to read will be heard differently by each reader, depending on his or her station in life. So I ask that you please read this chapter with an open mind to hear what God wants to impart to your life on this vital, life-giving subject of authority.

Every person on the planet — whether young, old, male, or female — is under some kind of authority. Being under authority is an inescapable part of life. Those who understand this truth and flow with it will find success. But life does not generally go well for those who disrespect authority or who try to sidestep its vital role in life. We can all think of individuals we know who have struggled with authority and whose negative response to it has resulted in bad circumstances in some aspect of life.

A key verse for understanding God's view of order and authority is First Corinthians 14:40. In that verse, God states that everything should be done "in order." The word "order" is the Greek word *taksis*, which the Jewish historian Josephus used to denote the *order* that the Roman army demonstrated in the way they erected their camps. The Roman army believed in order, right down to the smallest detail, and normally didn't engage in last-minute planning. Even when they erected their camps, they were set up in an *orderly* manner as opposed to something thrown together in an unthoughtful manner. For Paul to use this word in First Corinthians 14:40 to describe God's orderliness tells us that He is very serious when it comes to doing things in an orderly manner.

Being under authority is an inescapable part of life.
Those who understand this truth and
flow with it will find success.

Take a look at the world around you, and you'll see that science, nature, mathematics, and the very universe we live in reveal an undeniable order that is a significant part of everything God has created. A world without order would be a world in chaos, which is the direct opposite of anything made by God. This is why order can also be found in every level of human life as well. God has ordered government, society, family, church — even every organ of the human body — with a structure or an order that makes way for a peaceful, functional existence. And when that divine order is disrupted, it can result in confusion, in upheaval, and even in revolution.

God-established authority is so unquestionable that Romans 13:1 (*NIV*) says, "...The authorities that exist have been established by God." That word "authorities" is a translation of the Greek word *exousia* — a word that depicts *those who have received delegated power.* It could also denote *those who held public office or spiritual positions and wielded authority that had been entrusted to them.*

According to Romans 13:1, those entrusted with governmental, societal, family, or spiritual authority have been established by God, and as such, their positions of authority are to be respected. This remarkable verse that many struggle with, even today, was written when believers were suffering at the hands of wicked Roman rulers. But rather than encourage believers to ignore or overthrow Roman authority (which would have led to chaos), God instructed them to respect even *those* authorities who were treating them unjustly.

Order and authority is so important in human existence that every level of life is affected by it. For example:

- Children are under the authority of their parents.
- Wives are under the authority of their husbands.
- Husbands are under the authority of Christ.
- Employees are under the authority of their employers.
- Employers are under the authority of their superiors.
- Students are under the authority of their teachers.
- Teachers are under the authority of their school directors and superintendents.

- Citizens are under the authority of the rule of law and those government officials, police, and so forth, who enforce the law.

- Government is under the authority of its Constitution.

- Church members are under the authority of their pastor and elders.

- And on and on the list goes.

Every single person — at least in some measure — is under someone's authority in every season from the beginning to the end of life. And as already stated, those who disregard this inescapable fact often fall into trouble or are eventually even punished as lawbreakers.

By teaching our children, grandchildren, and others whom we love to cooperate willingly with authority, we give them a gift that will help them do well in life. How a person relates to authority — or how a person does *not* relate to authority — will eventually be one of the determining factors to gauge how high or low that person will go in life.

Theologian R. C. Sproul wrote, "The very word *authority* has within it the word *author*. An author is someone who creates and possesses a particular work. Insofar as God is the foundation of all authority, He exercises that foundation because He is the author and the owner of His creation. He is the foundation upon which all other authority stands or falls."[93]

In the beginning of time, Adam and Eve disregarded God's authority and defied His instructions. It was their attempt to sidestep God's authority that opened a door through which sin and death found its way into the human race. If Adam and Eve

---

[93] R. C. Sproul, "The Divine Foundation of Authority," *Ligonier Ministries*, https://www.ligonier.org/learn/articles/divine-foundation-authority/.

had respected God's authority and not tried to sidestep it, the chaos, bedlam, and anarchy we see in much of the world today never would have come about. But from the earliest pages of biblical history, the Scriptures demonstrate that tragic consequences occur when authority is disregarded, dishonored, sidestepped, or disobeyed.

How a person relates to authority
will eventually be one of the determining factors
to gauge how high or low that person will go in life.

THE NECESSITY TO GET ALONG WITH AUTHORITY

Understanding and getting along with all forms of authority is essential for any person to do well in life. It is also crucial for believers to submit to their spiritual authority in order to sustain their spiritual fire. Amos 3:3 demonstrates the indispensable nature of this key fuel: "Can two walk together, except they be agreed?"

Amos 3:3 implicitly means that it is impossible for two to walk together — to work together or to get anything done in any realm — if they are not in *agreement* with each other. This means for you to even get along with God — or to get along with *anyone else*, including all forms of authority — it is essential to "be agreed."

But what does "agreement" mean in this context? The Greek word that is most often translated "agree" or "agreement" in the New Testament is the word *sumphoneo*, which is a compound of the words *sum* and *phoneo*. The word *sum* means *with*, and the word *phoneo* means *to make a sound*. But when these two words are compounded to form the word *sumphoneo,* the new word depicts *a coming together to produce a blended sound.* The word *sumphoneo* means *agreement* or *concord of sound* and depicted *consonance* as opposed to *dissonance.* In fact, it is where we get the English word for a *symphony.*

Think of a *symphony* — that is, a large group of instrumentalists in an orchestra who play their various instruments at the direction of a conductor to create *a blended sound.* Although each musician is familiar with and can professionally play his or her part, the conductor is familiar with the entire piece being performed. He or she is the director who tells each instrumentalist when to play, how fast to play, or when to stop playing. Without a conductor to direct the orchestra, a host of conflicting sounds would be produced that assaults rather than soothes the listener's ear. As important as each player is to the finished musical production, the ability of the orchestra to produce a blended sound depends on a unified effort to follow the direction of a designated conductor.

As we've seen, our biblical example of the words "agree" and "agreement" is taken from the word *sumphoneo* — which depicts a symphony where every instrumentalist plays professionally, but each eye is focused on the directing hand of the conductor who leads, decides, and directs. If the various members of the orchestra choose to ignore or sidestep the conductor's direction, the result will be symphonic confusion and discord.

We can learn something vital from this illustration of the symphony (*sumphoneo*). The biblical meaning of being in "agreement" is having a cooperative attitude and learning to "play" one's part — to carry out one's assignment and fulfill one's role alongside others and in submission to the appointed authority in any sphere of life. For anyone to be a part of anything that produces a blended "sound," a person must learn to accommodate others who play their part alongside him or her and to come under the leadership of those who are in authority. Remember, two can't walk together unless they be "agreed" (*see* Amos 3:3) — in unity and cooperation with others called alongside and in submission to those who are leading the way.

> As important as each player is
> to the finished musical production,
> the ability of the orchestra to produce
> a blended sound depends on a unified effort
> to follow the direction of a designated conductor.

In this analogy, all of mankind are members of a great orchestra, and every human being is gifted to play his or her part in life. But for this orchestra to produce a powerful, blended sound, all must learn to cooperate with others and respect the various "conductors" in every sphere of life — family, workplace, school, church, etc.

Those who refuse to cooperate with the authority figures they are subject to will only add a discordant sound to the mix and will never play their part well unless they choose to change. And if they decide to stay discordant and continue to refuse to submit to authority, it is likely they will be uninvited from participating in the future.

> Those who refuse to cooperate with the authority figures
> they are subject to will only add a discordant sound
> to the mix and will never play their part well
> unless they choose to change.

Regardless of how gifted a person may be, no one wants to be a partner in life with someone who is defiant and insubordinate. We have read the words of the prophet Amos: "Can two walk together, except they be agreed?" (Amos 3:3). A person who cannot get in agreement with those who are entrusted with authority over them is unable to help produce the desired harmonious results.

This simple illustration of the words "agree" and "agreement" demonstrates that every one of us who wants to contribute to any level of life must learn to cooperate with and respect those who have been invested with authority, as well as learn to get along with others in life. In the majority of environments we live and work in — whether church, school, workplace, family, etc. — there is usually one who is the final authority, although there may be several others in a given area of life who are also in a position of authority over us (e.g., father/mother, senior pastor/pastoral team, employer/management team, principal/teachers, etc.). Regardless, we all must learn to work in harmony with whomever is over us in every situation.

God Himself is the ultimate Great Conductor who directs and decides. He is the One who has designed the biblical guidelines for family, church, society, government, and even creation itself. In each of these spheres, if His prescribed order runs afoul, it results in a discordant mess. This has been true from the beginning of time. When God's instructions are disrespected, ignored, or sidestepped, the result is anarchy, bedlam, chaos, and turmoil.

Theologian Abraham Kuyper eloquently stated it this way: "God built into the creation a variety of cultural spheres, such as the family, economics, politics, art, and intellectual inquiry. Each of these spheres has its own proper "business" and needs its own unique pattern of authority. When we confuse spheres, by violating the proper boundaries of church and state, for instance, or reducing the academic life to a business enterprise, we transgress the patterns that God has set."[94]

DISCORD AT THE END OF THE AGE

Because we live at the end of the age, we are witnessing a time when disregard for authority is pandemic across society. The disregard for God's authority that was first ceded by Adam and Eve in the Garden of Eden is now giving way to an unfettered harvest filled with a contagion of disrespect and dishonor. The Bible clearly teaches that as the prophetic clock ticks toward the final countdown, widespread disrespect for authority will grow even more out of control. In his book *Spiritual Authority*, Watchman Nee noted, "Authority in the world is being increasingly undermined until at the end all authorities will be overthrown and lawlessness shall rule."[95]

The disregard for God's authority that was first ceded by Adam and Eve in the Garden of Eden is now giving way to an unfettered harvest filled with a contagion of disrespect and dishonor.

As noted by Nee, the Bible unquestionably teaches that the last-days age will be filled with lawlessness, rebellion, and a demanding, clamorous cry for independence from every established moral norm. This lawlessness is spreading like gangrene

---

[94] Abraham Kuyper Quotes, "Christian Quotes," *ochristian.com*, http://christian-quotes.ochristian .com/Abraham-Kuyper-Quotes/.
[95] Watchman Nee, *Spiritual Authority* (New York: Christian Fellowship Publishers, 1972), p. 14.

in society today — and it has scattered its poison so widespread that we are now even living in a season when some children insist that their parents have no legal right to exercise parental authority over them! In some cases, parents who have endeavored to teach their convictions to their own children have been thrust into the legal jeopardy of having their children removed from their homes. Indeed, in certain Western countries, schoolteachers have observed parents teaching their own moral code to their children — and, as a result, those parents have had their children taken away from them. Scriptural parental influence is being contorted to implicate child abuse in these nations!

Who would have imagined that such nonsense could rule the thoughts of so many! But because rebellion is running rampant against every established form of authority, there is disrespect and dishonor for the authority of government, parents, police, and pastors — truly against nearly every facet of established authority.

Renowned British scholar and pastor John Stott said, "The modern world detests authority...." This is precisely what we are witnessing as we draw closer to the end of the age. The trend to throw off all forms of authority has reached such epic proportions that escalating numbers of people do not even want to accept the authority of biological anatomy — causing many to even rebel against their birth gender!

Rebellion to Authority — A Sign of the End Times

One day on the Mount of Olives, Jesus enumerated signs that would be evident as the age reaches its end. One sign Christ gave was that "iniquity would abound" before the end of the present age (*see* Matthew 24:12).

The word "iniquity" is a translation of the Greek word *anomia*. It is a form of the word *nomos*, which is the Greek word for *law*, used to depict *the standard of what is legally or morally correct*. But when an *"a"* is attached to the front of this word (the plural form in this case), it becomes *anomia*. That *a* has a *cancelling* effect. So rather than depict *law* or *a correct moral standard*, the word *anomia* holds the opposite meaning — that is, *without law*, *lawless*, or *no moral standard* — and it pictures *people who possess no fixed moral standards*.

Those who live this way are *void of standards*, *without law*, and *living in a state of lawlessness*. This word in Matthew 24:12 tells us that society will discard all age-old, biblically agreed-upon moral absolutes at the very end of the age. It will be a day when people will throw off authority as rebellion reaches a zenith in the heart of society in an end-time world.

In Second Thessalonians 2:3, Paul wrote about this when he said, "Let no man deceive you by any means: for that day shall not come, except there come a *falling away* first...." The words "falling away" come from the Greek word *apostasia*, a word that is also used in the Old Testament Greek Septuagint to depict *mutiny against authority*.

Paul used this word in this verse to explicitly depict a world-wide society in the end of the age that will be engaged in outright mutiny against the authority of God in the last of the last days. (In my book *How To Keep Your Head on Straight in a World Gone Crazy*, this is discussed in greater detail.) This end-time mutiny against God's authority — and against all previously established moral codes — is the reason that today we are seeing so many nonsensical developments in society. All restraints are being thrown off, and society is galloping on a collision course with the end of a lawless age. The closer we get to the end, this world will sink deeper and deeper into deception and depravity as it reaps the full harvest of disrespect for authority that began as a "first seed" in the Garden with Adam and Eve.

In Second Thessalonians 2:7, Paul stated that the "mystery of iniquity" would become an aggressive force in society at the very end of the age. This "mystery of iniquity" has been released with a vengeance and is working full steam in our age because we are nearing the end. The widespread disrespect for authority emerging in society is a sign that we are reaching the cusp of this end-time age. As Christians, we must be awakened to what God says about authority so we do not fall prey to the spirit of the age. Just because the world wanders astray does *not* mean we should wander with it.

The closer we get to the end, this world will sink
deeper and deeper into deception and depravity
as it reaps the full harvest of disrespect
for authority that began as a "first seed"
in the Garden with Adam and Eve.

Many years ago, I wondered what Peter and Jude were referring to when they wrote that people at the end of the age would engage in speaking "evil" against authorities (2 Peter 2:11,12; Jude 1:9,10). The word "evil" is a translation of the Greek word *blasphemeo,* which signifies *derogatory behavior that involves nasty, shameful, or disrespectful speech.* In these verses, Peter and Jude state that even angels do not dare to speak disrespectfully to established authorities — yet at the end of the age, people will dare to do what even angels will not do. In other words, a full venting of disrespect will be unleashed in society as people engage in railing against all forms of established authority.

As Christians, we must be awakened to what God says about authority so we do not fall prey to the spirit of the age. Just because the world wanders astray does *not* mean we should wander with it.

Friend, we are living in an hour when this is taking place. None of this is news to those of us who have been keeping up with the constant stream of ugly political discourse that populates our TV screens, computers, or mobile devices. Has there ever been a time in our age when political parties and various warring ideologies have been more uncivil? The public behavior of politicians and political parties has taken a steep downward slide from the days of respectful disagreement to a current ugly mess of intolerance and mudslinging. Add to that a widespread weaponizing of the media to perpetuate this indecent assault, and a clear example of the enemy's end-time strategy is revealed. People are railing against every imaginable position of authority, using every possible means of communication to bring a public platform to their fleshly rant.

Those who are in positions of authority today are under assault, and we must undergird them with prayer. From the highest to the lowest levels of authority — from the President, to our congressmen and senators, state governors, city mayors, police, schoolteachers, parents, and pastors — uncivil behavior is being unleashed in these end times on a ferocious scale. The fact is, we are living in a time prophesied by Jesus when a lost world — and often even a Church affected by the spirit of the age — will rebel against every form of established authority.

Everything you have read so far in this chapter is foundational to what you are about to read in its remaining pages. We will now turn our focus to *spiritual authority*. Here I'm referring to spiritual leaders in both the local church and in ministry beyond the walls of the local church. It's so important that we study what the Bible says about how God expects us to respond to our spiritual leaders, because where their authority is absent or sidestepped, spiritual confusion and chaos result. On the other hand, where spiritual authority is respected and honored, it brings a supernatural blessing to God's people.

Those who are in positions
of authority today are under assault,
and we must undergird them with prayer.

SPIRITUAL AUTHORITY

As believers — as followers of Jesus Christ — we are people who are under authority to Him first. Christ is the ultimate authority. In fact, submitting our lives to His authority is so fundamental that it is actually a requirement for any person to receive salvation. The apostle Paul made this clear in Romans 10:9:

> **If thou shalt confess with thy mouth the Lord Jesus, and shalt believe in thine heart that God hath raised him from the dead, thou shalt be saved.**

The word "Lord" in this verse is a translation of the Greek word *kurios*, which expresses the idea of *One who has ultimate and supreme authority in another's life.* This means our entrance into the Kingdom of God and our relationship with Christ are rooted in submission to His absolute authority.

Noted Christian author Elisabeth Elliot wrote, "Until the will and the affections are brought under the authority of Christ, we have not begun to understand, let alone to accept, His lordship."[96] When we recognize Jesus as Lord, we surrender to obey Him as the Supreme Master. We agree that we are continually submitting completely to His unquestionable authority and that we have yielded every realm of our lives — our will, emotions, passions, the way we conduct our lives — to His management, direction, and control. This is a spiritual commitment we make that leaves *no* part of our lives untouched by His authority.

When you are aligned under the authority of Christ, you become like a pipe that is cleared of all rubble and rubbish — a channel through which power can flow from Christ through you to the world around you. As we continue to discuss what is required to stay ablaze for God, it is essential for you to understand this key truth: *If you want the power and fire of God to flow through you, it is imperative that you are aligned under Christ's absolute authority.*

If anything in your life is out of alignment with Christ's rightful position of authority over you, it will disrupt the flow of Heaven through you into the earth. Hence, you must constantly be reassessing to make sure every area of life is aligned under Christ's authority. If you discover that any area is out of sync with Christ, you must put your attention to that area until it is back in divine alignment.

---

[96] Tyler Elliott, "In Memory of Elizabeth Elliott: 30 of Her Most Inspiring Quotes," *Logos Talk*, https://blog.logos.com/2015/06/in-memory-of-elisabeth-elliot-30-of-her-most- inspiring-quotes/.

When you are aligned under the authority of Christ,
you become like a pipe that is cleared of all rubble and
rubbish — a channel through which power can flow
from Christ through you to the world around you.

If you study the book of Acts, it will become quickly evident
to you that early believers understood spiritual authority and were
in submission to it. We read in Acts 2:42, "And they continued
steadfastly in the apostles' doctrine and fellowship, and in breaking of bread, and in prayers."

As noted in earlier chapters, the Greek word translated "steadfastly" means *to persevere consistently*. It carries the idea of *very
intense focus and hard work*. This tells us that when the early believers came together in those early meetings, they intentionally set
their hearts to listen and to learn from the apostles' teaching and
preaching the Word of God to them. The word for "steadfastly"
carries a strong meaning, actually signifying that those early
believers were *addicted* to the spiritual authority of the apostles to
the extent that they gathered to hear and receive from them every
day (*see* Acts 2:46).

The apostles themselves learned about spiritual authority by
their own submission to Jesus as they walked with Him. In the
King James Version of the New Testament, the 12 apostles are
often referred to as "disciples." This is a translation of the Greek
word *mathetes*, a word that depicts *a student who is in complete
submission to a teacher who has a master's influence in his life*. In
fact, the teacher has such a role of mastery in the life of a true
disciple that the disciple is bound to obey anything the teacher
requires.

So when we read of the apostles being Jesus' *disciples*, it means they both *followed* and *obeyed* Jesus and were committed to explicitly following His teachings and doing His bidding. All of these were requirements for a person to be a disciple. In other words, they were not mere followers — these were committed disciples who explicitly followed *whatever* Jesus asked of them.

This explains why Jesus told them, "Ye call me Master and Lord: and ye say well; for so I am" (John 13:13). The word "Lord" used in this verse is also the word *kurios*, which again expresses the idea of *One who has ultimate and supreme authority in one's life*. By making this statement, Jesus affirmed that the disciples literally called Him *kurios* — "Lord." And every time they called Him Lord, they were acknowledging who Jesus was in their lives.

Jesus was their Supreme Master. You could say that each of the 12 disciples was called to play his part alongside Him in the great symphony produced by His ministry — but Jesus was the indisputable Conductor who directed every step and every note they played. They were submitted to Jesus' authority and were committed to do anything and everything He ever asked of them. And because they were in submission to Him so completely, divine power was released to magnificently flow from Christ through them!

When Judas Iscariot decided to rebel against Christ's authority and go a different direction, he was eliminated from the team. To remain a viable part of Jesus' first team of 12 required total devotion, submission, and respect for the spiritual authority and leadership that God had entrusted Him to exercise over the disciples.

> The disciples were submitted to Jesus' authority and were committed to do anything and everything He ever asked of them. And because they were in submission to Him so completely, divine power was released to magnificently flow from Christ through them!

This is what the word "Lord" meant 2,000 years ago — and that is what the word "Lord" still means today for you and me. This means that every time you call Jesus the "Lord" of your life, you are saying: "You have absolute authority in my life, and I am submitted to You. I will obey whatever You will ever ask me to do. I am Your servant to command!"

So when the first 12 apostles — the "disciples" — called Jesus the "Lord and Master" of their lives, they literally meant that He was *Lord* and *Master* and they were His servants to command. Jesus was not an optional authority in their lives. He was the *ultimate* spiritual authority, and they were in complete submission to whatever being under His authority required of them.

Jesus was *over* the apostles; they were *under* Him; and they *obeyed* Him explicitly. And as a result of the apostles' submission to Jesus' spiritual authority, they would reap powerful benefits, both in this life and in the one to come.

LOCAL SPIRITUAL AUTHORITY

What was true for Jesus and the 12 was transferred to the entire Early Church as it was being established under spiritual authority. Again, Acts 2:42 states, "And they continued steadfastly in the apostles' doctrine...." This tells us that early believers really set their hearts to listen, to learn, and to be in submission to the spiritual authority of the apostles. Those early believers understood spiritual authority; in a real sense, they were addicted to it. And as a result, they were established in the power of God.

And today Christ — who is every believer's ultimate authority — continues to carry out His lordship over the Church, largely through the spiritual authority He has established *inside* the Church to help Him. The spiritual authority to which I refer are those whom He has called and anointed to lead the Church in various capacities.

These are leaders who have real voices that we can audibly hear and who are visible for us to see and to follow. Among those with spiritual authority are apostles, prophets, evangelists, pastors, and teachers — and any whom these leaders have chosen to work alongside them. All such leaders are to be in complete submission to Jesus as the supreme Head of the Church.

We as believers are going to produce the results God desires as we learn how to work with those whom God has set over us as our spiritual authority. When we are aligned under Christ's authority — and under the local spiritual authority He has set over us — that alignment enables us to be channels through which God's power can freely flow. On the other hand, if we are out of sync with God's established system, spiritual debris can accumulate to clog the channel, disrupt the flow of God's power, and ultimately snuff out our spiritual fire.

Consider again the illustration of a symphony. We must learn to play our part well according to the direction of the spiritual conductors to whom God assigns us. As we willingly recognize and respect our conductors' authority and follow their direction, we become part of a great symphony that produces a powerful, blended sound in the accomplishing of God's plan.

But we will produce the opposite effect if we ignore the direction of those God has called to lead the orchestra. If we become rebellious and choose to sidestep their spiritual authority and stay out of sync with their leadership, our unharmonious behavior will produce a discordant sound with detrimental consequences to us personally, to the others in the orchestra, and to the Kingdom of God.

If we are out of sync with God's established system,
spiritual debris can accumulate to clog the channel,
disrupt the flow of God's power,
and ultimately snuff out our spiritual fire.

A Lesson From Hebrews 13:7

As mentioned earlier, submission to authority is an inescapable part of life. This also includes submission to spiritual authority, which is a requirement for every Christian who intends to be a true disciple.

If we want to stay in sync with the ways of God's Kingdom and stay ablaze in our walk with Him, it is essential that we willingly submit to those whom He has established to exercise spiritual authority in our lives. In Hebrews 13:7, the Bible gives us guidelines to help us recognize who our spiritual leaders are and how we are to relate to them:

Remember them which have the rule over you, who have spoken unto you the word of God: whose faith follow, considering the end of their conversation.

The word "rule" tells us how to recognize those with spiritual authority over us. It is a translation of the Greek word *hegeomai*, which describes *one who has a leading or visible position of influence in your life*. In this context, it specifically describes those who have a visible position of spiritual authority or leadership. This tells us that those who have spiritual authority must be individuals with *significant influence* in our lives.

It is important to note here that no one is a perfect leader. However, those with spiritual authority over others must be those who allow the Holy Spirit to take them ever further, higher, and deeper in their walk with God. This is why Christian writer J. Oswald Sanders wrote, "A true leader influences others spiritually only because the Spirit works in and through him to a greater degree than in those he leads."[97]

Of course, this isn't to say that a younger, less seasoned spiritual leader might not be placed in authority over those who are more experienced in their walk with God. One whom God sets in authority may be younger or still growing in spiritual maturity compared to some of his more seasoned congregants — but that doesn't make him any less their leader. Spiritual authority is not about age — it's about assignment. It's about the spiritual stature a God-called leader carries and the anointing of the Holy Spirit that he operates in. It's about the giftings God equips him with to fulfill that divine call and the character he allows the Holy Spirit to cultivate within him to wisely steward that call.

The next element I want you to see in Hebrews 13:7 is the wording that describes these leaders as those who have "spoken unto you the word of God." This also points out that those whom God has sent to be a spiritual authority in your life are those who are tasked with regularly speaking the Word of God to you. It

---

[97] J. Oswald Sanders, *Spiritual Leadership* (Chicago: Moody Publishers, 1994), p. 28.

speaks of those who teach, preach, and instruct you most regularly in the Word of God. This means the one who has your ear is the one who has influence in your life.

But the scripture goes on to say that these must be those whose faith you are confident to "follow." The word "follow" is a translation of the Greek word *mimeomai*, which implies *an intentional study of the life, deeds, actions, and thoughts of another person in an attempt to fully understand that person and then to imitate or duplicate his attributes in one's own life.*

In other words, you should be so impressed by the faith and godly character of the spiritual leader who has your ear that you are willing to do whatever that person does to be *like* him or her! If you don't respect that leader enough to replicate his or her life of faith and character, you need to stop and find out why.

First examine yourself and make sure that the problem with lack of respect doesn't lie with *you*, the follower. But if your heart is clear in the matter and you still conclude that the leader's life in God and before man is not an example you desire to replicate in your own life, my question to you would be this: Why are you still committed to that church or still connected to that spiritual leader? If you can't respect that leader's life enough to replicate his or her example in your own walk with God, then that leader doesn't qualify to be a spiritual authority in your life.

A real God-given spiritual authority in your life will be a person whom you desire to follow and to imitate. In fact, Hebrews 13:7 says you are to "consider the end of their conversation."

The word "consider" means *to earnestly contemplate, to observe accurately,* or *to consider well.* The word "end" is a translation of the Greek word *ekbasis,* which literally describes how a person *steps forward* or *makes progress in life.* In essence, then, Hebrews 13:7 warns you *to earnestly contemplate, observe carefully, and consider well the way those who lead you are making progress in their own lives.* In other words, before you commit to submitting to these leaders' spiritual authority, look at their lives to make sure that what they are is what you want to be. You are to follow only those who have a faith and a life worthy of imitation!

There are no perfect leaders, so please don't look for one. Nevertheless, as you seek those whom God has assigned to have spiritual authority in your life, Hebrews 13:7 instructs you to look for those who have godly fruit in their lives — the very kind of fruit you want to see replicated in your own life. Do you respect them enough to replicate them? You should only be in submission to leaders whose lives you respect and whose faith you want to follow and imitate.

A KEY TO RECOGNIZING YOUR SPIRITUAL AUTHORITY

To emphasize the importance of selecting healthy spiritual leadership to exercise spiritual authority over your life, Hebrews 13:17 goes on to say:

> **Obey them that have the rule over you, and submit yourselves: for they watch for your souls, as they that must give an account, that they may do it with joy, and not with grief: for that is unprofitable for you.**

Notice again that the word "rule" also appears in this verse! It is again the Greek word *hegeomai,* the same word used in verse 7, which describes *one who has a leading or visible position of influence in your life.* By repeating this twice, God makes it abundantly clear that a true spiritual authority and leader in your life is whoever holds the greatest and most visible position of spiritual influence over you. When you are fully aware of who that person or that group of people is, Hebrews 13:17 says you are to "*obey* them that have the rule over you."

The word "obey" used in this verse is a form of the Greek word *peitho*, which depicts one who has become *convinced, coaxed,* or *swayed from one opinion to the opinion held by another.* It pictures *confidence.* It depicts *a rock-solid certainty.* This word is used to tell us that we need to have rock-solid certainty about who is supposed to hold a position of spiritual authority in our lives and to whom we are to be in submission. This is a very important issue, and we must each come to a place where we are *assured* that we are in submission to the correct person or persons. Then once that assurance is obtained, we are to submit to our spiritual leaders (*see* Hebrews 13:7).

This is such a key fuel in sustaining a life that remains ablaze for Christ. Yet submitting oneself to a God-ordained spiritual authority is a difficult subject for many to hear in this modern age. Today people generally do not want to be in submission to anyone's rule or to any established order.

We need to have rock-solid certainty about who
is supposed to hold a position of spiritual authority
in our lives and to whom we are to be
in submission. Then once that assurance
is obtained, we are to submit to our spiritual leaders.

Nevertheless, this word "submit" is clearly here in this verse. It is the Greek word *hupeiko*, and it means *to yield.* The use of this word indicates that submitting to spiritual authority is *voluntary*. But let's take our study of this word a little deeper.

The word *hupeiko* is a compound of the words *hupo* and *eiko*. The word *hupo* means *under*, and the word *eiko* means *to yield*, such as *a deliberate yielding of military forces to their commanders*. When *hupo* and *eiko* are compounded to form the word *hupeiko*, the new word depicts an individual who has willingly *placed himself under* authority, such as a soldier who understands that he is under the authority and the watchful eye of a commanding officer.

A soldier may not enjoy his commanding officer's personality or the orders he gives, but that is irrelevant. No soldier is required to *like* his officers — he is expected only to respect and to honor them. Whether or not the soldier likes the situation, the fact remains that the officer is *over* him and the soldier is *under* the officer. To disrespect a commanding officer is always out of order, and punishment follows such an attitude very quickly. This is so basic that every soldier early on learns how he is to relate to those in authority over him.

This illustration is important when we discuss the New Testament word "submit," for this example borrowed from a military environment is precisely the meaning of the word "submit" in the New Testament. Submission to authority occurs when a person respectfully recognizes his position under the leadership of one placed in authority over him — whether at work, at school, at church, at home, or in any other sphere of life.

But Hebrews 13:17 gives us another way to recognize those who hold a position of spiritual authority. Besides identifying the leaders whose lives are worthy of imitation (*see* Hebrews 13:7), you are given another way to recognize those who hold a position of spiritual authority over you in Hebrews 13:17. It says they are the ones who "watch for your souls." The word "watch" describes *constant watchfulness.* It pictures someone who is mindful about someone else. Christian leader and author J. Oswald Sanders said, "The true leader is concerned primarily with the welfare of others, not with his own comfort or prestige."[98] I cannot think of a more fitting word to describe one with spiritual authority in someone else's life.

The one to whom you submit spiritually should be one who carries an abiding sense of responsibility for you. If the leader doesn't have that sense of responsibility, he probably doesn't believe he is spiritually responsible for you in the way Scripture prescribes. Hebrews 13:17 says those with spiritual authority over your life "must give an account" to God. The words "give an account" mean *to give a full report* or *to be answerable to a superior.* This means that just as you will personally answer for how well you have followed those God has entrusted to have authority in your life, those He has called to lead you spiritually will also give account to Jesus Christ for the way they lead you!

"The true leader is concerned primarily with the welfare of others, not with his own comfort or prestige."
— *J. Oswald Sanders*

But Hebrews 13:17 also says that people can be a "grief" to lead. In fact, this verse commands you and me to obey and voluntarily submit to our spiritual leaders with joy so that the situation will not turn out to be a "grief" for those who are leading.

---

[98] J. Oswald Sanders, *Spiritual Leadership: Principles of Excellence for Every Believer* (Chicago: Moody Publisher, 1967, 2007).

The word "grief" is a translation of the Greek word *stenadzo*, which depicts *a groaning* or *a moaning*. What does this mean? Let me explain using firsthand experience.

There are some people God has asked me to lead who are difficult to lead because they do not yield or follow very well. They argue, challenge, fight, and rebuff those who are trying to help them. People who fit this description can be a "grief" to cover with spiritual authority.

Does the person God has assigned to hold spiritual authority in your life avoid you when he sees you? If so, let me tell you that this is not a good sign for you. In fact, Hebrews 13:17 goes on to say that if you nurture an inappropriate attitude toward that person's spiritual authority, it will be "unprofitable" for you. The word "unprofitable" means that your wrong attitude toward spiritual authority *will not be in your best interest.*

This issue of spiritual authority is vital to your spiritual health, to the strength of the Church, and to the strength of each individual believer who makes up the Church. Every person needs to be under spiritual authority. There is a miraculous mutual exchange of strength that occurs in such relationships.

AN EAR TO HEAR THE ONE WHO LEADS

One of the names the Bible calls Jesus is the *Good Shepherd* (*see* John 10:11), and He likewise refers to us as His *sheep*. In John 10:3 and 4, the "shepherd-sheep" relationship we have with Jesus is depicted. An important part of those verses say, "…The sheep hear his voice…and the sheep follow him: for they know his voice." In John 10:5, it adds, "And a stranger will they not follow, but will flee from him: for they know not the voice of strangers."

These verses teach that Jesus is the Shepherd and we are His sheep. As a part of His flock, we know the Good Shepherd's voice and will not follow any voice that is *not* His. In these verses, Jesus wanted us to truly grasp this "shepherd-sheep" concept, so He restated this principle throughout chapter 10. For instance, in John 10:14, He said, "I am the good shepherd, and know my sheep, and am known of mine." Then in John 10:27, He reaffirmed it when he said, "My sheep hear my voice, and I know them, and they follow me." In these verses, there is a principle about the "shepherd-sheep" relationship that will help you know who is supposed to exercise spiritual authority in your life.

In the natural world, sheep know the voice of their shepherd and do not follow the voice of anyone who is not their shepherd. Jesus used this principle to teach that believers are a lot like sheep and that there are spiritual leaders who have a shepherding influence in their lives. When the shepherd speaks, it is easy for the flock to follow him because the sheep relate to their shepherd and are tuned to hear his voice.

Christ is the Great Shepherd, and these undershepherds — spiritual authorities and leaders — are to guide those whom He has entrusted to them in their respective leadership assignments. God has given each believer an "ear" to hear whom they are supposed to be following.

For example, there are people who hear me at our church, who watch me on television, who read my books, and who deeply appreciate and respect me because they are supernaturally drawn to me. God has assigned these people to me, and they hear and follow my voice because God has appointed me to be a spiritual authority in their lives. But there are others who are *not* drawn to me because God has selected someone else to lead them and to have spiritual authority in their lives.

> God has given each believer an "ear" to hear
> whom they are supposed to be following.

God supernaturally connects people to mutually benefit each other. This is God's desire for all of His children — including you. He has called you to "be planted in the house of the Lord" and "flourish in the courts of our God" (Psalm 92:13). To be "planted" and "flourishing" is one of the greatest blessings of submitting to the spiritual authority under which God places you. If you do not have a spiritual authority to whom you are submitted, it is time you seek the Lord in prayer to direct and connect you with His choice for your spiritual leader.

IT'S TIME TO BE ABLAZE
WITH RIGHT RELATIONSHIP TO AUTHORITY

The issue of authority affects every one of us. At every age and stage of our lives, God has placed those over us to whom we are called and required to submit. From the cradle to old age, there will always be someone somewhere telling us what we need to do. So it's up to us to learn how to submit to, to be agreement with, and to cultivate appreciation for those God has placed over us.

It's so important for us to cultivate a passion for positioning ourselves correctly under divinely appointed authority. This is vital fuel for the Church and for each individual believer to stay strong and ignited for God both now and for generations to come.

If you are going to be on fire and stay on fire, you must learn how to come under the spiritual authority that God has established for your life. This is one reason why the Early Church experienced such power and spiritual fire! And now at the end of the age, God wants every believer — and this includes you and the church God has called you to be a part of — to come under the lordship of Christ and under the local spiritual authority whom He has sent to be a blessing.

It's so important for us to cultivate a passion
for positioning ourselves correctly
under divinely appointed authority.

Jesus required this type of "leader-disciple" relationship with His disciples, and they passed on the necessity of this divine order to the Early Church. Where there is proper functioning of spiritual authority, blessings flow today, just as they did then. Now at the end of the age — when lawlessness in society is throwing off all forms of authority and is screaming for independence — God is calling His people to come back into alignment with spiritual authority. He knows that when His house is in order, increase will come, promotion will come, protection will come, and provision will come — and the Church will come ablaze with the power and the fire of God!

THINK ABOUT IT

1. Authority establishes order. Order makes way for a peaceful and effectual existence. Lack of respect for authority results in chaos, which is the exact opposite of anything made by God. Amos 3:3 asks, "How can two walk together except they be agreed?" The harmony of agreement is achieved by the acceptance of authority. If you are going to be on fire and *stay* on fire, you must learn how to come under the spiritual authority God has established for your life.

   First of all, are you in complete submission to supreme authority — the lordship of Christ? Second, have you willingly positioned yourself — in attitude of heart, as well as in outward action — under the spiritual authority God has sent to be a blessing to you? Your relationship with and submission to spiritual authority is vital if you are to stay strong and on fire for the Lord both now and in the perilous times to come.

2. If anything in your life is out of alignment with Christ's rightful position of spiritual authority over you, it will disrupt the flow of Heaven through you into the earth.

   Do you make a regular practice of reassessing and course-correcting to make sure every area of your life is in proper alignment under the authority of Christ and His Word? Is there an area of your life that you recognize is out of sync with Him? How do you plan to rectify that area?

3. Are you assured that you are positioned under the appropriate spiritual authority for your life? Does that leader have your

attention to the degree that you are willing to do whatever that person does in order to be like him as he follows Christ?

Does the spiritual authority in your life demonstrate a constant watchfulness for your soul in prayer and in the preaching and teaching of the Word to secure your welfare? Does he or she express an abiding sense of responsibility to "give an account" to God for your life? And for your part — do you keep watch over actions, words, and heart attitudes so as not to give your spiritual leader grief by being difficult to feed spiritually or to lead in the ways of righteousness?

Remember, Jesus Christ, the Great Shepherd of the sheep, is paying close attention to the way those in authority lead — as well as to the way those in submission choose to follow.

CHAPTER 11

ABLAZE WITH THE FEAR
OF THE LORD

One thing is sure — God wants you to be a spiritual inferno that drives back darkness and brings warmth and light to the people who are around you. But as we've discussed throughout this book, you need spiritual fuel to keep your spiritual fire burning, just as a real fire needs fuel to keep burning continuously.

In this last chapter, I want to share a final type of fuel that needs to be injected into your spiritual fire to keep you burning for God till you finish your race on this earth. But before we explore the last fuel that will be discussed in this book, I first want to recap the nine fuels we have looked at so far that will help you keep your spiritual fire burning brightly for the rest of your life.

In previous chapters, we have seen that to stay on fire for God for years to come, we must be:

- Ablaze with God's Word
- Ablaze with prayer
- Ablaze with the Holy Spirit
- Ablaze with worship
- Ablaze with souls
- Ablaze with generosity
- Ablaze with holiness
- Ablaze with humility
- Ablaze under authority

As you ponder this theme of spiritual fuels, I'm sure you might think of other fuels that could be added to the list. But the last fuel I wish to insert into the conversation is the need for each of us to be ablaze with *the fear of the Lord*.

In Ecclesiastes 12:13 and 14, Solomon wrote, "Let us hear the conclusion of the whole matter: Fear God, and keep his commandments: for this is the whole duty of man. For God shall bring every work into judgment, with every secret thing, whether it be good, or whether it be evil."

According to Solomon, it is the *duty* of every believer to fear God. The need to *fear the Lord* is so important that the Scriptures command us to do it more than 300 times in various ways throughout the Old and New Testaments. And those who *do* fear the Lord are given great promises. For instance, Psalm 31:19 says, "Oh how great is thy goodness, which thou hast laid up for them that fear thee...."

The following represents a small sampling of amazing Bible promises for those who fear the Lord:

- Those who fear the Lord will be *greatly blessed* (*see* Psalm 112:1).

- Those who fear the Lord will find Him to be their *help and shield to protect them* in times of trouble (*see* Psalm 115:11).

- Those who fear the Lord will have *confidence*; their children will find a place of *refuge*; and they will have *a fountain of life* (*see* Proverbs 14:26,27).

- Those who fear the Lord will experience *riches, honor,* and *life* (*see* Proverbs 22:4).

This issue of *fearing the Lord* is of such importance that Psalm 147:10,11 tells us, "His [God's] delight is not in the strength of the horse, nor his pleasure in the legs of a man, but the Lord takes pleasure in those who fear him, in those who hope in his steadfast love."

According to this verse, when a person possesses a healthy fear of the Lord, God takes pleasure in him and ensures that this person experiences His steadfast love.

When the fear of God holds a healthy place in our lives, it *protects us* from sin, it *keeps us* from wrong behaviors, and it *saves us* from the effects of bad choices. When we have a healthy fear of the Lord, it *liberates us* from the fear of many things in life that would steal our peace. As Oswald Chambers wrote, "The remarkable thing about God is that when you fear God, you fear nothing else, whereas if you do not fear God, you fear everything else."[99] Charles Spurgeon made a similar statement years earlier when he wrote, "He who fears God has nothing else to fear."[100]

---

[99] W. K. Volkmer, *These Things: A Reference Manual for Discipleship* (San Antonio, TX: The Passionate Few, 2016), p. 38.
[100] C. H. Spurgeon, ed., *The Sword and the Trowel* (London Metrop. Tabernacle, 1867), p. 85.

When the fear of God holds a healthy place in our lives,
it *protects us* from sin, it *keeps us* from wrong behaviors,
and it *saves us* from the effects of bad choices.

But as important as the subject of the fear of the Lord is, it is also one of the most misunderstood. In his book, *The Fear of the Lord*, author John Bevere wrote, "Holy fear is the key to God's sure foundation, unlocking the treasuries of salvation, wisdom, and knowledge. Along with the love of God, it composes the very foundation of life.... We cannot truly love God until we fear Him, nor can we properly fear Him until we love Him."[101] (I highly recommend that you read John Bevere's book, *The Fear of the Lord*. It is an excellent resource on this subject that is so vital to our lives.)

WHAT IS THE FEAR OF THE LORD?

Many people struggle with the word "fear" in connection with the Lord; consequently, many Bible teachers and spiritual leaders have altered the phrase "the *fear* of the Lord" to "the *respect* for the Lord." I understand why many have done this. Pastors and spiritual leaders feel compelled to encourage people to *draw near* to the Lord, and it is difficult to draw near to a God one fears. So to stop people from running from God, spiritual leaders have replaced the word "fear" with "respect."

But although "respect" is *part* of the fear of the Lord, this word doesn't embody the full meaning of what the Bible refers to when it speaks of the *fear* of the Lord. There actually is a healthy fear of God, and as we will see in this final chapter — having a

---

[101] John Bevere, *The Fear of the Lord* (Lake Mary, FL: Charisma House, 1997, 2006), p. 3.

healthy fear of the Lord is something we all need to keep our spiritual fire burning!

Often Christians are fearful of what other people might *think* of them or of others' opinions or disapproval of what they are *doing*. In fact, Christians are often more concerned about what *people* think than they are of what the *Lord* thinks. This is why American theologian and author, Kevin DeYoung, wrote, "There is no sin so prevalent, so insidious, and so deep as the sin of fearing people more than we fear God."[102]

I am concerned that within the modern Church, in our efforts to compel people to draw near to a loving Heavenly Father (which God absolutely *is*), we have forgotten to bring the whole counsel of who He is to them. God is also a consuming fire who deals seriously with sin when it is in His household. Even though He has given the Holy Spirit to help His children overcome sin and evil, Christians invite negative consequences when they violate spiritual laws or willfully cooperate with sin or evil. This doesn't change the fact that He is a loving Heavenly Father, but He is also holy and He calls His people to live holy lives.

We have focused so much on the mercy and the love of God that we have failed to communicate the truth that negative consequences occur when we do wrong in His sight. Although we may be concerned about what others think of our actions or of their opinions about us, there are no eyes more important than God's eyes, and His eyes are on us all the time. First Peter 3:12 plainly says the eyes of the Lord are ever over us, and Hebrews 4:13 says everything we do is open and visible to God's eyes. When we do what is right, we please Him — but when we do what is wrong in

---

[102] Kevin DeYoung quote, "Best God-Fearing Quotes and Sayings," *Quotes Sayings*, https://quotessayings.net/topics/best-god-fearing/.

His sight, although He loves us, He is *not* pleased. And if we *persist* in those wrong behaviors, it will have negative consequences.

In our efforts to compel people to draw near
to a loving Heavenly Father (which God absolutely *is*),
we have forgotten to bring the whole counsel
of who He is to them.

Never forget that we serve a holy God who calls us to be holy. This is why First Peter 1:15-17 says, "But as he which hath called you is holy, so be ye holy in all manner of conversation; Because it is written, Be ye holy; for I am holy. And if ye call on the Father, who without respect of persons judgeth according to every man's work, pass the time of your sojourning *here* in fear...."

Notice that in the verse above, Peter wrote that God calls us to be holy in all manner of conversation. The word "conversation" is a translation of the Greek word *anastrophe*, which means *lifestyle* or *conduct*. It refers to a person's total conduct — rising up, sitting down, going in, going out — a total picture of one's life and behavior.

This means every aspect of our lives should reflect the holiness of God. But as Peter continued, he wrote, "And if ye call on the Father, who without respect of persons judgeth according to every man's work, pass the time of your sojourning here in fear...." In other words, Peter was saying, *"If you call on God as your Heavenly Father, that does not exempt you from consequences. You need to be serious about the way you live your lives."* The word "fear" in this verse depicts the need for us to take a *serious approach* to life and to conduct ourselves with the realization that *how we live has consequences.*

How well we conduct our lives and live in obedience to God's commands should be a concern for each of us. Why should we fear what others might think, yet not be concerned about what *God* thinks of our actions and attitudes? In the Church's attempt to make God approachable to people, Christians have diluted their concept of His holiness and their accountability to Him to live holy lives — to the point that holiness has been depreciated and nearly lost in the minds of many believers. Thus, many Christians conduct their lives in ways that are clearly displeasing to God with nearly no conviction about it.

Having a healthy fear of God is a very good thing, not a bad thing.

Why should we fear what others might think,
yet not be concerned about what *God*
thinks of our actions and attitudes?

In Psalm 34:11, the Psalmist wrote, "Come, ye children, hearken unto me: *I will teach you the fear of the Lord.*" This verse says we must be *taught* the fear of the Lord. The verses listed previously tell us that when we fear the Lord, we position ourselves to experience an abundant, long, and blessed life. Hence, we can conclude that if we want to see these types of blessings overtake us, the necessary prerequisite is to live with a healthy fear of the Lord.

But people struggle with the word "fear" in connection with the Lord. I understand this completely. Why should they fear the One who has washed them by the blood of His Son, forgiven and empowered them by His grace, and accepted them in the Beloved?

When we fear the Lord, we position ourselves
to experience an abundant, long, and blessed life.

When you search the meaning of the word "fear" in the dictionary, it is defined as *a distressing emotion aroused by impending danger*. My thesaurus gives these alternative words for "fear": *dread, anxiety, horror, distress, fright, panic, alarm, trepidation*, and *apprehension*. That is a terrible list of words! No one wants to experience dread, anxiety, horror, distress, fright, panic, alarm, trepidation, and apprehension in their relationship with God! *But does the Bible really mean that?*

To seek clarity, I turned to the Hebrew lexicon to obtain the Hebrew meaning of the word "fear" as it is used in context of the phrase "the fear of the Lord" in the Old Testament. Guess what I found? The word "fear" in the Hebrew Old Testament used in connection with *the fear of the Lord* means *fear, terror*, or *dread*!

But making this even more intriguing is First John 4:18, which tells us that if anyone is in Christ, he is perfected in the love of God and that this perfect love casts out fear. So if we are perfected in the love of God, as the Bible teaches, why then should we fear the Lord the way hundreds of verses in the Bible instruct us to do? And what in the world does the Bible mean when it tells us we are to possess a healthy *fear of the Lord*?

CONSEQUENCES ARE INEVITABLE

Let me help you understand the fear of the Lord with the following explanation. It is simply a fact that life has rules. If a person violates those rules, he will suffer consequences. For example, if a young person disrespects his parents or any other authority figure in his life, he will inevitably reap the negative results of disrespect toward authority. If a person disrespects the law — if he ignores it or tries to sidestep it — he will eventually get caught and pay the penalty for his disrespect.

Such a person gets a rude awakening when he learns from experience that the same police who are assigned to protect him are the very ones who also will arrest him for breaking the law. Violating any law or authority has consequences. (*See* Chapter 10, "Ablaze Under Authority.")

It is simply a fact that wrong behavior and wrong decisions eventually result in negative consequences. Should this knowledge of potential consequences make you afraid of living your life? Of course not! There is no reason to be afraid *unless* you are living your life contrary to God's spiritual laws found in His Word. In that case, you need to wake up and make a change to avoid negative repercussions of your poor choices. Understanding the spiritual law motivates you to make wiser decisions about living in accordance with that law so you can experience a blessed life — not one that is in a constant state of jeopardy.

Let me use electricity as an example of what I want to convey to you. The innovation of electricity changed the world. It moved us into the age of technology and improved every aspect of life. Electricity produces light, energy, heat, and air-conditioning. It powers up computers, microwaves meals, energizes equipment — and the list goes on endlessly.

What electricity has brought to the human race is simply *amazing* and beyond the ability to exaggerate. But this electrical power that has added so many benefits to life and has brought us into the age of technology can also be *deadly* if handled incorrectly.

Wrong behavior and wrong decisions
eventually result in negative consequences.
Understanding this spiritual law motivates you
to make wiser decisions about living in accordance
with that law so you can experience a blessed life —
not one that is in a constant state of jeopardy.

When I was a young man, my father was working on something in our attic when he accidentally took hold of an electrical cord in an incorrect way. When he mishandled that electrical power, the charge in the electrical line flowed into him like a river on fire and knocked him clear to the back of the attic.

When my father emerged from the attic, he was not only badly shaken, but his hands and face were burned. He was trembling with fear from the realization that by mishandling that electricity, he could have been killed. Later that day, my father looked at me intently and said, "Rick, take this as a lesson never to mishandle electricity." What I saw on my father's face in that moment made an indelible impression on me. Years later when I became a parent and then later a grandparent, that memory was still so vivid in my mind as I strictly warned my own sons and grandchildren about the necessity of being careful with electricity.

There is nothing fearful about electricity if it is *respected* and *handled correctly*. But on that day when my father was injured, I learned that if handled improperly, electricity should be feared. The same electrical current that brings blessing to our homes and to every aspect of our lives can produce negative results as well.

Should this knowledge make us *fear* the use of electricity? No, but it should help us know to *respect it* and to *handle it correctly* to avoid its negative side. The problem is not electricity. The problem is *how* electricity is handled. If one understands and respects electricity and handles it correctly, he has no need to be afraid of it. But for the one who has no understanding of or respect for electricity, it can be a deadly force.

This same principle can be carried over into our subject of the fear of the Lord. God's Word is absolute truth that rules every aspect of life, and His power is more real than the electrical current that is so pervasively available in modern civilization. If you cooperate correctly with God's Word and respect His power, both of these spiritual forces will bring blessings into your life. But if you disrespect God's Word, violate His clearly stated principles, or live out of sync with His power, you will experience the backside of those forces in a negative way.

You see, friend, the fear of the Lord is *foundational* to everything else in life.

THE FEAR OF THE LORD IS FOUNDATIONAL TO EVERYTHING

Proverbs 9:10 declares, "The fear of the Lord is the beginning of wisdom: and the knowledge of the holy is understanding."

According to this verse, the fear of the Lord is the *beginning* of wisdom. This truth is so vitally important that the Holy Spirit inspired it to be written almost word for word in other verses as well. For example, Psalm 111:10 tells us, "The fear of the Lord is the beginning of wisdom: a good understanding have all they that do his commandments: his praise endureth forever." And Proverbs 1:7 says, "The fear of the Lord is the beginning of knowledge: but fools despise wisdom and instruction."

The fear of the Lord is *foundational*
to everything else in life.

Like the example of electricity I just used, God's Word and His awesome power are amazing! Both of them bring life, light, illumination, healing, and deliverance. Both quicken the dead to come alive again and improve our lives in ways that are indescribable. Yet if God's Word and His power are mishandled — that is, if they are exploited for any impure motive or treated casually, disrespectfully, or irreverently — the consequences can be very negative.

Just as we have no need to fear electricity if it is handled correctly, we never need to be afraid of God *if* we are living in obedience to His Word and responding properly to His mighty power. We need to be afraid only of the consequences we will reap if we are deliberately living in disobedience to the principles of His Word or if we mishandle His power.

The spiritual realm has laws — and when spiritual laws are broken, negative consequences result. And Christians are not exempt. When a Christian who is indwelt by the Holy Spirit knowledgeably transgresses and violates God's holy presence in his life, that person is probing into realms that will produce negative consequences.

God's Word and His awesome power both quicken
the dead to come alive again and improve our lives
in ways that are indescribable. Yet if they are treated
casually, disrespectfully, or irreverently,
the consequences can be very negative.

I am personally convinced that one reason believers violate spiritual laws is simply that they have not been taught or don't fully understand what a profoundly grave violation it is to transgress against God's presence in their lives. If they did, they wouldn't do it so casually. But because of a lack of knowledge, many Christians sin with no conviction or pain to their conscience at all. This is why A. W. Tozer wrote, "When men no longer fear God, they transgress His laws without hesitation."[103]

On the positive side, God promises that we will reap blessing when we walk in obedience to His Word and respect His power and presence in our lives. We are guaranteed that this will bring tremendous benefits to us.

THE EARLY CHURCH
POSSESSED A FEAR OF THE LORD

The Early Church understood the need to walk in the fear of the Lord. To see this more clearly, let's turn our attention once again to Acts 2:42,43.

> **And they continued steadfastly in the apostles' doctrine and fellowship, and in breaking of bread, and in prayers. And fear came upon every soul: and many wonders and signs were done by the apostles.**

Notice that verse 43 says, "And *fear* came upon every soul...." It does not say, "*Respect* came upon every soul" — it says *fear*. Just as the early believers cultivated a passion for God's Word and for prayer, they also nurtured a healthy fear of the presence and power of God. This verse says fear of the Lord came upon every soul in the Early Church. Because they handled the Word of God

---

[103] A. W. Tozer, *Knowledge of the Holy* (Zeeland, MI: Reformed Church Publications, 2015), p. 65.

and the power of God with such awe, respect, and godly fear, they experienced the positive side of His mighty power. Acts 2:43 tells us that the power of God flowed among them "...and many *wonders* and *signs* were done...."

Not only did the fear of the Lord release the power of God to produce supernatural signs and wonders, but it also produced supernatural generosity among these early believers. Let's see what the Bible tells us in Acts 4:32:

> **And the multitude of them that believed were of one heart and of one soul: neither said any of them that aught of the things which he possessed was his own; but they had all things common.**

From this verse, we see that there was a mighty move of God's presence among the people. It was so powerful that they began to generously give to fellow believers to ensure everyone had what he or she needed. So when God's Word and power were handled correctly, so much power moved among the people that selfishness seemingly evaporated.

Acts 4:34,35 begins a scenario that shows us the importance of the fear of the Lord, with the full story carried over into Acts 5:

> **Neither was there any among them that lacked: for as many as were possessors of lands or houses sold them, and brought the prices of the things that were sold, and laid them down at the apostles' feet: and distribution was made unto every man according as he had need.**

The generosity of the believers in the Early Church graduated from small possessions, such as food, clothing, and household goods, to big-ticket items like lands and houses. And one man's gift was so huge that it was engraved in the historical account in Acts 4:36,37:

And Joses, who by the apostles was surnamed Barnabas, (which is, being interpreted, The son of consolation,) a Levite, and of the country of Cyprus, having land, sold it, and brought the money, and laid it at the apostles' feet.

Stay with me, for in this biblical account, we will find an example of what happens when there is no fear of the Lord and when God's principles and presence are handled incorrectly and with no fear of consequences.

In the above verses, we read that a man named Joses had a valuable piece of land that he sold; then he brought the entire price he received for the land and laid it at the apostles' feet. It was an enormous freewill offering given from his heart with no strings attached. Joses was obviously moved to give, and he trusted the apostles to use the money to provide for the needs of other believers who were experiencing financial struggles. So he sold his valuable possession and graciously gave at a time of great need.

The Church had just been birthed, and thousands of members from all backgrounds had various types of financial and material needs. Then suddenly Joses' gift was placed at the feet of the apostles. His gift was the largest offering ever given in the Early Church to that point. In fact, the apostles had never seen anything like it.

The gift was such an enormous blessing of encouragement that the apostles changed Joses' name to Barnabas, which means *encourager*. They must have said something like this to Joses: "Up until now you have been known you as Joses, but you have encouraged us so much that we're officially changing your name to 'Barnabas' — the son of encouragement."

In Proverbs 18:16, we are told, "A man's gift maketh room for him, and bringeth him before great men." Although this man originally named Joses was previously unknown, his magnificent gift brought him before the apostles and made room for him. And as a result, everyone in the Early Church began to rejoice about what Barnabas — this amazing encourager — had done and the great sacrifice he had made. In a short period of time, Barnabas quickly became known in the Church, nearly like a celebrity, because he had graciously given a massive financial gift from his heart at a time of great need.

These details are important to keep in mind as we continue the account in Acts chapter 5 to see what happened next.

Enter Ananias and Sapphira

What happened immediately after Barnabas gave his enormous, generous gift and laid it at the apostles' feet is eye-opening. It is a divine wakeup call regarding what happens when a person lacks the fear of the Lord.

Acts 5:1 begins this part of the story:

But a certain man named Ananias, with Sapphira his wife, sold a possession, and kept back part of the price, his wife also being privy to it, and brought a certain part, and laid it at the apostles' feet.

At first, it sounds like Ananias and Sapphira did exactly what Barnabas had done in Acts 4:36,37. But when you read deeper into the text, it is clear that this act of giving was not the same at all. Barnabas' gift was given freely from his heart with no strings attached and with no secret motives.

Ananias and his wife Sapphira saw the notoriety that Barnabas attained as a result of his giving. They watched what happened when this unknown Joses sold his land and gave his huge gift. In their minds, it seemed he had reached overnight stardom and celebrity status in the Church — something they obviously longed to possess themselves.

I can just imagine the conversation Ananias and Sapphira had behind closed doors. "Look what happened to Joses when he gave his gift. He became famous in the Church. This is the key to our becoming famous too." Ananias likely said something like this to Sapphira: "They even changed Joses' name to Barnabas, the encourager, and now everyone is talking about him and what he did. So if we sell a piece of our property and give some of the proceeds to the Church, the apostles will notice us and we'll become celebrities too!"

Although the exact conversation between this husband and wife is not recorded in Scripture, we know that they had ulterior and impure motives in their giving. The Bible tells us plainly that they "kept back part of the price" of the land. There was nothing wrong with their selling the land and giving a portion of the sale to God. It was their land and their money, and they had the right to keep a part of the sale for themselves. The problem was that Ananias and Sapphira misled everyone to think they had given the entire profit to God when in reality they did not.

In effect, Ananias and Sapphira told the apostles and the multitude, "We are giving everything we received from the sale of our land just like Barnabas did when he sold his land and gave his huge gift." The couple's plan was to make everyone think that they gave the full amount they received for the land. They wanted to make it look like they were as generous and sacrificial as Barnabas — maybe even more. But secretly, they decided not to let it be known that they were going to keep part of the sale for themselves. The image that Ananias and Sapphira were projecting was *untrue* and their motivation was *impure*.

In this situation that occurred in the infant stages of the Early Church, God was about to demonstrate what happens when the fear of the Lord is absent in someone's life. This couple clearly mishandled the power and presence of God, and it produced a negative result. In a short period of time, the same divine power that flowed mightily in the Church to heal, deliver, and save was about to flow as judgment to those who mishandled God's principles and power in their midst.

Peter knew by the Spirit that this was a charade, so he addressed Ananias:

> **...Why hath Satan filled thine heart to lie to the Holy Ghost, and to keep back part of the price of the land? While it remained, was it not thine own? And after it was sold, was it not in thine own power? Why hast thou conceived this thing in thine heart? Thou hast not lied unto men, but unto God.**

Peter asked, "Why did you plan this charade in your heart?" He explained, "You lied to the *Holy Spirit*." Then in Acts 5:4, Peter clarified, "You lied unto *God*."

In these two statements, Peter communicated clearly that the Holy Spirit is not just a partial representation of God — He is *fully* God. In fact, Acts 5:3,4 may be the clearest and earliest revelation of this vital truth to the Early Church, who taught emphatically that the Holy Spirit *is* God.

In a short period of time, the same divine power
that flowed mightily in the Church to heal,
deliver, and save was about to flow
as judgment to those who mishandled
God's principles and power in their midst.

EXIT ANANIAS AND SAPPHIRA

What happened to Ananias and Sapphira as a result of their lying to the Holy Spirit? Their fate is recorded in Acts 5:5,6:

And Ananias hearing these words fell down, and gave up the ghost: and great fear came on all them that heard these things. And the young men arose, wound him up, and carried him out, and buried him.

By the time Peter finished speaking, Ananias' body had stopped breathing and his lifeless body had collapsed to the ground. A group of young men wrapped him up, took him outside, and buried him. Acts 5:5 says this event caused "great fear" to come on all who heard what happened.

Notice that the Bible does not say, "Great *respect* came on all those who heard what happened." It says *great fear*. The people were stunned and astonished, even speechless, as they witnessed this act of mishandling God's presence and power. The outcome provided such a clear demonstration of how imperative it is that one relates to the Holy Spirit correctly.

When people heard what had happened to Ananias and the words that Peter had spoken to him just before he died, a great fear came upon the entire Church. That fear was accompanied by a new, profound understanding that the Holy Spirit *is God* and that He is to be feared, respected, and related to correctly.

The outcome provided such a clear demonstration
of how imperative it is that one relates
to the Holy Spirit correctly.

But the story continues in Acts 5:7, where we are told:

And it was about the space of three hours after, when his wife, not knowing what was done, came in. And Peter answered unto her, Tell me whether ye sold the land for so much? And she said, Yea, for so much.

When Ananias' wife and partner in this charade returned, Peter asked her, "Did you sell the land for this amount?" Sapphira in essence answered, "Yes, *exactly* for that amount." When those words exited her lips, she became guilty of lying to the Holy Spirit as well — and God viewed Sapphira's actions as impure as her husband's. Acts 5:9 tells us:

Then Peter said unto her, How is it that ye have agreed together to tempt the Spirit of the Lord? Behold, the feet of them which have buried thy husband are at the door, and shall carry thee out.

This verse clearly says that Ananias and Sapphira agreed to "tempt" the Spirit of the Lord. The word "tempt" is the Greek word *peiradzo*, which in this case means *to challenge God by impious, irreverent, sinful, or wicked conduct.* By using the term *peiradzo*, Peter essentially said what I've been communicating to you all along — that Ananias and Sapphira broke spiritual laws and disrespectfully mishandled how they related to the Spirit of God.

Remember what we discussed regarding electricity? If you handle electricity correctly, it will bring a multitude of blessings into your life, but if you handle it incorrectly, it will bring negative repercussions. Because Ananias and Sapphira insulted and disrespectfully mishandled the presence and power of God, Ananias dropped dead — and Acts 5:10 tells us that the same thing happened to Sapphira:

> **Then fell she down straightway at his feet, and yielded up the ghost: and the young men came in, and found her dead, and carrying her forth, buried her by her husband.**

The fact that Ananias and his wife Sapphira conspired to carry out this scheme reveals their utter lack of the fear of God and of His power and presence. However, the final outcome of this event is revealed in Acts 5:11, where it says the news of what happened caused a great increase in godly fear wherever believers heard of it.

> **And great fear came upon all the church, and upon as many as heard these things.**

This verse tells us that *the fear of the Lord* came upon *the entire Church.* Everyone was talking about the sudden deaths of Ananias and Sapphira, about their lying to God, and about their improper handling of the Holy Spirit. Truly, this event sent shock waves throughout the Early Church!

As a result of what happened to this couple, every believer understood more than ever that, if disrespectfully mishandled, the power and presence of God could bring divine punishment. From that moment forward, the Early Church recognized and comprehended the serious role of the Holy Spirit and began walking in a deeper respect and a greater healthy fear of the Lord.

From that moment forward, the Early Church recognized and comprehended the serious role of the Holy Spirit and began walking in a deeper respect and a greater healthy fear of the Lord.

DIVINE DISCIPLINE: IT HAS HAPPENED BEFORE

What happened to Ananias and Sapphira was not the first time someone experienced divine punishment for disrespectfully mishandling the presence of God. There are examples in the Old Testament as well.

For instance, Second Samuel 6:3 tells us what happened when King David and the people of Israel attempted to bring the Ark of the Covenant back to their homeland: "And they set the ark of God upon a new cart, and brought it out of the house of Abinadab that was in Gibeah: and Uzzah and Ahio, the sons of Abinadab, drove the new cart."

King David and the people were thrilled at the thought of having the Ark of God back in Israel, so they sang and played their harps, lyres, cymbals, and tambourines in worship as they marched home. This was a mighty display of celebration before the Lord!

Then something unexpected happened. Second Samuel 6:6,7 says, "When they came to Nachon's threshing floor, Uzzah put forth his hand to the ark of God, and took hold of it; for the oxen shook it. And the anger of the Lord was kindled against Uzzah;

and God smote him there for his error; and there he died by the ark of God."

To truly grasp the full impact of what happened, one must understand that the Ark of God represented the presence and power of God — which He demanded be treated with reverential fear. Through Moses, God had instructed how the Ark of the Covenant was to be handled. He had clearly communicated that it was to be carried only by the Levite priests who used special, gold-plated poles that slid through golden rings attached to the Ark (*see* Numbers 3:27-32; Deuteronomy 31:9,24,25). But David and his leaders had not heeded these instructions, so in their zeal, they failed to handle the Ark correctly as God required.

When Uzzah was struck dead, it was a consequence of this mishandling of the Ark — which, again, represented the presence and power of God. Second Samuel 6:9 says that as a result of Uzzah's death, "David was afraid of the Lord that day, and said, How shall the ark of the Lord come to me?"

When David witnessed the divine power that was present within and flowing from the Ark of the Covenant that day, he was overwhelmed. The fear of the Lord literally came upon him as never before. It was so strong that he decided to abandon his mission, and he placed the Ark of God at the nearest home he could find — which was at the home of Obed-edom. There the Ark of God remained for three months (*see* 2 Samuel 6:11).

Later David got word of how the presence and power of the Lord had mightily blessed the home of Obed-edom where the Ark of God was residing, so once again he decided to bring it to the city of David. There is an amazing truth revealed in this part of the biblical account: The same divine presence and power that killed Uzzah through wrongful mishandling brought blessing to the house of Obed-edom — because in the second location, *it was handled correctly.*

However, this time David took extreme care in the way he and the other leaders handled the Ark that represented the Lord's presence. Second Samuel 6:13 (*NLT*) says, "After the men who were carrying it had gone six steps, they stopped and waited so David could sacrifice an ox and a fattened calf." With a new understanding and a deep sense of the fear of the Lord, David offered sacrifices to God and displayed great honor and respect for His holy presence.

For the remainder of David's life, he treated the Ark of the Covenant with reverential fear and great respect and taught the people to do likewise. The demonstration of God's power in judgment permanently branded the fear of the Lord into David's heart.

A Fresh Influx of God's Power

In each situation in the Bible where God's power brought a negative effect, it was nearly always as a result of someone improperly handling His presence and power. But in each instance, the fear of the Lord came upon God's people as a result, and their understanding increased that God's power and presence are to be treated with great honor and respect. Each incident reminded the people to never improperly handle God's presence and power. As they received this message and once again walked in the reverential fear of the Lord, their obedience released a fresh influx of His power and blessing.

For David, the fear of the Lord brought him and the nation of Israel unprecedented military victories. Biblical history records that after the Ark of God had been respectfully transported back to Israel, David was empowered to subdue the Philistines. He conquered the Moabites and made them his servants. He destroyed the forces of Hadadezer, defeated the Arameans, and took control of Damascus, their capital city. David became highly respected and greatly feared by neighboring kings from that time forward (*see* 2 Samuel 8).

Each incident reminded the people
to never improperly handle God's presence and power.
As they received this message and once again walked
in the reverential fear of the Lord, their obedience
released a fresh influx of His power and blessing.

For believers in the Early Church, the reverential fear of the Lord came upon them at the time of Ananias and Sapphira's deaths and released a fresh flood of His signs and wonders! Immediately after the deaths of Ananias and Sapphira, Acts 5:12 reveals that "many signs and wonders wrought among the people...." Acts 5:15,16 goes on to relate details of what happened immediately following this event and the fresh fear of the Lord that fell upon the Church as a result:

> ...They brought forth the sick into the streets, and laid them on beds and couches, that at the least the shadow of Peter passing by might overshadow some of them. There came also a multitude out of the cities round about unto Jerusalem, bringing sick folks, and them which were vexed with unclean spirits: and they were healed every one.

These early believers had received the revelation that God's power and anointing is to be feared! His presence is to be treated with reverence and respect. In the end, such power erupted in the midst of God's people that in a short period of time, He added to their number "multitudes both of men and women" (v. 14).

What Does All This Mean for You?

Friend, you need the fear of the Lord in your life. You need it just as David needed it to experience God's best as king of Israel and just as the early believers needed it to experience God's power in the newly birthed Church.

Never forget — there are spiritual laws that must be obeyed if you want to be blessed. If you respect and handle God's Word and His power correctly, you will receive great blessing as a result. But if you choose to disobey, ignore, sidestep, or disrespect His truth, His presence, and His power, the same power that could help you may bring you a severe correction or even judgment. This is simply the way it works.

When you truly know and believe that you will give an account to Jesus Christ for your life, that knowledge greatly affects the way you live. Conversely, if you *don't* know or *don't* believe that one day you will give an account to Jesus for your life, that also affects your behavior — but in a negative way. Essentially, it reduces you to living merely for temporary matters, having no concern for eternal consequences.

People who live on that low level reveal a dangerous deficiency in the fear of the Lord. Remaining in such a state will have negative consequences for any of God's children who neglect to maintain this healthy fear of God.

As I said at the beginning of this chapter, many Christians today have a disturbing, lopsided view of who God is. They see Him only as a God of love and mercy, and they actually assume He will ignore their wrong behaviors and choices and will never *really* hold them accountable.

When you truly know and believe that you will give an account to Jesus Christ for your life, that knowledge greatly affects the way you live.

This causes people to behave and live irresponsibly. They lose a healthy fear of God and develop a casual attitude toward Him and toward the prospect of judgment. As a result, it's just a matter of time before they begin to conduct themselves in ways that violate God's moral code. And they will do it blatantly — with no fear of accountability for their actions.

PRACTICAL ADVICE FOR DEVELOPING A HEALTHY FEAR OF THE LORD

You must continually guard your heart from ever losing a healthy fear of the Lord. If you ever grow deficient in godly fear, you will find yourself becoming irreverent and disrespectful of God's presence and power at some level.

I encourage you to ask yourself — and to honestly answer — these important questions:

- *Do I truly reverence the presence and the power of God in my life?*

- *Do I show that I am respectful of God's presence and power by my daily actions and choices?*

- *Do I really walk in the fear of the Lord as the Bible commands me — or have I become too casual with God? Have I slipped in my understanding of His mighty power and the holy life He has called me to live?*

Answering these questions will help you gauge where you are in regard to this key fuel that you need to keep spiritually ablaze throughout your life. As you take time to reflect on these questions, the Holy Spirit will show you any areas in which you may have slipped. When He does, your part is to take Him seriously and *deal with those areas*. Repent before God, and pray for the fear of the Lord to be recultivated in your life. If you respect and reverently handle God's holy presence, you will cause His power to flow mightily into your life to bring blessings that will make you grow and flourish.

I would also encourage you to pray for the ability to see God in a balanced way. Realize that the same divine power and holy presence that can improve your life can also bring negative consequences if God is disrespected and His power is wrongly handled. Yes, He is a kind and loving Heavenly Father. But He is also Almighty God — holy, righteous, and just. He desires that you show Him the respect that is due Him.

The Holy Spirit will show you any areas
in which you may have slipped. When He does, your part
is to take Him seriously and *deal with those areas*.

Keep your eyes on Jesus and live to please Him every day. Make His Word the guide for your life, and never permit yourself to become so casual in your approach to God that you forget that one day you will stand before the Judgment Seat of Christ to give an account for your life (*see* 2 Corinthians 5:9,10; Romans 14:10-12). Keeping this truth in your mind will help you live in a way that is pleasing to God.

Friend, the Word of God is full of promises for those who reverently fear Him. The fear of the Lord is a powerful blessing for you!

The blessings that result from walking in the fear of the Lord include:

- Angelic protection and deliverance (*see* Psalm 34:7).
- Strong confidence (*see* Proverbs 14:26).
- Divine direction (*see* Psalm 25:12).
- Having what you need without lack (*see* Psalm 34:9).
- The Lord's good pleasure (*see* Psalm 147:11).
- God's great mercy and compassion (*see* Psalm 103:11-13).
- Long life (*see* Proverbs 10:27).

I like what Leonard Ravenhill said about the fear of the Lord. He noted, "He who fears God fears no man."[104] It's true — when you have a healthy fear of the Lord, you are so secure, so safe, and so shielded in God's refuge, that there is no need to be afraid of any man or any other thing!

Having this fear of the Lord is the tenth vital fuel that I pray you will inject into your spiritual fire. It will cause you or any believer — or any church — to burn brightly now and for the rest of your life.

---

[104] Leonard Ravenhill, *Why Revival Tarries* (Minneapolis: Bethany House, 1959, 1987), p. 34.

"He who fears God fears no man."
— *Leonard Ravenhill*

So ask the Lord to give you this healthy fear of the Lord. It would also be good to ask God to forgive you for any irreverent attitude you've had in the past or for any way that you have disrespectfully handled or responded to His Word, His power, and His presence in your life. As you grow in your understanding of the fear of the Lord, there is no question that it will release the power of God like a surging flood that brings the miraculous into every sphere of your life!

Remember Ecclesiastes 12:13, where Solomon wrote, "Let us hear the conclusion of the whole matter: Fear God, and keep his commandments: for this is the whole duty of man. For God shall bring every work into judgment, with every secret thing, whether it be good, or whether it be evil." And never forget that Psalm 31:19 says, "Oh how great is thy goodness, which thou hast laid up for them that fear thee…"

This means everything good awaits those who are ablaze with the fear of the Lord.

In Conclusion

At the beginning of this book, I asked:

- How do you stoke the embers of the fire within you so that it begins burning red-hot in your heart again?

- Once you have that fire burning hot and bright, how do you sustain and *grow* the intensity of that inner fire for the rest of your time on this earth?

In this book, I have given you ten different kinds of fuel you need to stay spiritually ablaze. Now that you have read this book, it's time to put what you've read into practice. If you'll inject these ten key fuels into your spiritual flame on a consistent basis, they will reignite the fire in your heart. These fuels will not only cause your spiritual passion to burn brightly as it once did, but they will also cause your heart to burn brighter than you have ever known before!

In Second Timothy 1:6, Paul wrote, "Wherefore I put thee in remembrance that thou *stir up* the gift of God, which is in thee by the putting on of my hands." Now it's time for you to do just that — *to be enthusiastic, to be fervent, to be passionate, to be vigorous, to be wholehearted,* and *to be zealous* about stirring up the fire of God in your heart!

If you sense that the fire in your heart has ebbed to embers or is on a low burn, begin to passionately and rigorously *stoke* and *stir up* the gift of God in your life. Just as one would stoke the embers of a fire in a hearth or fireplace, reach within yourself and begin *to rekindle* the fire in your heart until you are once again a raging inferno that burns with the power of God.

Just as one would stoke the embers of a fire in a hearth or fireplace, reach within yourself and begin *to rekindle* the fire in your heart until you are once again a raging inferno that burns with the power of God.

Remember, you can't depend on someone else to do the stoking and stirring for you. You must take responsibility to look inside yourself, determine your fuel supply, and do whatever you must to stir your spiritual embers and keep your fire burning.

If you'll ask the Holy Spirit, He'll show you how to open the door to your heart and apply the fuels you've read about in this book to your inner fire. The Spirit of God has a full supply of every kind of fuel that you need to fortify your reserves. So take the initiative. Determine today that you're never going to let up on fueling your fire so that you can remain a blazing inferno for Jesus on this earth till the day He returns!

THINK ABOUT IT

1. God is indeed a loving Heavenly Father who longs to manifest the glory of His goodness in our midst. He is also an all-consuming fire who deals seriously with sin and evil — especially within the household of His saints. Scriptures abound with examples of how the lack of reverential fear toward God and His presence invites negative consequences.

   Does the fear of God hold a healthy place in your life? Can you think of instances in your life when the reverential fear of the Lord rescued you from the consequences of acting outside of His will in a situation? Would you describe your walk with God as a journey into greater intimacy? Do you maintain an abiding desire never to knowingly earn His displeasure? Why or why not?

2. The book of Acts shares numerous accounts of how the fear of the Lord releases a fresh influx of supernatural power and generosity. How have you experienced the "cause and effect" of this spiritual reality in a personal way?

3. In Ecclesiastes 12:13 and 14, Solomon wrote, "Let us hear the conclusion of the whole matter: Fear God, and keep his commandments: for this is the whole duty of man. For God shall bring every work into judgment, with every secret thing, whether it be good, or whether it be evil."

   The eyes of the Lord see all, and He will require us to give an account for every word and deed. Repeated violation of spiritual laws or willful cooperation with sin and evil results in self-deception and a potentially seared conscience, which can lead to disastrous consequences.

Do you deeply reverence the written Word of God? Do you esteem as precious the promptings of the Holy Spirit to guide you? As you examine your own heart, what are some of the ways you can fuel your fervency toward God with greater reverence?

PRAYER TO RECEIVE THE BAPTISM IN THE HOLY SPIRIT

The baptism in the Holy Spirit is a free gift to *everyone* who has made Jesus Savior and Lord of his or her life (*see* Acts 2:39).

After you made Jesus your Lord at the time of the new birth, the Holy Spirit came to live inside you, and your old, unregenerate spirit was made completely new. This subsequent gift is the "baptism into," or *an immersion in*, the Holy Spirit.

The baptism in the Holy Spirit supplies the supernatural power of God for witnessing about Christ, for enjoying a deeper, more intimate relationship with the Holy Spirit, and for victorious Christian living.

Receiving this precious gift is easy. Before you pray to receive the infilling of the Holy Spirit, you might want to read and meditate on the Scripture references I provide on the next page. Then expect to receive what you ask for *the moment* you pray!

If you would like to be baptized in the Holy Spirit and speak with new tongues (*see* Acts 2:4), simply pray the following prayer and then act on it!

Lord, You gave the Holy Spirit to Your Church to help us fulfill the Great Commission. I ask You in faith for this free gift, and I receive right now the baptism in the Holy Spirit. I believe that You hear me as I pray, and I thank You for baptizing me in the Holy Spirit with the evidence of speaking with a new, supernatural prayer language. Amen.

As a result of praying this prayer, *your life will never be the same*. You will have God's power working through you to witness, to operate in the gifts of the Holy Spirit, and to experience Jesus' victory as a living reality every day.

Rick Renner

Scripture References for Study and Review: Mark 16:17; Luke 24:39; Acts 1:4,5,8; 2:4,39; 10:45,46

Prayer for a Life Ablaze

If your heart is crying out to be *a life ablaze*, I encourage you to join your faith with this prayer as you pray it right now:

Father, I come to You in Jesus' name to say thank You for speaking to me through the pages of this book. After reading it, I am stirred to ask You to help me add the right fuels to my heart to keep the fire of God burning in me for the entire balance of my life on this earth. Many good years lie before me, and for me to do everything that You have planned for me to do, I need to be ablaze with the power of the Holy Spirit. So I ask You to loose Your power inside me and to help me do those things that are necessary to keep myself burning like a spiritual inferno for years to come.

And as we approach the end of the age, help me take my place within the ranks of the end-time army of believers that You are calling to take the blazing light of God's Word and power into darkness to further Your Kingdom and accomplish Your purposes. I know that the power of the Holy Spirit resides within me, but please help me consistently do those things that cause my spiritual fire to burn more radiantly.

Father, my heart's response to this book and my prayer today is that I will never stop being a life ablaze for You all the days of my life.

I pray this prayer in Jesus' name!

ABOUT THE AUTHOR

RICK RENNER is a highly respected Bible teacher and leader in the international Christian community. Rick is the author of a long list of books, including the bestsellers *Dressed To Kill* and *Sparkling Gems From the Greek 1* and *2*, which have sold millions of copies in multiple languages worldwide. Rick's understanding of the Greek language and biblical history opens up the Scriptures in a unique way that enables readers to gain wisdom and insight while learning something brand new from the Word of God.

Rick is the founding pastor of the Moscow Good News Church. He also founded Media Mir, the first Christian television network in the former USSR that broadcasts the Gospel to countless Russian-speaking viewers around the world via multiple satellites and the Internet. He is the founder and president of RENNER Ministries, based in Tulsa, Oklahoma, and host to his TV program that is seen around the world in multiple languages. Rick leads this amazing work with his wife and lifelong ministry partner, Denise, along with the help of their sons and committed leadership team.

Contact Renner Ministries

For further information
about RENNER Ministries,
please contact the office nearest you,
or visit the ministry website at:
www.renner.org

**ALL USA
CORRESPONDENCE:**
RENNER Ministries
P. O. Box 702040
Tulsa, OK 74170-2040
(918) 496-3213
Or 1-800-RICK-593
Email: renner@renner.org
Website: www.renner.org

MOSCOW OFFICE:
RENNER Ministries
P. O. Box 789
101000, Moscow, Russia
+7 (495) 727-1470
Email: blagayavestonline@ignc.org
Website: www.ignc.org

RIGA OFFICE:
RENNER Ministries
Unijas 99
Riga LV-1084, Latvia
+371 67802150
Email: info@goodnews.lv

KIEV OFFICE:
RENNER Ministries
P. O. Box 300
01001, Kiev, Ukraine
+38 (044) 451-8315
Email: blagayavestonline@ignc.org

OXFORD OFFICE:
RENNER Ministries
Box 7, 266 Banbury Road
Oxford OX2 7DL, England
+44 1865 521024
Email: europe@renner.org

Books by Rick Renner

Build Your Foundation*
Chosen by God*
Dream Thieves*
Dressed To Kill*
The Holy Spirit and You*
How To Keep Your Head on Straight in a World Gone Crazy*
How To Receive Answers From Heaven!*
Insights to Successful Leadership
Last-Days Survival Guide*
A Life Ablaze*
Life in the Combat Zone*
A Light in Darkness, Volume One,
    Seven Messages to the Seven Churches series
The Love Test*
No Room for Compromise, Volume Two,
    Seven Messages to the Seven Churches series
Paid in Full*
The Point of No Return*
Repentance*
Signs You'll See Just Before Jesus Comes*
Sparkling Gems From the Greek Daily Devotional 1*
Sparkling Gems From the Greek Daily Devotional 2*
Spiritual Weapons To Defeat the Enemy*
Ten Guidelines To Help You Achieve
    Your Long-Awaited Promotion!*
Testing the Supernatural
365 Days of Increase
365 Days of Power
Turn Your God-Given Dreams Into Reality*
Why We Need the Gifts of the Spirit*
The Will of God — The Key to Your Success*
You Can Get Over It*

SPARKLING GEMS FROM THE GREEK 1

In 2003, Rick Renner's *Sparkling Gems From the Greek 1* quickly gained widespread recognition for its unique illumination of the New Testament through more than 1,000 Greek word studies in a 365-day devotional format. Today *Sparkling Gems 1* remains a beloved resource that has spiritually strengthened believers worldwide. As many have testified, the wealth of truths within its pages never grows old. Year after year, *Sparkling Gems 1* continues to deepen readers' understanding of the Bible.

1,048 pages
(Hardback)

To order, visit us online at: **www.renner.org**

SPARKLING GEMS FROM THE GREEK 2

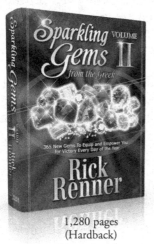

Rick infuses into *Sparkling Gems From the Greek 2* the added strength and richness of many more years of his own personal study and growth in God — expanding this devotional series to impact the reader's heart on a deeper level than ever before. This remarkable study tool helps unlock new hidden treasures from God's Word that will draw readers into an ever more passionate pursuit of Him.

To order, visit us online at: **www.renner.org**

1,280 pages
(Hardback)

DRESSED TO KILL
A BIBLICAL APPROACH
TO SPIRITUAL WARFARE AND ARMOR

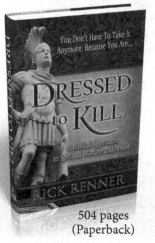

504 pages
(Paperback)

Rick Renner's book *Dressed To Kill* is considered by many to be a true classic on the subject of spiritual warfare. The original version, which sold more than 400,000 copies, is a curriculum staple in Bible schools worldwide. In this beautiful volume, you will find:

- 504 pages of reedited text in paperback

- 16 pages of full-color illustrations

- Questions at the end of each chapter to guide you into deeper study

In *Dressed To Kill*, Rick explains with exacting detail the purpose and function of each piece of Roman armor. In the process, he describes the significance of our *spiritual* armor not only to withstand the onslaughts of the enemy, but also to overturn the tendencies of the carnal mind. Furthermore, Rick delivers a clear, scriptural presentation on the biblical definition of spiritual warfare — what it is and what it is not.

When you walk with God in deliberate, continual fellowship, He will enrobe you with Himself. Armed with the knowledge of who you are in Him, you will be dressed and dangerous to the works of darkness, unflinching in the face of conflict, and fully equipped to take the offensive and gain mastery over any opposition from your spiritual foe. You don't have to accept defeat anymore once you are *dressed to kill*!

To order, visit us online at: **www.renner.org**

Book Resellers: Contact Harrison House at 800-722-6774 or visit **www.HarrisonHouse.com** for quantity discounts.

HOW TO KEEP YOUR HEAD ON STRAIGHT IN A WORLD GONE CRAZY

DEVELOPING DISCERNMENT FOR THESE LAST DAYS

400 pages
(Paperback)

The world is changing. In fact, it's more than changing — it has *gone crazy*.

We are living in a world where faith is questioned and sin is welcomed — where people seem to have lost their minds about what is right and wrong. It seems truth has been turned *upside down*.

In Rick Renner's book *How To Keep Your Head on Straight in a World Gone Crazy*, he reveals the disastrous consequences of a society in spiritual and moral collapse. In this book, you'll discover what Christians need to do to stay out of the chaos and remain anchored to truth. You'll learn how to stay sensitive to the Holy Spirit, how to discern right and wrong teaching, how to be grounded in prayer, and how to be spiritually prepared for living in victory in these last days.

Leading ministers from around the world are calling this book essential for every believer. Topics include:

- Contending for the faith in the last days
- How to pray for leaders who are in error
- How to judge if a teaching is good or bad
- Seducing spirits and doctrines of demons
- How to be a good minister of Jesus Christ

To order, visit us online at: **www.renner.org**

Book Resellers: Contact Harrison House at 800-722-6774 or visit **www.HarrisonHouse.com** for quantity discounts.

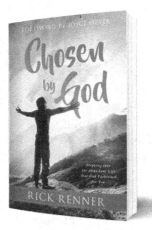

BUILD YOUR FOUNDATION

Six Must-Have Beliefs for Constructing an Unshakable Christian Life

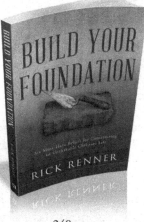

248 pages
(Paperback)

A building contractor has a top priority every time he begins a construction project: *to get the foundation right.* He knows that's the key to the stability of the structure he is building. If the foundation is laid incorrectly, the rest of the building might look good — but it will always have problems and will possibly never fulfill its purpose for being constructed in the first place.

That same principle is true as you build your life in Christ. You will never last long in your quest to fulfill what God has put you on the earth to accomplish *unless* you first focus on laying your spiritual foundation *"rock-solid"* on the truths of His Word.

In this book, author Rick Renner provides the scriptural "mortar and brick" that defines the six fundamental doctrines listed in Hebrews 6:1 and 2 — the exact ingredients you need to lay a solid foundation for the structure called your life in Christ.

Topics include:

- An Honest Look at the Modern Church
- Let's Qualify To *'Go On'*
- Remorse vs. Repentance
- The Laying on of Hands
- Three Baptisms and Three Resurrections
- The Great White Throne Judgment
- The Judgment Seat of Christ
- *And many more!*

To order, visit us online at: **www.renner.org**

Book Resellers: Contact Harrison House at 800-722-6774 or visit **www.HarrisonHouse.com** for quantity discounts.

Connect with us on

f Facebook @ HarrisonHousePublishers

and **[O]** Instagram @ **HarrisonHousePublishing**

so you can stay up to date with news

about our books and our authors.

Visit us at **www.harrisonhouse.com**

for a complete product listing as well as

monthly specials for wholesale distribution.

The Harrison House Vision

Proclaiming the truth and the power
of the Gospel of Jesus Christ with excellence.
Challenging Christians
to live victoriously,
grow spiritually,
know God intimately.